MW00472247

Civil War Citizens

CIVIL WAR CITIZENS

*Race, Ethnicity, and Identity in
America's Bloodiest Conflict*

EDITED BY

Susannah J. Ural

NEW YORK UNIVERSITY PRESS
New York and London

NEW YORK UNIVERSITY PRESS
New York and London
www.nyupress.org

© 2010 by New York University

Library of Congress Cataloging-in-Publication Data

Civil War citizens : race, ethnicity, and identity in
America's bloodiest conflict / edited by Susannah J. Ural.
p. cm.
Includes index.
ISBN 978–0–8147–8569–0 (cl : alk. paper) — ISBN 978–0–8147–8570–6
(pb :alk. paper) — ISBN 978–0–8147–8571–3 (ebook)
1. United States—History—Civil War, 1861–1865—Participation, Immigrant.
2. United States—History—Civil War, 1861–1865—Participation, German
American. 3. United States—History—Civil War, 1861–1865—Participation,
Irish American. 4. United States—History—Civil War, 1861–1865—Participation,
Jewish. 5. United States—History—Civil War, 1861–1865—Participation, Indian.
6. United States—History—Civil War, 1861–1865—Participation, African American.
7. United States—History—Civil War, 1861–1865—Social aspects. 8. Minorities—
United States—Social conditions—19th century. 9. Immigrants—United States—
Social conditions—19th century. 10. United States—Social conditions—
19th century. I. Ural, Susannah J.
E540.F6C49   2010
973.7'1—dc22   2010023623

New York University Press books are printed on acid-free paper,
and their binding materials are chosen for strength and durability.
We strive to use environmentally responsible suppliers and materials
to the greatest extent possible in publishing our books.

Manufactured in the United States of America
c 10 9 8 7 6 5 4 3 2 1
p 10 9 8 7 6 5 4 3 2 1

*For my colleagues in the Center for the Study
of War and Society at Southern Miss —
I cannot recall another group with whom
I have worked* and *laughed so hard.*

CONTENTS

INTRODUCTION

Susannah J. Ural

On September 10, 1861, applause shook the walls of Institute Hall in Charleston, South Carolina. The audience cheered its local men, most of them German-born, who had volunteered as soldiers for the Confederacy. Having enjoyed a "stirring and patriotic address in the tongue of the Faterland [sic]," it was the gift from the German Ladies Society of Charleston that brought the audience to its feet. The women had sewn the company flag with the colors of the United States on one side and the colors of their homeland on the other. As Captain W. K. Bachman raised the banner and turned to address his men, the ladies rained flowers down from the balcony, which the young volunteers placed in their muskets. Addressing the enthusiastic crowd, Bachman cried out, "Comrades. This is our flag. Under it you are to go to take your place in the contest. . . . Recollect at all times who made [this] flag. All that they ask in return is that you will never bring dishonor upon their own loved German name."[1]

Twelve days earlier an even larger crowd had gathered in Jones's Wood in New York City. Irish revolutionary Thomas Francis Meagher, a Captain in the 69th New York State Militia Regiment, spoke to a crowd gathered to honor the Irish men who had fallen the previous month in defense of the Union at the Battle of First Bull Run. The Wood, a *New York Times* reporter observed, "was crowded to an excess which can scarcely be described without apparent exaggeration." Meagher cast his voice over the audience and called on the listeners to join him in honoring with "proud regard and duty . . . those whose husbands and fathers, fighting in the ranks of the Sixty-ninth, were slain in battle, sealing their oath of American citizenship with their blood."[2]

Despite the wealth of scholarship on the U.S. Civil War, especially regarding how individuals and communities responded to the conflict, there is no comprehensive study of immigrants and nonwhites in the North and South during this era, who constituted nearly 15 percent of the U.S. population in 1860. Despite their numerical significance, as well as their influence on military and political policies and their active role in the armies and navies engaged, these groups have received relatively little attention from historians. Scholars have long used, and criticized, Ella Lonn's classic books on immigrant service in the Union and the Confederacy. More recently, historians enjoyed William Burton's study *Melting Pot Soldiers: The Union's Ethnic Regiments* and Lawrence Kohl's excellent series of edited memoirs and letter collections relating to soldiers in the Irish Brigade. Since 2000, Walter Kamphoefner and Wolfgang Helbich published *Germans in the Civil War: The Letters They Wrote Home*, and Fordham University Press reprinted Grace Palladino's study *Another Civil War: Labor, Capital, and the State in Anthracite Regions of Pennsylvania, 1840–1868*, addressing ethnic responses to war on the home front, as well as Christian Keller's *Chancellorsville and the Germans: Nativism, Ethnicity, and Civil War Memory*.[3] Still, scholars lack a work that ties all this material together.

Historians need a book that highlights the complexity of the ethnic and religious responses to America's bloodiest war. Such a work can show that there is no single "Irish" or "Jewish" reaction. Just as native-born white communities responded in different ways due to their social makeup or their economic infrastructure, immigrants, Native Americans, African Americans, and Jews also responded at times with one voice, and at other moments differed greatly, including within their own communities. Scholars understand this through individual studies, but not in a work that examines these groups side by side. That is what *Civil War Citizens: Race, Ethnicity, and Identity in America's Bloodiest Conflict* offers. Contributors challenge the idea of immigrants and nonwhites volunteering to prove their loyalty while recognizing their frustration when such rewards were not forthcoming. They underscore the different expectations these groups had of citizenship and what they expected from their sacrifices for the survival of the Union or the Confederacy. The wartime responses of immigrants and nonwhites reveal an acute awareness that whatever actions their communities took would be carefully scrutinized not only by the dominant white Anglo-Saxon Protestant Americans but also within their own populations. This collection examines the momentous decisions made by these communities in the face of war, their desire for full citizenship, the complex loyalties that shaped their actions, and the inspiring and heartbreaking results of their choices that still echo through the United States today.

While the excellent historiography of particular ethnic soldiers, politicians, and communities has been beneficial to scholars, *Civil War Citizens* is the first effort to gather into one book the wartime experiences of groups that fell outside of the dominant white Anglo-Saxon Protestant citizenry of mid-nineteenth-century America. For the sake of brevity, this volume collectively refers to these immigrant and nonwhite communities as "outside groups," which is how they often saw themselves while also fighting against that image. Their efforts to secure the full rights of citizenship united immigrants and nonwhites in nineteenth-century America, even when they approached this goal in different ways and faced different obstacles. As Andrea Mehrländer shows in her chapter on the Southern German response to the war, the reactions of Richmond's Germans differed greatly from those of New Orleans's Germans, and the Germans of Charleston had an equally unique story. Similarly, William McKee Evans highlights the complexity within the response of the Western Cherokee community, which differed from the Eastern Cherokees' mobilization for war. At the same time, however, these groups had shared motivations with each other and even with the native-born white population. They saw the war in terms of how it impacted their homes, their communities. Their mobilization, then, becomes a powerful tool with which scholars can interpret the values of these ethnic and religious populations and how they defined their place in America. By looking at the Northern African American response to the war, for example, Joseph Reidy is able to demonstrate the powerful motivation of citizenship that blacks would not simply request but would take for themselves. Thus this book highlights the different and similar approaches that ethnic, religious, and racial communities took in their internal battle for citizenship during America's larger Civil War.[4]

Two key themes thread through this work to explain the actions of the groups under study, which include Irish, German, African, and Jewish Americans, as well as Native Americans. The first theme involves outside groups' efforts to obtain the full rights of citizenship; the second theme investigates their shared loyalties to the Union or to the Confederacy, as well as to their homelands. These two factors of citizenship and loyalty shaped outside groups' responses to the war, which evolved along with the conflict, sometimes sustaining while at others times challenging immigrants' and nonwhites' actions.

Concepts of citizenship and individuals' relationship with government were central to the Civil War. Even individuals born in the United States, such as free blacks, Native Americans, and the Catholic or Jewish children of immigrants, struggled to exercise rights stripped from them by legislation, court rulings, and the prejudices that defined the age. The guns of Sumter offered outside groups a unique opportunity to redefine their place in America, and many rushed into the contest. This was, after all, Meagher's message to his audience when he spoke of Irish soldiers "sealing their oath of American citizenship with their blood." The master orator portrayed men who took for themselves that most coveted American right, the one from which all other rights stemmed in the nineteenth century. Citizenship was the prize of the age, and nonwhites and immigrants recognized the opportunity this war offered them to stop requesting or insisting on their rights and to seize these for themselves.

This situation occasionally led to heated conflicts within the larger war. In his study *Minorities and the Military*, sociologist Warren Young observed that during hostilities, "minority-military service can take the theme of 'quid pro quo,' that is, full support of the war effort on the part of the minority and its leadership in return for full citizenship rights or other benefits for minority-group members."[5] The trouble with this, he observed, was that all sides did not always agree on what was expected in return for service. Governments and dominant social groups did not always wish to bestow the full rights of citizenship that minorities demanded, and minority communities did not always agree on what they sought through service. Miscommunication, accidental and purposeful, surfaced within ethnic and racial communities, and between them and the federal government, as they debated the rights and responsibilities of citizenship, including military service and a federal draft. Citizens and noncitizens waged this ideological struggle at home and on the battlefield, and that debate is key to scholars' understanding of this era.

"Loyalty," a word indicating constancy yet subject to various interpretations, is another thread woven through this collection. Like citizenship, loyalty is a central issue in any war, but it becomes more complex when one considers the experiences of outside groups. Most scholars accept that, as James McPherson argued, cause and comrades inspired Civil War soldiers to volunteer and to continue their fight. This does not, however, sufficiently explain the motivations of immigrant and nonwhite soldiers, whom McPherson noted were underrepresented in his study of Civil War soldier motivations in *For Cause and Comrades*.[6]

Many immigrant communities had shallow, if any, roots in the country in 1860, and the years immediately preceding the war, dominated by nativism, severely challenged their ties to America. Free and enslaved African Americans and native tribal groups had a longer history within the United States, but their relationship with the government was scarred by years of abuse, misunderstandings, and enslavement. Their troubled pasts in America put an entirely new twist on scholars' understanding of these Civil War soldiers' motivations and the experiences of their home front communities. Some responses to the war were shared between white and nonwhite or immigrant and native communities. They fought to preserve the Union or for the rights, limited though they were, that they enjoyed within the country. Others were defending a nation's right to break away from an abusive federal power. But every individual working in an Irish Catholic neighborhood, worshiping in a synagogue, or serving in a black regiment had a unique set of shared loyalties to their past and their present that influenced their response to the war. Scholars cannot apply the motivations of white native-born soldiers to all soldiers in the conflict. Nor should historians look at the ethnic responses to the war in isolation. Their responses are unique, but there are common traits between these outside groups. Our failure to carefully consider this created a major void in the historical understanding of the war, and *Civil War Citizens* seeks to fill it

To address these complexities, each chapter of this book focuses on a particular outside group responding to America's defining crisis. They have been selected because they were some of the largest immigrant or racial groups in the country (Irish Americans, German Americans, and Northern African Americans, for example) or because they are an understudied ethnic population in the Civil War era (Southern Jews and Native Americans). The largest immigrant groups of the age, Germans and Irish, had populations in the North and South that were significant enough in size to raise whole companies, regiments, and even brigades. Irish and German communities also wielded significant political power. President Abraham Lincoln recognized the sociopolitical influence that the 1.6 million Irish and 1.3 million German immigrants living in the United States could exert, along with their children, when he appointed ethnic generals like Franz Sigel and Thomas Francis Meagher.[7] While the majority of America's immigrant populations lived in the

North, the Southern cities of Charleston, Richmond, and New Orleans had sufficient Irish and German populations that single chapters on these unusually large ethnic populations would suffer from overgeneralizations. Thus this collection includes individual essays on Northern Irish and Southern Irish, as well as Northern German and Southern German communities and their responses to the war.

Susannah Ural's chapter on the Northern Irish Catholics' response to the war highlights the dual loyalties that ran through their communities. Every action was grounded in their ties to Ireland and their more tenuous links to America. They saw the war through these lenses and supported the Union cause when it supported their own interests. When that cause came to include emancipation and conscription, however, Irish Catholics largely abandoned the Union war effort, which they believed had abandoned them. David Gleeson shows similar motivations and responses among Irish men in the South. Here, however, Gleeson highlights the postwar influence of Irish Catholics on the "Lost Cause" and their success in placing their story into that myth. In both chapters, readers can see how Irish men, North and South, struggled to secure their place in America and to define for themselves their role as citizens.

Andrea Mehrländer and Stephen Engle found similar responses within the Southern and Northern German responses to the war. Mehrländer's chapter emphasizes the vast differences in communities' experiences as the focus shifts from Richmond to Charleston and to New Orleans. Economy and geography proved major factors in shaping the participation of Southern Germans in the war and their struggle to define that role. Stephen Engle highlights similar complexities in Northern German communities' responses. He notes, though, the greater political power that Northern Germans could wield due to their large populations that would not always unite but would come together when they believed that native-born whites were harming their communities. Like every group in this study, Germans mobilized in hostile and sometimes violent responses when they saw the Lincoln administration and its supporters infringing upon the rights Germans claimed for themselves.

In a book examining outside groups' reactions to this conflict, it is instructive to include a study of tribal groups that the United States actively placed in a position as outsiders. America's longest military struggle focused on the suppression of these groups, and Native Americans' efforts to protect their interests within a civil conflict offer fascinating insights into their communities. As contributor William McKee Evans notes, "In 1861, Native Americans . . . had few illusions about being on the winning side. . . . After the American victories [in the War of 1812], General [Andrew] Jackson . . . punished the pro-British Creeks by confiscating half of their lands . . . [and then he] confiscated half of the lands of the pro-American Creeks." Evans shows how the memory of such betrayals, not simply to the Creeks but to other tribal groups as well, influenced responses to the war. Focusing on the western Cherokee, the eastern Cherokee, and the Lumbee of North Carolina as case studies, Evans argues that Native Americans served to receive recruitment bounties or as hired substitutes, and "more than the white poor, they acted from pressure from some powerful patron or protector."

Free blacks were in a similar position to redefine their place and rights within the United States, not only as free men and women but also as those most closely linked by the color of their skin to the institution of slavery, as historian Edmund Morgan has argued. Like immigrants and Native Americans, free African Americans, who constituted 488,000 of the 4.4 million blacks in the United States in 1860, recognized the unique opportunity provided by the war to seize their rights as citizens.[8] As Joseph Reidy explains in his chapter, they defined citizenship in their own terms through their complex loyalties to the free black communities in which they lived, to the slave communities to which many Northern blacks had close ties, and to the dominant white society that influenced their lives.

In a chapter on the often-overlooked Southern Jewish experience in the Civil War, Robert Rosen offers insights into the ethnic and religious traditions of the United States and how Jews, especially in the South (historically viewed as intolerant of non-Protestant beliefs), adapted to the dominant traditions while preserving their heritage. He discusses their successes and failures in navigating the prejudices of the day and their ability to secure their own interests in such tumultuous times.

Taken together, these chapters present a wide variety of motivations linked to two key factors: loyalties shaped by ties to the Old World and the New, and each group's ability to secure the rights and powers of citizenship. While the United States was no longer a republic by 1860, its roots were firmly planted in that tradition, and the groups studied here were aware of that fact. Their motivations varied between and within communities as factions responded in different ways to the war. The pro-slavery Ridge Party, for example, chose to rapidly support the Confederacy (and increased its power by doing so), whereas the Cherokee National Council was far more hesitant to do so and lost power within the tribe. Similarly, "Gray" Germans in the North, most of whom were conservative Democrats, challenged the more radical "Green" German immigrants' support for the Republican Party, particularly its reform wing. Some Eastern Cherokee were more motivated by tribal loyalties than any ties to the Confederacy that they defended, just as some Irish Catholic volunteers fought more for Ireland than they did for the Union. The thread running through all their actions, however, links a desire to protect the community's interests while promoting their rights within the United States or the Confederacy.

Despite the racial and ethnic themes threading through this book, this is not a racial or ethnic history of the war, nor is it a traditional military history of the era. This book lays between the home front and the battlefield; between the dominant white traditions of nineteenth-century America and the minority communities that insisted on their place in that story. The authors offer insights into the complex motivations that shaped ethnic communities' responses to the Civil War and the impact these decisions had on them as well as the larger nation. Thus there is a significant racial and ethnic aspect to this book that is inextricably tied to an examination of cultures in conflict.

A Note on Sources

In each chapter, readers will note that specific individuals—usually leaders of the ethnic families, villages, and neighborhoods—often influenced a group's decisions and actions. The focus on leaders is due in part to the fact that some of these groups suffered from high rates of illiteracy, which makes the source base small. It is also the result, however, of the recognition that leaders spoke for their communities: as elected officials or as individuals that the community unofficially recognized as leaders, perhaps for their economic or other influence within the group. Whether politicians, tribal leaders, or even in some cases military officers (appointed for their political influence), they represented the will of the people. When they failed to do this, the community, tribe, or faction replaced them. Thus, this work embraces social historians' call for history from the bottom up while also recognizing the significant influence of community leaders on outside groups' responses in this conflict.

Similarly, newspapers are a common source utilized by the authors. Editors could not stay in business if they failed to address the interests of their communities. Thus when source materials are limited, racial and ethnic newspapers are a valuable measure of a group's hopes, fears, and frustrations. The authors also incorporate letters, diaries, and other traditional primary source material into this book to integrate the voices of less prominent members of these communities. Through intense research in consular records, church archives, tribal treaties and other negotiated agreements with local, state, and federal governments, newspapers, and private collections, the contributors reveal how the sometimes silent members of these ethnic groups supported the opinions more frequently expressed by their political, military, and social leaders.

NOTES

1. *Charleston Mercury*, September 11, 1861.
2. *New York Times*, August 30, 1861.
3. Ella Lonn, *Foreigners in the Union Army and Navy* (Baton Rouge: Louisiana State University Press, 1951); Lonn, *Foreigners in the Confederacy* (Chapel Hill: University of North Carolina Press, 1940); William L. Burton, *Melting Pot Soldiers: The Union's Ethnic Regiments* (New York: Fordham University Press, 1998); Walter Kamphoefner and Wolfgang Helbich, eds., *Germans in the Civil War: The Letters They Wrote Home*, trans. Susan Carter Vogel (Chapel Hill: University of North Carolina Press, 2006); Grace Palladino, *Another Civil War: Labor, Capital, and the State in Anthracite Regions of Pennsylvania, 1840–1868* (New York: Fordham University Press, 2006); Christian B. Keller, *Chancellorsville and the Germans: Nativism, Ethnicity, and Civil War Memory* (New York: Fordham University Press, 2007). Lawrence F. Kohl has edited a number of letter collections and memoirs written by Irish American soldiers. See his Irish in the Civil War series with Fordham University Press. Also, there have been excellent articles and essays on this subject over the last decade, such as Randall Miller's chapter "Catholic Religion, Irish Ethnicity, and the Civil War," in *Religion and the American Civil War*, ed. Randall M. Miller, Harry S. Stout, and Charles Reagan Wilson (New York: Oxford University Press, 1998); Kurt Hackemer's study of immigrant enlistment patterns in Kenosha County, Wisconsin; and Russell Johnson's work on the impact of Civil War military service in Dubuque, Iowa. All the authors in this volume have contributed to the historiography of race and ethnicity in the Civil War era.

4. Total U.S. population in 1860 was 31.4 million. Four million immigrants are included in that total, approximately 500,000 free African Americans, and at least 40,000 Native Americans tallied in the 1860 census, though that number is far undercounted due to census-taking methods and definitions at the time. *Population of the United States in 1860; Compiled from the Original Returns of the 8th Census, under the Direction of the Secretary of the Interior,* by Joseph C. G. Kennedy, Superintendent of Census (Washington, DC: Government Printing Office, 1864), 598–99.

5. Warren L. Young, *Minorities and the Military: A Cross-National Study in World Perspective* (Westport, CT: Greenwood Press, 1982), 255.

6. James M. McPherson, *For Cause and Comrades: Why Men Fought in the Civil War* (New York: Oxford University Press, 1998).

7. Campbell J. Gibson and Emily Lennon, "Table 4: Region and Country of Area of Birth of the Foreign-born Population, with Geographic Detail Show in Decennial Census Publications of 1930 or Earlier: 1850 to 1930 and 1960 to 1990," in "Historical Census Statistics on the Foreign-born Population of the United States: 1850-1990," Population Division Working Paper No. 29, U.S. Bureau of the Census, Washington, D.C., February 1999, http://www.census.gov/population/www/documentation/twps0029/tab04.html (updated January 18, 2001).

8. Campbell Gibson and Kay Jung, "Table 1: United States—Race and Hispanic Origin: 1790 to 1990," in "Historical Census Statistics on Population Totals by Race, 1790 to 1990, and by Hispanic Origin, 1970 to 1990, for the United States, Regions, Divisions, and States," Population Division Working Paper Series No. 56, U.S. Bureau of the Census, Washington, D.C. September 2002, http://www.census.gov/population/documentation/twps0056/tab01.pdf.

YANKEE DUTCHMEN

Germans, the Union, and the
Construction of a Wartime Identity

Stephen D. Engle

For all the debate about states' rights and slavery being the cause of the American Civil War, the actual conflict was fought between military communities, no matter how large or small, no matter what their ethnic complexion. "This is essentially a People's contest," explained Abraham Lincoln in his July 1861 message to Congress. As such, immigrants, along with their fellow Americans, needed to embrace the notion that they were preserving a Union that was favorable to their plight, and perhaps in some way make inroads into establishing themselves as more acceptable to Americans. As Phillip Shaw Paludan so wonderfully argues in his work *"A People's Contest": The Union and Civil War, 1861–1865*, Northerners came to understand the meaning of the Union more substantively. Never before had Americans participated in such a cause that forced them to travel more miles, over more landscapes, endure more hardships, and meet more people of ethnically diverse backgrounds than in the years of the Civil War. By joining the military, Northerners came to appreciate more fully the ethnically diverse nature of their Union. In some cases, such exposure to other groups during the war affected the way native-born Americans saw themselves.[1]

Because the war created small military communities at the regimental level that reflected the Northern population, it was no surprise that Americans were more likely to come into contact with Germans because of their presence in the military. While most Germans in the United States would agree that they were as uniquely different as were Americans (or any other ethnic group) and had yet to develop any singular "German identity," Americans nonetheless typically perceived them as the same ethnically because the sole characteristic binding Germans to one another was language. Whether the war forced Anglo-Americans to accept or reject the ethnically diverse society they discovered in the ranks, those soldiers serving to preserve the Union at least came to recognize, because of the presence of their German comrades, that they were living in an ethnically diverse society, even if their views about the Germans did not change the kind of Union they wanted to preserve.[2]

Of all the ethnic groups that dotted the American landscape before the Civil War, none were more "generally distributed over the United States as were the Germans," noted Ella Lonn in her seminal work *Foreigners in the Union Army and Navy.*[3] Whether Germans settled into urban communities or the rural confines of states, by 1861 they had made a distinct impression on certain regions of the Northern landscape, adding significantly to the color and character of American culture. Wherever they resided, their customs, language, and cultural traditions stood out distinctly and, in many respects, provided Americans with their first exposure to ethnic difference, largely because it was the first time many Americans heard a language other than English. James Bergquist notes, for example, that the nineteenth-century Germans "were one of the most successful ethnic groups in establishing a tangible presence in American cities that went beyond a mere collection of institutions to advance ethnicity and became instead a community in the fullest sense." Few Americans recognized the diversity within German communities that included Catholics, Lutherans, Reformed, Jewish, Freethinkers, old settlers, newcomers, farmers, artisans, businessmen, or simple laborers. Most Americans saw them as ethnically different first and foremost because of language.[4]

By 1861, Germans who had felt the need to belong to a German community had established German neighborhoods in many American cities. Whether in New York, Philadelphia, Cincinnati, St. Louis, or Milwaukee, *Kleindeutschlands* (Little Germanies) had become a significant and influential feature of the North, particularly in the urban areas. New York's *Kleindeutschland* was the third-largest German-speaking community in the world behind Berlin and Vienna and was the first of the large ethnic urban settlements that came to distinguish American cities in the antebellum period. In Cincinnati, St. Louis, and Milwaukee, Germans constituted roughly one-third of the population. Other Northern cities such as Baltimore, Chicago, Indianapolis, and Buffalo absorbed sizable portions of America's German population; these Germans typically segregated themselves into ethnic neighborhoods, which more often than not were "more uniform in their origins than they were in the blocks they inhabited."[5] This urban concentration of Germans quite often gave them a "disproportionate weight in many important centers of population and industry." Fredrika Bremer, for example, described Milwaukee, or "German Town," before the war as a place where "one sees German houses, German inscriptions over the doors or signs, German physiognomies." "Here are published German newspapers," she added, "and many Germans live here who never learn English, and seldom go beyond the German town."[6] Noted British reporter Edward Dicey, on assignment in America while walking the streets of New York City's *Kleindeutschland,* observed the same characteristics of the German population, concluding that the Germans in that city "evidently [retain] the strongest individuality of any foreign class."[7]

Other than New York, Milwaukee, and St. Louis, Cincinnati was perhaps the most German of all cities in the Civil War era. Strolling the streets of Cincinnati in the spring of 1862, Dicey remarked that what struck him most about the "Queen City of the West," or "Over the Rhine" (as the Germans called it), was "the German air of the place and people." It was hard to believe, he observed, "that you were not in some city of the old German vaterland." Indeed, at least one-third of Cincinnati's roughly 70,000 residents were German. "Almost everybody that you meet is speaking in the harsh, guttural, German accents," remarked Dicey. "The women, with their squat, stout figures, their dull blue eyes, and fair flaxen hair, sit knitting at their doors, dressed in the stuffed woollen petticoats of the German fashion," he noted, and "the men have still the woollen jackets, the blue worsted pantaloons, and the low-crowned hats one knows so well in Bavaria and Tyrol." Here the old country prevailed. "There are *'Bier Gartens,' 'Restaurations,'* and *'Tanz Saale,'* on every side," noted Dicey. "There are German operas, German concerts, and half a dozen German theaters," and it was "here, in the free West, the Germans have asserted their right to spend Sunday as they like; and so 'across the Rhine,' the dancing gardens are open, and the *Turner* Feasts take place, and the first representations of the opera are given on Sunday as in their native land."[8] Still, Dicey noticed perceptively that despite this strong German identity in Cincinnati, "the German element was being merged in the American."[9]

One of the distinguishing features of this assimilation or "merging," as Dicey called it, was the presence in these German neighborhoods of the German American Turnvereine. In the tradition of Friedrich Ludwig Jahn's work in Germany, these organizations were not only geared toward gymnastics and physical education but also served as "vehicles for German immigrants to continue their cultural endeavors" in America. They provided Germans outside of Germany with a local channel for maintaining their cultural heritage while embracing American culture and customs. The leaders of the Turnerbund (National Coordinating Organization) encouraged political activism and, by the time of the Civil War, had been responsible for encouraging Germans to engage in the political culture, join the Republican Party, and vote for Abraham Lincoln. Living abroad, Germans could espouse their disdain for politics in Germany without fear of persecution, while the Civil War provided them a chance to express their patriotism for the Union.[10]

When the war broke out, the approximately 150 Turnvereine were instrumental in marshaling and organizing Germans for the Union army. Inspired to serve by the Turnerbund, Turners were among the first Germans to volunteer. Within days of President Lincoln's call for 75,000 volunteers, German Turners from Philadelphia, Louisville, Baltimore, Boston, Cincinnati, Indianapolis, Kansas City, St. Louis, and other cities enlisted to support the Union army. In Cincinnati alone, some 300 Turners from across the state came together in a few days and formed the Ohio Turner Regiment, officially known as the 9th Ohio Volunteer Infantry. In his work on the German Turners, Eugene Miller argues that the day after Lincoln's call for volunteers, some 2,000 Kentucky Germans crossed the Ohio River into Cincinnati and volunteered for the army. In Chicago, more than 100 Turners organized the Turner Union Cadets shortly after President Lincoln's call for volunteers, and in New York, Turners immediately came together and formed the 20th New York (Turnerschuetzenregiment, or Turner Rifles) led by Max Weber. Members of the Turnvereine in St. Louis followed suit and formed the Westliches Turnerregiment, officially known as the 17th Missouri Volunteers. Although Carl Wittke argued that in 1861 some 10,000 Germans were members of Turnvereine in America and that between 5,000 and 6,000 men enlisted in the military, Annette Hofmann contends that the number was considerably lower. Yet, the significance of their presence in the Union army was more important to the German community than the numbers of Turners who enlisted, as expressed by one German Turner who acknowledged "the spirit of 1848 has once more awakened."[11]

Although Bruce Levine suggests that in 1860 "the average German immigrant was almost three and a half times as likely as the average U.S. Citizen to live in one of the country's major cities," many Germans tended to settle on rural lands and earned their livelihood from tilling the soil, as Kathleen

Neils Conzen has observed in her work on nineteenth-century Germans. Traveling through rural villages of Indiana before the war, an Austrian tourist recalled that he journeyed sixty to eighty miles through an area he recalled was "inhabited . . . exclusively by Germans."[12] The small Hoosier village of Ferdinand, he remarked, was "a completely Catholic German village protected and governed by the church that crowns the hilltop."[13] Rural Germans, noted Conzen, typically settled on lands that gave them not only economic and social independence but also easy access to markets, as well as access to nearby German settlements.[14]

More recently, Christian Keller has contributed to our understanding of the rural German populace in Pennsylvania. Keller argues that Germans who had migrated to that region in the eighteenth century had established farming communities and distinct identities as the "Pennsylvania Dutch" apart from those Germans who arrived in the decades before the Civil War. "The urban world of 'Gemütlichkeit,' of beer gardens, voluntary societies, and the Turnverein," notes Keller, "held no appeal for the rural-dwelling Dutch, who felt no bond with the immigrant Germans."[15]

Like their American counterparts, the bulk of the Germans who joined the rank and file of Union soldiers came from the farming and laboring classes. Pulled to the United States by the hope of economic opportunity, thousands of Germans had departed the fatherland years before the war and had managed to establish a cultural identity in their newfound communities. As William Burton insightfully observes in his classic work *Melting Pot Soldiers: The Union's Ethnic Regiments*, it was not the radical, the intellectual, or the political leader but Germans like Nikolas Greusel of Aurora, Illinois, who made up the bulk of German Americans who came into the Union ranks. Greusel had migrated to America with his parents in 1834 and at the time of the Civil War was working for the Chicago, Burlington, and Quincy Railroad.[16]

From these German urban enclaves and farm communities came enthusiastic volunteers eager to join the Union army and become part of the cause. Many of the Germans who arrived in the North prior to the conflict were of military age and without jobs; they believed that life in America meant freedom, and life in the army meant full citizenship, which was attractive since it was financially worthwhile to enlist. Karl Wesslau of New York, for example, boasted to his family during the war that "these are very good times for people in Germany who want to come over here, it's easy enough to find well-paid employment."[17] Obviously, the reasons for enlistment in the Union army were as varied for Germans as for any group, but many Germans desired some degree of assimilation and considered the military an opportunity to provide a bridge toward that goal. Hoosier commander August Willich, for example, wrote to the *Freie Presse von Indiana* shortly after the War Department had authorized Governor Oliver P. Morton to form an all-German regiment from Indiana. Willich argued that military service would provide Germans the opportunity to "really prove that they are not foreigners, and that they know how to protect their new republican homeland against the aristocracy of the South."[18]

German enlistees typically felt a strong sense of comradeship among themselves, despite religious, economic, and political differences. The opportunity to participate in a great contest stirred the interest and excitement of Germans, particularly those who had been cast aside, rejected, or defeated during the German revolutions of 1848–49. The war inspired Germans to express a loyalty to their adopted country and, by their military participation, provide a manifestation of their strong allegiance to the kind of republic many had hoped to establish in Germany. In their wonderfully rich collection of edited and translated German letters entitled *Germans in the Civil War: The Letters They Wrote Home*, Walter D. Kamphoefner and Wolfgang Helbich observed that the "immigrants' opinions on Americans issues were closely tied to their democratic aspirations for Germany and the rest of Europe."[19] Fritz Anneke of Wisconsin represented the typical attitude of the German Forty-Eighter volunteer in urging his fellow German Badgers to join the Union army and take part in a "second fight for freedom."[20] Albert Krause, who left Germany in the summer of 1861, concurred, writing to his family in July that, "as far as I am concerned, I am off to the fire filled with courage and enthusiasm." "The United States have taken me in," he confided, "I have earned a living here, and why shouldn't I defend them, since they are in danger, with my flesh and blood?!" "I don't want to go back to Germany," he continued, "I have tasted freedom, and it tastes too good to trade it in again for a dungeon. I don't think I could take it there for even one day, I would feel too miserable.— Long live freedom!"[21]

Germans were like other foreign-born enlistees, sensitive to the fact that their newfound freedoms in America were now bound to the successful preservation of the Union. Whether they were from the city or the farm, when the conflict erupted in April 1861, Germans considered the war an opportunity to demonstrate their deep affection for their adopted home and its constitutional freedoms. For those who had fled Germany out of fear of political persecution or simply to find new economic opportunities in America, the war heightened their awareness of the kinship that existed between people and place. Corporal Ludwig Kühner of Ohio perhaps said it best, writing to his brother in 1861 that although it was hard to leave his wife and children and march into battle, "there's nothing else we can do if we want to preserve freedom for ourselves and our children."[22] As Germans had loved the fatherland, now the time had come to demonstrate their love for their new home. In the process, many hoped to advance their status in the American mainstream. As Edward Dicey put it, the names of Franz Sigel, Carl Schurz, and John Fremont were as important to the Germans in this cause as Jefferson, Hamilton, and Madison had been to the War of Independence. "They [the Germans] are attached to the Union," he noted, "because it secures the prosperity and development of their new country, and because it has proved a good Government to them, or rather has allowed them the unwonted privilege of governing themselves."[23]

Like the American press, the German newspapers that chronicled the daily lives of their countrymen rarely spoke with one voice, but their editors influenced readers by reasoning that preserving the Union was synonymous with preserving American freedoms. Although race was not typical among the reasons to volunteer among Germans, the German press translated the war into a political and noble cause, and as such German American intellectuals and political, civic, and journalistic leaders took the lead in helping to promote this feeling within the German community. "America and its people are the vanguard of the great mission of the nineteenth century," proclaimed the *St. Louis Westliche Post* in May; "on its flags are written the magic formula of the future, which is 'Liberty and Fraternity for all Free People.'"[24]

Naturally, some Germans distinguished themselves as leaders either by group association, such as the Turners or the Forty-Eighters, or simply by using their pens, their political status, or their military experience. Among them were community leaders, shopkeepers, craftsmen, teachers, doctors, farmers, intellectuals, journalists, and old revolutionaries from the 1848–49 German revolutions collectively known as the Forty-Eighters. In many cities where German Turner Societies abounded, their members volunteered en masse. Because an inordinate proportion of Germans who had fought in the

German revolutions of 1848–49 came to America to escape political persecution and had become leaders in their respective communities, they, too,
found themselves on the forefront of encouraging Germans to participate
in the war effort. As members of the Lincoln administration reached out to
immigrant communities, these prominent revolutionaries were some of the
first Lincoln contacted. For his work in the development of the Republican
Party in Wisconsin and in advancing the German votes for Lincoln in 1860,
Carl Schurz was appointed minister to Spain. Other political and social leaders, including Friedrich Hecker, Franz Sigel, Adolphus Engelmann, August
Willich, Friedrich Kapp, Rudolph Lexow, Oswald Ottendorfer, Henry and
Joseph Kircher, Caspar Butz, and Gustave Körner, would follow similar paths
to prominence.[25]

Despite the feeling of union in the early spring of 1861, the Northern states
remained a place of ethnic distinctions. Germans could not escape this, and
in some cases refused to abandon their cultural distinctions. Chicago busi-
nessman Johann Dieden, for example, wrote to his family before the war that
"the Germans in the United States, as I wrote earlier, have been winning more
and more honor and fame in the last several years [because of German cultural organizations] and since the revolution in Germany in 1848, the position
of the Germans in the United States has really improved remarkably, since
in that year many intelligent and educated people left the old fatherland."
He added that "despite all the efforts of the educated Germans to promote
Germanness here, there still are some who, as soon as they have become a
bit used to things, want to throw off everything that's German probably just
because they don't want to be a *Dutshman* [*sic*]." "All in all," he concluded,
"they [Americans] don't distinguish between different German nationalities in
a foreign land, here there are no Prussians, Austrians, Bavarians, Hanoverians,
or Hessians anymore—but only Germans." He noted that while Americans
were quick to misjudge the "shy, undemanding, modest outward appearance
of the Germans," they were still at a disadvantage, he argued, because they
had the terrible habit of "criticizing what someone knows or does."[26]

Yet, the fact that some Germans had mastered the English language did not
negate the fact that some still spoke limited English, and with a coarse accent,
and their manners and customs could hardly go undetected by Americans.
Their visibility was made more acute by the perception that the one thing
they all had in common was their love of *bier*. As Roger Daniels argues in his

excellent work, *Coming to America: A History of Immigration and Ethnicity in American Life*, "it is true that saloons and beer gardens, where families went to drink beer, socialize, and listen to music, proliferated in German American neighborhoods and cities."[27] In Cincinnati alone in 1860, "there were two thousand places where drinks were sold . . . more than one for every hundred residents."[28] Publicly, Germans' cultural distinctions easily identified them as foreigners despite how long they had lived in the United States; for example, their attitude toward drinking beer was, in Daniels's view, "one of the crucial points of friction between Germans and some of their neighbors, between continental and Puritan ways of spending a Sunday, between a relaxed attitude toward alcohol and a crusade against it."[29] In his work *Chancellorsville and the Germans*, Christian Keller agrees that Germans considered beer "a necessity of life." Because German units were allowed beer in their camps (while most regiments were not), Keller argues that "once word spread that a certain German regiment had a new supply of beer, soldiers from every division in the army would suddenly descend on the Germans and drink beer with them."[30]

Their sizable population and visibility in society made Germans appear to Anglo-Americans perhaps more politically powerful than they were in the mainstream political culture. In 1860, out of a total of 31.2 million Americans, the census recorded 1,301,136 native-born Germans living in the United States, with 1,229,144 Germans residing in the Northern states (more than three-quarters of the German population lived in New York, New Jersey, Pennsylvania, Ohio, Illinois, Indiana, Michigan, Wisconsin, and Iowa), and some 200,000 living in the border states of Missouri, Delaware, Maryland, and Kentucky. The remaining 71,992 Germans lived in the states that formed the Confederacy. Moreover, during the war years, 1861–65, it is estimated that an additional 100,000 Germans migrated to the United States. Indeed, the *New York Times* reported in October 1864 that Germans abroad were worried about the decline in their population so much so that books and newspapers attempted to portray the horrors of American society due to the war. Although they were not the largest immigrant group in the United States in 1860, the Germans constituted the largest foreign-born group in the Union army; historians have estimated that between 180,000 and 216,000 German soldiers appear on the muster rolls.[31]

While the census numbers reveal that Germans joined the military in large numbers in 1861, their ethnicity made those numbers appear disproportionately high. Although some historians have observed that German Protestants entered the Union military in larger numbers than German Catholics, Walter Kamphoefner and Wolfgang Helbich take the view that this was partly because "Republican immigrants enlisted more eagerly in the Union army than did Democrats."[32] Most historians would agree that Catholics were more committed to the Democratic Party, which might explain why in some states with large German populations, such as Indiana, so few Germans enlisted. The perception existed among Northerners (and many Southerners) that the Northern armies contained large numbers of Germans in their ranks, in part because the military brought more Americans into contact with more Germans than ever before. Although most of the Germans were foot soldiers, many were assigned to the artillery and engineering units, and many were officers, which gave them a higher profile in the eyes of Americans than in the society from which they came. The fact that many Southerners possessed antiforeign feelings toward immigrants, and in particular toward the Germans, no doubt led many Confederates to believe that there were more Germans in the ranks than there actually were. St. Louis, Missouri, for example, had a population of 160,733, and the Germans constituted more than one-third of that city's population, which were, in many cases concentrated into regiments and scattered throughout the army.[33]

Many of the German units came from the same American cities and neighborhoods and shared essentially the same values, experiences, and historical memories. These shared experiences, coupled with the shared fervor to preserve the Union, served to strengthen unit cohesion, which frequently led Germans to self-segregate their units from American units and rename them with German titles. Many Germans insisted on forming their own companies and regiments and carried the individual flags of their homeland along with the Union flag into battle. This military cohesion reflected a similar degree of cohesiveness in their communities. The editor of the *Providence Daily Journal* cited an example of this patriotic fervor among the Germans, acknowledging that the intelligent German engravers and lithographic printers at the H. F. Wallings Map Establishment in New York simply decided to enlist en masse (including the girls in charge of the editing room), so much so that it crippled the business.[34]

Those Germans who wanted to segregate themselves from Americans did so in part, and understandably, because they feared nativist hostility in the ranks, and in part because with their military skill and education they considered themselves better suited to command soldiers and had contempt for American military officers. Although a Philadelphia schoolteacher, Carl Hermanns nonetheless encouraged his sister Laura to come to America because he was "truly satisfied" to be in America and argued that "the Germans are always the ones who are the most honest and fight the best, and the bravest fighter of all is the German General Major [Franz] Sigel."[35]

Though German soldiers in the Union army wanted to fight to preserve the Union, many wanted to fight under a commander who understood their German traditions. A reporter for the *Illinois Staats-Zeitung* summarized the sentiment of the Illinois Germans when he wrote that it had been the contention of his readers that a German corps needed to be organized under German leadership because they believed that "many more Germans would share in the struggle, [and] that the unity of the command would attain greater results."[36] William Burton argued that Chicago Germans such as Caspar Butz, George Schneider, Anton Hesing, and Lorenzo Brentano came to believe in this notion of unity and greater results, and made efforts to organize a German unit and pressured Illinois governor Richard Yates to adopt the idea. So voluminous were the petitions to support the all-German unit that Governor Yates was forced to employ a German-speaking translator to handle the correspondence. But the idea of all-German units was common to several Northern cities with sizable German populations. The all-German Milwaukee 26th Wisconsin Infantry, for example, led by Colonel William Jacobs, named itself the "Sigel Regiment," after Franz Sigel, or "Unser Deutches Regiment" (Our German Regiment). Ludwig Blenker at one point even decided to rename his German 5th Division of the Mountain Department "Blenker's Division." Such distinctions heightened the presence of the Germans fighting for the Union; indeed, signs that read "German Spoken Here" further sharpened perceptions of these distinctions.[37]

Perhaps the most distinguished group among the Germans in the Civil War were the Forty-Eighters, who were extremely articulate, highly visible, and colorful intellectual leaders who took up pen, political gauntlet, and in some cases the bayonet to influence their countrymen. It was in this group of Germans, according to Wilhelm Kaufmann, that "there was far more German self-consciousness . . . than in the other German immigrants."[38]

These "Greens," as they were dubbed, were zealous reformers who were appalled by and critical of America's political and cultural life, and who, in Ella

Lonn's estimation, were "determined to remake the world and who thought to begin by making the United States the center of a world of republics." These "Greens" came in conflict with the older, more established Germans, known as "Grays," who had emigrated to America before 1848 and typically settled into farming in Ohio, Illinois, Missouri, and Wisconsin. Known as "Latin Farmers," because these German farmers were also interested in education and politics, the "Grays" viewed the newcomers as youthful, but reckless, zealots who might instigate trouble for them. As both groups of Germans became more politically active in the years before the Civil War, many viewed the Democratic Party as the friend of the immigrant. The rise of the Republican Party posed a serious challenge to the ethnic allegiance to the Democrats, and as they fought off nativist tendencies, many of the Forty-Eighters became political activists for the new party inside and outside the German community. Still, as Martin Öfele, in his excellent study of German officers of black troops, correctly cautions, "Despite the Forty-eighter's highly articulate visibility, one must be careful not to overemphasize their impact on German-American identity building and their ability to shape ethnic public opinion in favor of Lincoln."[39]

Although many Germans were concentrated in the urban areas and formed whole units in which only German was spoken, and because they wanted to fight alongside their native comrades, most Germans came from small communities where their numbers were too few to constitute an entire regiment. Thus, the bulk of the Germans served in units in which they we outnumbered by their American counterparts. Nonetheless, it must be noted that even in the most recent work that examines ethnic groups in the Civil War, Dean Mahin disclaims in his book *The Blessed Place of Freedom: Europeans in Civil War America*, that "there is no precise definition of a 'German' regiment and no agreement on the number of such regiments or the number of Germans who served in them."[40]

This fact has been true since scholarly research began on the Germans in the Civil War. In her prodigious yet often criticized study, Lonn confessed that it was "discouraging to the scholar when he has to admit that despite the most laborious research, no claim can be made for complete accuracy of the data presented."[41] Like any Civil War unit, according to Lonn, "the personnel of companies and regiments was constantly being changed by death, resignation, expiration of term of enlistment, and the addition of new recruits."[42] In

1869, Benjamin A. Gould of the U.S. Sanitary Commission published a statistical study, which concluded that more Germans served in the Union army than any other foreign-born group, and that the ratio calculated that one in every five soldiers was of German descent. Still, the best estimates suggest that at least 125 (and perhaps as many as 145) units (militia, regiments, batteries, cavalry, companies, etc.) in the Union army were composed of all, or nearly all, German soldiers. The cumulative estimation of the relevant studies cited suggests that seventeen states contributed German units to the Union's war effort: New York (24 units), Missouri (18 units), Illinois (18 units), Ohio (15 units), Wisconsin (13 units), Indiana (6 units), Pennsylvania (6 units), Minnesota (4 units), Kentucky (4 units), New Jersey (3 units), Iowa (3 units), Connecticut (3 units), Massachusetts (2 units), Maryland (2 units), Kansas (2 units), West Virginia (1 unit), and Texas (1 unit). These mostly German regiments accounted for 20 to 25 percent of the Germans in the Union army.[43]

In their work *Germans in the Civil War*, Kamphoefner and Helbich provide an insightful analysis of German recruitment among the states based upon Gould's statistics and Wilhelm Kaufmann's pioneering study, *Die Deutschen im amerikanischen Bürgerkrieg*. They note that Germans in New York and Pennsylvania showed rather high recruitment quotas, "despite largely Democratic affiliations," but the states of Indiana, Iowa, and Michigan, where there were mainly rural Democratic populations, produced few German soldiers, when compared with their German populations. Recently arrived Germans, they argue, particularly those arriving to eastern seaboard cities, had a higher recruitment percentage, as in the case of the Germans in New England, New Jersey, Delaware, and the District of Columbia, than those who had been here a few years. Missouri Germans were the strongest Republican supporters, Kamphoefner and Helbich observe; therefore, it is not surprising that they also had far and away the highest level of Union army participation. The fact that Franz Sigel was also located in St. Louis at the beginning of the war was certainly a factor in attracting recruits to the Union in that critical border state. It is not surprising that slave states such as Kentucky and Maryland, where the Republican Party had made little progress in attracting Germans, had the smallest number proportionally of Germans in the ranks. Of all the Union states, however, Kamphoefner and Helbich see Wisconsin—the most German state in the Union—as the anomaly in German military participation. Although the Badger Germans "outnumbered those in Missouri by 40 percent, and made up twice as large a share of their state's population, they supplied half as many troops."[44] To help explain some of these anomalies, Kamphoefner and Helbich conclude, "There can be no doubt that political affiliation weighed heavily in such varying enthusiasm for the Union cause."[45]

Some of the more prominent German units that fought for the Union included the 24th Illinois Infantry, known as the Hecker Jäger Regiment for Friedrich Hecker, and the 82nd Illinois Infantry, also commanded for a time by Hecker. Both of these regiments were drawn from the Chicago area. The 43rd Illinois Infantry, known as the Körner Regiment in honor of Gustave Körner, who helped raise the regiment, was drawn from downstate Illinois in the Belleville–East St. Louis area. Adolphus Engelmann, Körner's brother-in-law, took over command of the regiment at Shiloh when its colonel was killed. His letters home are among the most voluminous and most insightful of any German's in the war. Although more than half of Indiana's immigrants were German, and Indianapolis was the center of the largest German population, the state mustered in surprisingly few German units, in part because of politics and discontentment with the war aims or commanders. Yet, among the most distinguished of all German regiments in the war was the 32nd Indiana, made up from Germans across the Hoosier State and commanded for a time by the colorful Forty-Eighter August Willich, who led the regiment at the Battle of Shiloh, April 6–7, 1862. The 32nd Indiana and its colonel went on to have a distinguished career in the war. With the largest German population in the United States, New York of course had the most German units, and certainly one of the most notorious.[46]

As William Burton concluded in *Melting Pot Soldiers*, of all the New York regiments, Louis (Ludwig) Blenker's "First German Rifles," or the 8th New York Regiment, was the most infamous of all German units in the war and one that fostered a negative persona from which Germans could hardly escape. When journalist Dicey visited Blenker's camp in 1862, he noted that the unit was "filled with the black sheep of every nation under the sun," and that commands "had to be given in four different languages."[47] This regiment was known for its disreputable manner and conduct; its looting drew the attention and wrath of the German and American press and bore a legacy that significantly outlasted its tour of duty, as did the unit's commander. In early 1862, for example, the editor of an Anglo-American newspaper, the *St. Paul Pioneer and Democrat*, was so upset by the perception Blenker had created of the Germans that he wrote an article defaming the commander and eulogizing Sigel. While the "Germans of the whole country almost adore Gen. Sigel," he declared, "a large number of their prominent organs bitterly denounce General Blenker," and there were "curious doings in his command."[48] He made it clear that Sigel, as commander of the revolutionary forces, had been so disgusted by Blenker's activities during the German revolutions of 1848 that at one point he dispatched an order "depriving him [Blenker] of all his command, declared him to be a 'cowardly plunderer and traitor to his country' and authorized anybody to arrest him at once and bring him to headquarters."[49] The perceptions of this unit no doubt contributed to the negative perceptions of all Germans in the army. As Kaufmann observed, Germans "would have liked to have had a fine, educated German officer as a leader of the sole German division." "The fact that Blenker received that rank," Kaufmann concluded, "negatively influenced the role that our people were called to play in the Civil War."[50]

Cincinnati Germans, mostly Turners, were the first to organize a regiment in Ohio as the 9th Ohio, which initially, and surprisingly, was commanded by non-German-speaking Robert McCook; the unit's command was later given to August Willich. Alexander von Schimmelfennig, a noted Forty-Eighter, commanded the 74th Pennsylvania made up mostly of Pittsburgh Germans and won notoriety for his role at the Battle of Gettysburg in 1863. Forty-Eighter Franz Sigel inspired the Missouri Germans, some 31,000 strong, and when the members of the 3rd Missouri Infantry mustered into service, they chose Sigel as their leader, commencing his long but controversial stint as commander. Sigel's admirers would come to sing "I fights mit Sigel," and the German press and German communities throughout the North followed closely his rise to the rank of brigadier general.[51]

Many of the German regiments were in brigades and divisions commanded by German officers. Dean Mahin has identified at least seventy Germans who were regimental commanders and ten Germans who, excepting Carl Schurz, rose from the rank of colonel to general, including Ludwig Blenker, Henry Bohlen, August, V. Kautz, Karl L. Matthies, Peter Osterhaus, Frederick Salomon, Alexander Schimmelfennig, Franz Sigel, Adolph Wilhelm August von Steinwehr, and August Willich. The largest and most prominent unit of Germans in the war was by far the 11th Corps of the Army of the Potomac. In a broader sense, no other unit in the Union army provided more Americans with more exposure to ethnic difference than did the 11th Corps, in large measure because of the language difference. Most recently, Mark Dunkelman has done some fine work with the 154th New York Infantry Regiment and the 11th Corps. Known throughout the army as the ethnic unit (it was supposedly composed of mainly German Americans as fifteen of the twenty-eight infantry regiments were primarily German), the 11th Corps had a relatively undistinguished history in the war, as a corps that was routed at the battles at Chancellorsville and Gettysburg. Indeed, after the Union defeat at Chancellorsville some Northern papers considered the entire Union debacle the fault of the Germans and "talked of shooting the entire Corps." The Germans of this corps, noted Ella Lonn years ago, "were condemned as a worthless lot, coming from the scum of a vicious population."[52]

Dunkelman's work on the 154th Infantry, which was assigned to the 11th Corps, provides a window into the experiences of a native-born regiment serving in the noted "Dutch Corps." His work reveals that there were indeed ethnic tensions among the men and that these tensions were "an internal problem as well as an external problem for the Eleventh Army Corps."[53] He examines the prejudices against the Germans from other units outside the corps as the "outsider outfit that had never fought alongside the older troops" and the routine frustration of Americans of having to serve with Germans who spoke with coarse accents and had very different cultural manners, which Dunkelman illustrates "had a negative effect on the unit's esprit de corps and morale."[54] Yet, so significant was this unit's esprit de corps that when General Carl Schurz endeavored to obtain the command of the Germans in the corps and to have them ordered to Kentucky, General Adolph von Steinwehr wrote to General Oliver O. Howard, the commander of the 11th Corps, that "neither myself nor the Germans under my Command have any desire to be detached from this Corps."[55]

In this same vein, Christian Keller offers an insightful analysis of the Germans of the 11th Corps, arguing that the Battle of Chancellorsville "has always been considered a watershed for German-Americans." "The attack and rout of the Eleventh Corps by Confederate General [Thomas J.] 'Stonewall' Jackson's flanking columns late in the afternoon and evening of May 2, 1863," he contends, "set the stage for the strongest nativist and anti-German backlash since the rise of the Know Nothing Party in the previous decade."[56] According to Keller, "It is not an exaggeration to say that the North's German-born population never got over what happened in the Virginia woods in May 1863"; he argues that this battle brought all Germans closer together as they "suddenly lost their ardor for the war and began to look to one another for support rather than a Union which seemed to despise them and disdain them for their sacrifices."[57] In describing the months following the battle, Keller reconstructs "how and why Chancellorsville became the key event of the nineteenth century for the nation's largest ethnicity," pointing out that the American reaction to Germans "heightened their ethnic consciousness of ethnic identity at the expense of Americanization."[58]

Yet the debate over the precise number of whole German units overlooks the real significance of the ethnic dimensions of the Civil War for the Germans. For all their efforts in fighting to preserve the Union, Germans, who fought in many of the major battles quite often seemed to be on the receiving end of considerable prejudice, in large measure because Americans linked the performance of these Germans in battle to what they thought of Germans in general. Sometimes this criticism was deserved and sometimes it was undeserved, yet in the end Germans typically came to be known as the "Damned Dutch," a degeneracy of Deutsche (German). It was not surprising that the German officers, and later ethnic historians, often praised lower-ranked comrades, arguing that the Germans "gave to the army a conservative, stabilizing force," and that they were "patient, philosophical, plodding men" who were "well disciplined, persevering, and inspired by some idealism," and while "slow in response," were nonetheless "solid in battle."[59] Indeed, when compared with American soldiers, for whom Germans occasionally expressed contempt, some Germans came to believe themselves "generally far more faithful, conscientious and zealous than the native-born American," as did, for example, Gottfried Rentschler of the 6th Kentucky. "The German soldier," he remarked, "is obedient and loyal to duty without regard to reward or punishment."[60]

Naturally, Germans were apprehensive about nativism among Anglo-Americans and Anglo-American concerns about German Catholics and Freethinkers, as well as beer drinkers. It was hard not to be, since Germans had been among the targets of the semisecret nativist Know-Nothing movement to alienate them years before by discriminating against them in the workplace, the social sphere, and the political culture. It was not surprising that such nativism followed them into the ranks. Although prejudice was a fact of life in general, army life made Germans easy targets for abuse. A frustrated Sergeant Wilhelm Francksen of Milwaukee commented to his father about such animosity in society and in the ranks that "you make sure that you get along with yourself and with a few good friends, and you leave in peace the arrogant *Yankees* who think Germans are only good enough to work for them, but otherwise pay them less respect than a Negro."[61]

Quite often Americans associated all Germans with the noted German Forty-Eighters, who created friction and attracted attention to their ethnicity in a manner that drew the ire of the American soldier. "America can curse the day that a dutchman joined her army," remarked Edward C. Hubbard of the 13th Illinois. "I used to think any white man was better than a negro, but I had rather sleep or eat with a negro than a dutchman."[62] Germans routinely complained that Americans treated them unfairly, that they went without the latest weapons and the best rations, and too often found themselves in the thickest combat. John Henry Otto of the 21st Wisconsin, for example, explained years after the war that the treatment and characterization of the Germans were in his mind akin to those directed at "Mudsills," or the lowest class of society. Private Gottfried Rentschler of the 6th Kentucky wrote, "If an entire company is required for rough service, e.g., several days or several weeks as Train-Guard, a German company will be ordered wherever possible." "As a rule," he remarked, "the German has to wade through the mud, while the American walks on the dry road." "The German," Otto concluded, was "a 'Dutch Soldier' and as a 'Dutchman' he is, if not despised, disrespected, and not regarded or treated as an equal."[63]

True or not, Germans came to believe they were frequently on the receiving end of ethnic prejudice. They were mistreated, passed over for promotions, and denied access to adequate supplies and food. Christian Keller argues that in the case of Pennsylvania Germans, officers combated ethnic prejudice by "dispensing favoritism to other Germans and prejudice against non-Germans, thus ridding the ethnic regiments of much influence from non-German leadership, even at the end of the war."[64] Most Germans simply decided to seek out the company of other Germans before that of Anglo-Americans. Carl Uterhard, a surgeon from New York, who had been captured during the war and spent a few weeks in a Southern prison, commented that it was during his incarceration that he learned more English than ever before because he was around only English-speaking soldiers. Once he was released, however, he soon forgot all that he had learned because he associated only with Germans. As a result, he concluded, "I don't have much hope of being promoted, since the Americans loathe all the Germans and slight them whenever they can."[65] In his recent work, *German-Speaking Officers in the U.S. Colored Troops, 1863–1867*, Martin W. Öfele makes the case that many Germans who sought an officer's commission in the U.S. Colored Troops did so because they had already served and experienced nativism and considered serving with black troops an improvement over serving with nativist whites. They received "better pay, higher status, improved accommodations, and a higher chance of survival."[66]

In the border states, Germans were doubly cursed, or so they believed, which might also help to explain why so few Germans from the Union's slave states enlisted in the military. Confederate sympathizers who detested them reinforced this animosity toward Germans by creating exaggerated stories, which portrayed them as not simply demeaning and disreputable but as demeaning and disreputable Germans fighting against the Southern cause. In Missouri, the Camp Jackson affair in May 1861 highlighted the animosity Southerners felt toward Germans loyal to the Union. In that episode, the Germans participated in the Union's forced surrender of the Missouri State Guard, which resulted in a scuffle that led that city's Southern population and newspaper corps to demonize the Germans. The press immediately published outrageous stories that led people to believe that the Germans were barbarians who "would murder people in their beds," which encouraged some Missouri families to leave. Gottfried Rentschler, a border state German, observed that the very same abolitionists who argued to free the slave condemned Germans because they "had no business to bear arms and become soldiers because they value the country so little."[67] As Adolf E. Schroeder argues in his classic work *The German Contribution to the Building of the Americas*, this kind of animosity toward Germans in the ranks helped to elevate a sense of identity among the Germans, particularly in the border states such as Missouri.[68]

Although Germans were often blamed for "problems common to the whole army," as Bruce Levine acknowledges, some Germans did loot and rob civilians, thereby undermining any positive reputation gained in camp or on the battlefield.[69] Their language and demeanor, more often than not, made them appear far too serious for the American volunteer, yet their affinity for *bier*, which had the affect of perhaps loosening them up, came to be seen as a weakness in their character. Perhaps no other unit more than Blenker's provided Americans with a substantive window through which many Americans perceived Germans, and while the colorful German proved he was capable of organizing and preparing his men for combat, he was nonetheless, according to Carl Wittke, "vain and loved pomp and circumstance."[70] The editor of the *St. Paul Pioneer and Democrat* was so disillusioned by Blenker's actions in 1862 that he wrote a letter denouncing Blenker as *the* typical representative of the German element, arguing that most Germans and German newspapers bitterly denounced the corrupt commander. Of course, Germans were not the only soldiers committing such atrocities, but Americans had almost come to expect this kind of behavior, so when it occurred, it merely confirmed for them what they wanted to believe about Germans.[71]

Perhaps more than anything that added to the character of the German war experience and how Americans came to view Germans was the experience of those who distinguished themselves from the masses and who managed to highlight, for good or bad, some of the qualities that many Americans came to associate with the "Damned Dutch" or the "Flying Dutchmen." Ethnic leadership was a significant feature of the German role in the Union army as it had been in Northern communities. Either as regimental commanders or as brigadier generals commanding departments or large divisions, German officers managed to distinguish themselves, which in many cases led to advancement in the ranks. Numerous Germans distinguished themselves as leaders during the Civil War, including Henry Bohlen, Alexander von Schimmelfennig, Franz Sigel, Peter Osterhaus, Adolph August von Steinwehr, August Willich, and Carl Schurz. Schurz was quite popular among the Germans, and in 1862 he resigned his minister post to join the military. Although Germans and Americans questioned Schurz's military competence, Lincoln made him a brigadier general, making his rise to higher rank seem politically engineered and undeserved. Öfele's work on German officers in the U.S. Colored Regiment contends that some Germans sought advancement in the ranks so desperately that they were willing to serve as leaders of all-black units. By comparing the military careers of Peter Osterhaus and Franz Sigel, Earl Hess, for example, provides another analysis of distinct paths for advancement. Whereas Osterhaus relied on few lobbyists in Washington and a "quiet execution of assignments," in his pursuit of a brigadier general's commission, Franz Sigel's "meteoric" rise was due to "sensationalized public relations" and numerous political connections in Washington, as much as the commander's self-promotion to gain advancement. As Hess contends, Osterhaus's experience in the war represented German loyalty and served as a "positive counterweight to the negative image the ethnics only partially deserved."[72]

Part of this fortune, or in some cases misfortune, in advancement was caused not only by the meritorious conduct of the officers but also by the German press. Many Forty-Eighters had assumed a journalistic leadership before the war and had established papers such as the *St. Louis Anzeiger des Westens*, the *Illinois Staats-Zeitung*, and the *Philadelphia Demokrat*, and others such as the *Cleveland Wächter am Erie*, the *St. Louis Westliche Post*, and the *Davenport Demokrat*. As young contemporaries, according to James Bergquist, the Forty-Eighters took their shared influence of the 1848 German Revolution into the Civil War and the German press was "no longer merely an isolated voice speaking from a separate culture, but was indeed an American press published in the German language."[73]

Nonetheless, the German press's close following of their comrades in the ranks helped to foster an image of Germans in general, whether positively or negatively, largely because the Anglo-American press tended to ignore the Germans in their columns. Therefore, the North's German American newspapers kept the home front informed about life in the Union army, chronicled the events of the soldiers, and seldom missed the opportunity to connect the prejudices the soldiers confronted with the larger ethnic implications of being German in America. These papers rallied Germans to the cause, politicized the war, provided an outlet for Germans opposed to the war, and allowed editors the opportunity to debate the administration's prosecution of the war. Joseph Reinhart, for example, has done some yeoman's work by bringing to light sixty letters written by the soldiers and officers of the 32nd Indiana Regiment, to the *Louisville Anzeiger*, *Cincinnati Volksfreund*, and *Freie Presse von Indiana* confirming the German soldiers' use of the press.[74]

The editors of these papers, like many other German editors, published these letters clearly to link home front to battlefront. The circulation of German newspapers increased dramatically at a time when the influx of Germans had decreased. Oswald Ottendorfer's Democratic *New Yorker Staats-Zeitung*'s readership increased because New York City Germans wanted to follow what was happening in the war. A special German weekly called *Das Archiv*, which appeared in the summer of 1861, chronicled the activities of German soldiers and units. Rudolph Lexow's *Criminal-Zeitung und Belletristisches Journal* provided Germans of New York City a detailed study of the causes of the war and weekly reports of battles, commanders, and operations. Karl Heinzen's *Boston Pioneer* also increased in readership, in part because he was perhaps the most outspoken German critic of the German press and used his paper to combat what he believed were unmerited stories. He was highly critical of Blenker in the early part of the war and followed Franz Sigel's rise to prominence in the military, denouncing it as ill-gotten gain. Still, through the press, German soldiers and officers emerged as noble figures fighting for two causes—to preserve the Union and their German honor.[75]

Although the press and the public wanted to believe in the noble cause and that the German population was unified by its participation in it, the fact remains that the bulk of Germans were deeply divided politically during the war. Because the government and nobility in the fatherland had oppressed many Germans, they became supporters of the Democratic Party that spoke to the white victims of society before the war, and many remained in the party throughout the war. The editor of the *Hartford Daily Times* remarked in the fall of 1862 that the Germans of New York, who had apparently voted for Lincoln in 1860, were so disillusioned by the prosecution of the war and treatment of Germans that they were coming back to the Democratic Party. "They all declare that they have been humbugged and deceived," remarked the editor, and "that they shall hereafter remain true to the Democrats." So alarming was the shift that at one point, Frederick Rauchtuss, editor of the *New Yorker Abend-Zeitung*, urged Lincoln to provide his paper some funds to allow him to expand his circulation to be able to cut into the German Democratic contingent in New York. "We have to compete here," he argued with a "very dangerous and by no means unimportant foe," referring to the *New York Staats-Zeitung*, which was a well-known "copperhead organ" in the city.[76]

With the rise of the Republican Party, coupled with the growing animosity over slavery, Germans came to view the new party and Lincoln's election as an opportunity to fundamentally change the character of the United States by breaking the shackles of slavery and adopting more fully the ideas that allowed all Americans to pursue wealth freely. Once the war started, however, and the Union's effort evolved into a massive undertaking that required dramatic steps to conquer the Confederacy, such as the Emancipation Proclamation and conscription, German radicals came to view these measures as necessary. Still, many Germans joined the millions of Americans in protest of these actions. Certainly, the timing of the Emancipation Proclamation and the national draft inspired an otherwise complacent German populace to react. Although many German Republicans supported Lincoln's expansive war measures, some Germans protested fighting a war to end slavery, but even more, they resisted an inequitable conscription system to do it. The impact of these wartime measures on the German community, coupled with the perceived prejudice in the ranks, was simply demoralizing. German Democrats and Radical Republicans had protested Lincoln's handling of the war because in their view slavery had been the sole cause of the war, and Lincoln had been slow to interpret the war in this manner. Yet, German Democrats disliked the war measures because they represented the centralization of government, which was bullied by a powerful Republican Party. Typically, these Germans protested passively, but occasionally they engaged in active resistance, for example, by contesting conscription in Wisconsin and Pennsylvania in 1862. Yet, these protests were separate concerns for the Lincoln administration that believed the German radicals could do far more damage to his campaign for reelection. German Forty-Eighter Caspar Butz of Illinois, for example, perhaps best expressed the sentiment for his disgruntled radical countrymen by characterizing Lincoln as "the weakest and worst man that ever filled the Presidential chair."[77] His discontented German friends condemned the president for removing John C. Fremont in 1861 after he ordered slaves in Missouri emancipated, and by 1864, the more radical Germans from both parties supported Fremont's nomination for the presidency and moved "heaven and earth" to defeat Lincoln. In the end, the Fremont campaign dissolved, and Germans turned to the radical elements within the Republican Party to advance their cause. In his memoirs, Gustav Körner, Lincoln's Illinois friend, apologized that "so many Germans were found in opposition to Lincoln," but it was not unexpected. As Dean Mahin observes, in 1864 "many Germans and others voted against McClellan, rather than for Lincoln."[78]

What Germans and Americans came to believe about themselves through the experience of the Civil War was that Germans more than any other ethnic group exposed Americans to ethnic difference, if simply by speaking a different language. Whatever politics had done in the antebellum period to assimilate Germans into the American mainstream (thereby shaping a degree of ethnic tolerance among Americans) was made more acute during the war by the

Germans' physical presence in the rank and file. It was through the military that Germans were more engaged by contact with the American populace than ever before. As they left their ethnic neighborhoods and joined the ranks of Americans, the military produced new communities of social, political, and cultural significance. Even if ethnic stereotyping, nativism, hostility, and resistance toward Germans remained present in the war's aftermath, Americans learned firsthand that they were different in some respects and, for better or worse, came to deal with Germans and vice versa during the four-year conflict. Though the bulk of Germans who fought for the Union served in units in which Americans greatly outnumbered them, significant influences such as language, camaraderie, community pressure, location, and, above all, the persuasion of ethnic leaders and the press encouraged some Germans to enlist in German-only units. Those states with large German populations held even more ethnic and political currency if they were border states. Lincoln understood the significance of the ethnic dimension of building a national army that reflected its demography. The president recognized from the very beginning of the war that as a border state, Missouri's ethnic makeup made it much more complicated to deal with than Maryland or Western Virginia and just how important it was to capitalize on the Germans' loyalty to keep Missouri in the Union.[79]

In many ways the ethnic struggles of the German soldiers reflected the ethnic political battles in the larger social context. Editors, politicians, and civic leaders of the *Turngemeinden* and *Arbeitervereine*, for example, attempted to capitalize on discontent in the ranks by emphasizing the mistreatment and neglect of the German soldiers to heighten the social and political alienation shared by many noncombatant Germans. Whatever the level of their involvement, their participation in the war gave German Americans considerable visibility in American society. Indeed, as Martin Öfele observes in his work, some German officers sought commissions in the U.S. Colored Troops because they considered military service a venue for recognition in American society, much like the black troops they led.[80]

In its broadest yet simplest context, the Civil War was a catalyst for change. For Germans, like other immigrant groups, it raised their ethnic consciousness. Some Germans, whether using the pen or the sword, sought to heighten Germans' awareness of their place in society and how the war could serve to elevate that status. Some Germans found elements of service, combat, and

political life valuable to the self-construction of a German identity by emphasizing their *Deutschtum*—in particular they linked the home front to the
battlefront. It was not so much that this emphasis stemmed from communal
settlements and institutions that bound group members to one another, but
rather from a common cultural maintenance that took shape as those citizens
went to war. The war encouraged a "multiculturalist" emphasis on *Deutschtum* and a reliance upon the devices of ethnocultural maintenance. For
example, when the German American press and other publicists stressed the
role of German Americans in the military effort to preserve the Union, they
were claiming a bigger slice of the American pie—clearly an assimilationist
goal. They wanted to be recognized as Americans, not as immigrants with
questionable loyalties. Yet, their accents and customs unmistakably identified
them as foreign-born, as newcomers, and they could not escape that. As Ella
Lonn observed decades ago, "The German soldier, perhaps unconsciously,
felt that at the same time he was fighting for preservation of the Union he
was fighting for the honor of the German people, a fact which explains, of
course, his desire to serve in a German unit."[81] Indeed, it was, as August Willich remarked, "at the beginning of the war I had different intentions than
only taking part in it." "I wanted to show everyone," declared Willich, "who
believes that you can only be a worthy citizen of the republic if you were born
here, that we as Germans are also republicans [members of the republic]. I
wanted to help the immigrant gain a right that they [Americans] kept from
him or sought to diminish."[82]

Still, the war provided Germans with new ways of expressing ethnic identity as both soldiers and citizens, since it called for a renegotiation of Germanness with respect to its meaning and its relations both to Americans and
to other ethnic groups participating in the war. As Jörg Nagler perceptively
argues, Germans actively stressed their *Deutschtum* and saw the war as an
opportunity to reapply a familiar shield of identity to new circumstances. The
solidarity produced by witnessing how the involvement of German soldiers
aided the Union also had ethnic connotations, since Germans attempted to
unite their fragmented ethnic group in a political fight for the Union and in
support groups to help their soldiers. The creation of the German Hospital of
Philadelphia by Germans, for example, represented the kind of ethnic awareness that heightened their identity in the urban communities. "No experience
had struck so deep into the life of German-Americans," concluded Lonn,

"and never before had there existed such unity among them."[83] Whether or not Lonn's conclusion is accurate, some Germans certainly attempted to capitalize on this unity and attempted to advance their ethnicity. The attempt by some German commanders such as Franz Sigel to enhance their military standing took the form of ethnic construction. Germans who felt unappreciated by Americans employed their Germanness to promote the interests of their military leaders and give Americans an opportunity to appreciate them not simply because of what they did but also because of who they were.[84]

Of all the Germans in the war, Franz Sigel, for better or worse, was the symbol of the German effort in the military, and he increasingly became aware of his position and stature among the Germans in the army as well as at home. As a soldier and officer, he recognized the ethnic significance of German participation in the war and viewed it as an opportunity to redefine the status of Germans. But while Sigel engaged in the self-promotion of his cause, he had help along the way, a fact that suggested he was something more than just a German Union commander.

Prominent political leaders also understood his importance. Virginia representative from Wheeling, John S. Carlisle, wrote to Salmon P. Chase, secretary of the Treasury, that based on what Sigel had done in the West, he was just the commander they needed in the East, commenting that "Siegel [sic] is the man we want. I would not give him for 50 Rosencranz's or 100 Fremonts'."[85] Massachusetts Senator Charles Sumner concurred, recognizing Sigel's worth as early as the fall of 1861. When Lincoln was searching for a replacement for Fremont in St. Louis, Sumner informed Lincoln that Sigel had "many of the conditions which you are seeking for the command West of the Mississippi. As a German he would be most acceptable in St. Louis, where there are so many of that nation."[86]

Sigel soon became aware of the product the German press had created in him. His role and status in the war were an extension of his place in the German American community, and he represented the link between the home front and the battlefront perhaps more successfully than any other German in the war. Because Sigel was a symbol of the German community, his role magnified the worth of the German community in American society, and his wartime experience forced him to recast his own ideological formation and construction as a German. As Bruce Levine concluded, the North's German communities followed their countrymen in arms with "great and touchy pride." The German press created in Sigel an instrument with which to promote their cause and rail against prejudice, and Sigel came to recognize himself as the product the German American community had created and was successful in consolidating support for his cause.[87]

Whatever value historians have placed on Franz Sigel's worth to the Union war effort, his role in the Civil War and his resignation from the army illustrated for his contemporaries the importance of the ethnic dimensions of the conflict. No other German American was more the "Damned Dutch" to Americans, and yet no other German American military leader possessed his enormous, albeit perplexing, popularity. The German American community would produce numerous outstanding soldiers and commanders, but none measured up to Sigel in his overall significance. Despite his undistinguished military endeavors, Sigel was, according to Hans L. Trefousse, "still the darling of the Germans."[88]

From the beginning of the conflict many Germans throughout the North wanted to fight under Sigel because he represented something larger to them; his near-legendary status as a passionately devoted and militarily skilled revolutionary made him all the more attractive as a commander. In the summer of 1861, Germans from Pittsburgh, Pennsylvania, were willing to trek all the way to St. Louis just to join his regiment. He was the instrument of their solidarity in the war. The phrase "I fights mit Sigel," used by German soldiers throughout the war, represented more than just military allegiance. "His soldiers will follow him even if he goes with one against a dozen," declared Henry Kircher to his father; "it never occurred to any of us to be afraid for himself because of this or that," wrote Kircher, "he did not teach us to know fear, only to obey him blindly and to win."[89] A Hoosier army correspondent for the *Indianapolis Sentinel* corroborated this sentiment, writing from Missouri in 1861 that "everybody except envious regular officers loves Sigel." "The soldiers of his command adore him," he declared. "Thoroughly conversant with all the details of modern warfare," he acknowledged, "he preserves order and all necessary discipline, and yet retains the enthusiastic love of his men." The correspondent went on to say that Sigel's "commands are obeyed, not through slavish fear, but because nobody doubts their propriety. 'Sigel said so,' stops all debate. The dispute is ended. An emanation from superior being has settled the controversy. The *esprit du* [*sic*] *corps* is a fixed institution in his division. To be able to say 'I'm mit Sigel,' is the pride with us, and when said is accompanied with a look of pity to the listener, saying intelligibly, 'Poor fellow, I'm sorry for you that you are not mit Sigel.'"[90] Captain Theodore Howell of the 153rd Pennsylvania perhaps summed it up best announcing that he "would rather fight under Sigel than any other Gen'l in the army."[91]

Although not all Germans were of the same positive opinion regarding Sigel, it was evident that many were, and fighting with Sigel became symbolic of their desire to fight together as Germans in solidarity—a solidarity that extended beyond the battlefield to the community. Whenever he passed through a Northern city, the German American press made sure his followers knew when he was to arrive and where he would be staying, and hundreds, if not thousands, of civilians flocked to shake his hand, greet him, or simply listen to one of his stirring speeches. Because he was a symbol of their participation in the war, Germans were extremely sensitive about the treatment of their esteemed general. Whenever he was abused by the press or mistreated by superiors, the German community took it personally. Indeed, as the *St. Louis Daily Missouri Democrat* observed, Sigel was "*the* representative of the German element," a fact that numerous papers highlighted in their reprints of this assessment. Thus, when he resigned on two occasions and when his requests for more significant commands were denied, it injured a community of Germans that transcended the battlefield and linked the battlefront to the home front.[92]

His first resignation in late December 1861 was prompted over what appeared to be a misunderstanding regarding military protocol in the appointment and replacement of commanders. Sigel thought his replacement by General Samuel Curtis had been an attempt by General Henry W. Halleck, his anti-immigrant superior, to eliminate him from command, based on his fear that Sigel's prominence among the Germans in the West posed a threat to the Union. Halleck had concluded that the Germans commanded by Sigel and other foreign adventurers constituted a "dangerous element in the army." Lack of evidence and President Lincoln's tactful handling of the affair, including the promotion of Sigel to major general, encouraged the general to rescind his resignation in January 1862 and satisfied the German community that their interests had been served. Sigel's resignation in March 1863 grew out of his dissatisfaction that his 11th Corps, widely known as the German Corps, was the smallest in the Army of the Potomac and that it should be enlarged. When Halleck responded to Sigel's request by quipping that he "should do the best he can with it," Sigel again hastily resigned from the army.

At the urging of the German community, Sigel rescinded his resignation and planned to return to his unit, but when he returned to Washington, Halleck had no use for him. After several months without a command, Sigel was finally sent to an obscure military department in Pennsylvania. But because neither Sigel nor the German community was satisfied with his position, they both pressured Lincoln to give him a more significant command. In February 1864, Lincoln acquiesced, and Sigel was sent to command the Department of West Virginia. Given Sigel's notoriety, the president was cognizant of the commander's worth on and off the field in an election year, acknowledging on one occasion that the "gist of the Sigel difficulty" was that the commander "would never forget that he and his Germans are step-sons."[93]

What was important about Sigel's resignations from the military and what set him apart from Blenker, Schurz, Schimmelfennig, and other Germans was not only that his behavior exposed a vain and self-absorbed commander who probably deserved his misfortunes, but also that his resignations caused a stir that created a sense of solidarity in the German American community. Part of this stir came from the Germans within the ranks. Summing up the status of Sigel in the army, one private in the 154th New York remarked when Sigel resigned from the 11th Corps, "The grand 11th corps has lost its idol."[94]

Outside the military, Sigel's resignations swelled into national proportions. "The German community . . . is greatly exercised just now about the resignation [of Sigel]," wrote an Illinois resident to Senator Lyman Trumbull.[95] Throughout the West in early 1862, the battle cry of the Germans was "We fight with Sigel!" Even Sigel's military failures had not soured "Dutch" enthusiasm for the German. The *Delaware Republican*, a paper that generally was not interested in German affairs, noted that Sigel had been unjustly superseded. The *Providence Daily Journal* published an article that reported that German residents as far away as San Francisco had raised $1,000 to procure a testimonial for presentation to Sigel (the gift was a golden eagle wreathed with laurels and set with diamonds). Part of the reason that German newspapers throughout the North had come to his defense when he resigned was that they understood that his soldiers adored him because they had written editors countless letters for publication. One officer on Sigel's command wrote a letter to his wife in early 1862 that was published in the *Cincinnati Commercial* and then picked up by several papers. He related that after reading the New York papers detailing the events surrounding Sigel's resignation, some twenty officers from throughout the command felt compelled to pay the general a visit at his headquarters. They crowded into his small tent and made known just how much they favored him. "We left the General," the writer remarked, "with a unanimous feeling that a better man than Franz Sigel is not now in command in the vast army of the Union."[96]

The press played a crucial role in emphasizing Sigel's worth as a German linking the home front to the battlefront, despite the near unanimity among editors (German as well as American) regarding his worth as a commander. Several German papers established a clear link between the nativism Germans had experienced before and during the war with the nativism Sigel was experiencing as a commander. Germans at home personalized his affair and made him a martyr for their rejection in American society. Prominent St. Louis lawyer and banker Peter A. Ladue wrote to Francis P. Blair Jr. in early 1862 that in Sigel's resignation "the Union cause loses a most important man." "Sigel is a representative man," he stated, and "the whole German element among us clings to and adores him." "A blow struck at Sigel," he warned, "will be considered a blow at the whole German people, not only in Mo. but throughout the Union."[97] Blair endorsed the opinion and sent it on to Lincoln. The editor of the *Anzeiger des Westens* argued that since Sigel was the highest-ranking German officer at the time, "he has to bear the cross of Germany."[98] Although the editor also observed that this was unfortunately true, he did not "wish to stoke the fires of alienation and make the gap between ethnic groups even greater than it is." The editor of the *St. Louis Westliche Post* perceptively summed up the sentiment toward Sigel in the German communities throughout the North, saying that a "loyal population of four million citizens of German birth and extraction in the north, will make the supposed sacrifice of Sigel their own grievance."[99]

Although there were differences of opinion among Germans about Sigel, the commander's affair actually gave them the opportunity to generally unite behind his cause. The German community also pressured its political leaders to make Sigel's affair the affair of all Germans, soldiers and citizens. Sigel's first resignation prompted Illinois congressman Isaac N. Arnold, leader of a pro-Sigel group in Congress, to send the president a petition demanding that Sigel be made a major general. The combined propaganda media of the German community and political pressure influenced the Lincoln administration to transfer Sigel in 1862 and to give him another more significant command in 1864. Joseph Medill of the *Chicago Tribune* wrote to Lincoln in February 1864, urging that Sigel be restored to active command. "The Germans of all classes are deeply offended at the treatment received by Sigel," he confided. "The German regiments and soldiers are not re-enlisting," he wrote, "they are wounded in feeling, and sore and mad. They feel ill treated."[100] M. A. Jacobi, proprietor of the *Cincinnati Daily Volksblatt* and a delegate to the National Union Convention in Baltimore, wrote to Lincoln in September that "if there is a name which has obtained a firm and immoveable hold on the minds and the hearts of my German-American fellow citizens, it is that of Gen. Sigel." "If there is a man in whose success and in the recognition of whose services they feel proud and elated and gratified, it is Gen. Sigel."[101] Carl Schurz, too, clearly recognized the connection between Sigel and the German community. In February 1864, he wrote Lincoln approvingly, noting that placing Sigel in command of the Department of West Virginia was a "very judicious measure in every respect."[102]

More important than Sigel's military significance in the war was the fact that the German presence in society was made more complete by Germans' participation in the Civil War. Germans entered the military community and exposed their ethnicity, for better or worse, to people who had never before had contact with Germans, and Sigel's career had been the most publicized example of this exposure. In politics alone, Sigel was a force. Ben Field, a New York merchant and philanthropist, for example, was secretary of the Union State Central Committee who urged Lincoln in the fall of 1862 to consider allowing Sigel a furlough from the field to come to New York to give a few speeches to the Germans, which "would make several thousand votes difference in the results." While the Democrats were making "superhuman efforts to elect their ticket," wrote Field, Sigel's presence in the state "would take the Germans by storm."[103]

At home, Germans supported the war like Americans did. German ladies' aid societies sprang up in the German enclaves in cities, as did German hospitals and other benevolent organizations. German women enlisted as nurses, went to work in factors, organized into support groups, such as the Turner Sisters, and made linen for bandages, regimental flags, and clothes and a variety of other goods. The German Society of New York City organized the Patriotic Central-Assistance Association and assumed the responsibility of creating and overseeing a fund to support German families in need of relief, thereby establishing a model association that other German communities emulated. In his work on Pennsylvania Germans, Christian Keller provides some insights into the connection between these community efforts and the ethnic identity, concluding that the assistance of these purely German aid societies in Philadelphia, for example, was the "result of the antebellum growth of *Deutschtum*, in which the German immigrant's ethnic identity became entwined with that of the greater German community." The same could be said for most cities in the Union with sizable German populations.[104]

In the end, the war exposed overwhelming numbers of Germans and Americans to one another who under no other circumstances would have come into such contact, and both groups came to learn more about themselves and just how similar and how different they really were than ever before. Arguing that the Civil War completed a phase in the development of an ethnic identity in America among Germans, Kathleen Conzen stresses that German leaders rejected the notion of complete assimilation and instead recognized a stronger ethnic solidarity established in the war that took the form of a cultural maintenance in postwar years. Keller's work on Pennsylvania Germans confirms Conzen's assessment of the war years, and his conclusions can no doubt be applied to most German Yankees. The German ethnic consciousness and growth of a German identity grew out of the fear that Germans might lose their ethnic identity during the war. Whether it was cultural maintenance through ethnic solidarity or fear of losing it, there is certainly no denying the simple fact that La Vern Rippley perceptively concluded years ago: "The Civil War probably did as much for the Germans in America as the Germans in America did for the Union."[105]

NOTES

1. Roy P. Basler, ed., *The Collected Works of Abraham Lincoln* (New Brunswick, NJ: Rutgers University Press, 1953), vol. 4, 438; Phillip Shaw Paludan, *"A People's Contest": The Union and Civil War, 1861–1865* (New York: Harper and Row, 1988), 3–31.

2. Ella Lonn, *Foreigners in the Union Army and Navy* (Baton Rouge: Louisiana State University Press, 1951), 8; James M. Bergquist, "German Communities in American Cities: An Interpretation of the Nineteenth-Century Experience," *Journal of American Ethnic History* 4 (Fall 1984): 10–11; Bergquist, "Germans and the Cities," in *Germans in America: Retrospect and Prospect*, ed. Randall M. Miller (Philadelphia: German Society of Pennsylvania, 1984), 37–56; Christian B. Keller, "Germans

in Civil War–Era Pennsylvania: Ethnic Identity and the Problem of Americanization (Ph.D. diss., Pennsylvania State University, 2001), 20; see also Keller's book from the dissertation entitled *Chancellorsville and the Germans: Nativism, Ethnicity, and Civil War Memory* (New York: Fordham University Press, 2007), 2–23. Because some quotations in the dissertation appear either differently or not all in the published work, I have cited both.

3. Lonn, *Foreigners in the Union Army and Navy*, 8.

4. Bergquist, "German Communities in American Cities," 9–15; Edward Dicey, *Six Months in the Federal States* (London: Macmillan, 1863), vol. 1, 13; Stanley Nadel, *Little Germany: Ethnicity, Religion, and Class in New York City, 1845–80* (Urbana: University of Illinois Press, 1990), 1–8; Dean B. Mahin, *The Blessed Place of Freedom: Europeans in Civil War America* (Washington, DC: Brassey's, 2002), 2–3. It should be noted that Mahin cites Edward Dicey, *Spectator of America* (London, 1863; Chicago: Quadrangle Books, 1971), for his quotations which appear in somewhat different fashion than in Dicey's work cited here in this essay. See also Bruce Levine, *The Spirit of 1848: German Immigrants, Labor Conflict, and the Coming of the Civil War* (Urbana: University of Illinois Press, 1992), chaps. 1–3, for an excellent analysis of the German population in the United States and its location and influence before the Civil War.

5. Bergquist, "German Communities in American Cities," 9–15; Nadel, *Little Germany*, 1–8; Mahin, *Blessed Place of Freedom*, 2–3.

6. Fredrika Bremer, *The Homes of the New World* (New York, 1864), vol. 1, 615–16; Richard N. Current, *The History of Wisconsin: The Civil War Era, 1848–1873* (Madison: State Historical Society of Wisconsin, 1976), 123–24; Levine, *Spirit of 1848*, 58–59; Bergquist, "German Communities in American Cities," 9–15; Lonn, *Foreigners in the Union Army and Navy*, 9; David A. Gerber, *The Making of an American Pluralism: Buffalo, New York, 1825–1860* (Urbana: University of Illinois Press, 1989), 163–235.

7. Dicey, *Six Months in the Federal States*, vol. 1, 13;.

8. Ibid., vol. 2, 53–56.

9. Ibid., 56.

10. Annette R. Hofmann, "The Turners' Loyalty for Their New Home Country: Their Engagement in the American Civil War," *International Journal of the History of Sport* 12 (December 1995): 153.

11. Annette R. Hofmann, "One Hundred and Fifty Years of Loyalty: The Turner Movement in the United States," *Yearbook of German-American Studies* 34 (1999): 63–81; Joseph R. Reinhart, trans. and ed., *August Willich's Gallant Dutchman: Civil War Letters from the 32nd Indiana Infantry* (Kent: Ohio: Kent State University Press, 2006), 9; Eugene C. Miller argues that the 32nd Indiana Infantry was a Turner regiment. See Miller, "The Contribution of German Immigrants to the Union Cause in Kentucky," *Filson Club Historical Quarterly* 64 (October 1990): 466–69; Levine, *Spirit of 1848*, 91–95, quote on 256; Gerber, *Making of an American Pluralism*, 198;

see also Robert Knight Barney, "Knights of Cause and Exercise: German Forty-Eighters and the Turnvereine in the United States during the Antebellum Period," *Canadian Journal of the History of Sport* 13 (Spring 1982): 62–79; and Robert Knight Barney, "German-American Turnvereins and Socio-Politico-Economic Realities in the Antebellum and Civil War Upper and Lower South," *Stadion* 10 (1984): 135–81; see also John Charles Bodger Jr., "The Immigrant Press and the Union Army" (Ph.D. diss., Columbia University, 1951), 96–97; and Mary Elizabeth McMorrow, "The Nineteenth Century German Political Immigrant and the Construction of American Culture and Thought" (Ph.D. diss., New School for Social Research, 1982), 21–24; and Lonn, *Foreigners in the Union Army and Navy*, 96–102. For an excellent analysis of the Turnvereine in America, see Carl Wittke, *Refugees of Revolution: The German Forty-Eighters in America* (Philadelphia: University of Pennsylvania Press, 1952), and Henry Metzner, *History of American Turners* (Rochester, NY: National Council of American Turners, 1974); C. Eugene Miller and Forrest F. Steinlage, *Der Turner Soldat: A German Soldier in the Civil War: Germany to Antietam* (Louisville, KY: Calmar Publications, 1988); *Indianapolis State Journal*, August 16, 1861. Franz Sigel wrote to the editor of the *New York World*, which was published in several newspapers, that the Turners of Pittsburgh offered to enter his Missouri Regiment.

12. Levine, *Spirit of 1848*, 58–59; Emma Lou Thornbrough, *Indiana in the Civil War Era, 1850–1880* (Indianapolis: Indiana Historical Society, 1965; reprint, Bloomington: Indiana University Press, 1991), 548; Josephine Goldmark, *Pilgrims of '48: One Man's Part in the Austrian Revolution of 1848 and a Family Migration to America* (New Haven, CT: Yale University Press, 1930), 222; Kathleen Neils Conzen, "Germans," *Harvard Encyclopedia of American Ethnic Groups* (Cambridge: Harvard University Press, 1980), 415; see also Conzen, *Immigrant Milwaukee, 1836–1860* (Cambridge: Harvard University Press, 1976), and Conzen, "Patterns of German-American History," in Miller, *Germans in America*, 14–36.

13. Thornbrough, *Indiana in the Civil War Era*, 548; Goldmark, *Pilgrims of '48*, 222.

14. Conzen, "Germans," 415.

15. Keller, "Germans in Civil War–Era Pennsylvania," 36–37; Keller, *Chancellorsville and the Germans*, 2–23; Conzen, "Germans," 415.

16. William L. Burton, *Melting Pot Soldiers: The Union's Ethnic Regiments* (New York: Fordham University Press, 1998), 1–9; Nadel, *Little Germany*, 13–41; Roger Daniels, *Coming to America: A History of Immigration and Ethnicity in American Life* (New York: HarperCollins, 1990), 151–52.

17. Walter D. Kamphoefner and Wolfgang Helbich, eds., *Germans in the Civil War: The Letters They Wrote Home*, trans. Susan Carter Vogel (Chapel Hill: University of North Carolina Press, 2006), 67. These editors have done an outstanding job in editing and translating more than 340 letters from seventy-eight Germans, both soldiers and civilians.

18. Reinhart, *August Willich's Gallant Dutchman*, 22–23; see also Kamphoefner and Helbich, *Germans in the Civil War*, and Keller, *Chancellorsville and the Germans*, who speak to the many reasons for German enlistment.

19. Kamphoefner and Helbich, *Germans in the Civil War*, xiii.

20. E. B. Quiner, *The Military History of Wisconsin in the War for the Union* (Chicago: Clarke, 1866), 91–92.

21. Kamphoefner and Helbich, *Germans in the Civil War*, 195–99.

22. Ibid., 293.

23. Dicey, *Six Months in the Federal States*, vol. 2, 167–68; see also Reinhart, *August Willich's Gallant Dutchman*, 22–23; see the letter in the *Freie Presse von Indiana*, August 25, 1861, in which August Willich observes that volunteering in the army "will really prove that they [the Germans] are not foreigners and that they know how to protect their new republican homeland against the aristocracy of the South." Lonn, *Foreigners in the Union Army and Navy*, 78.

24. Steven Rowan and James Neal Primm, eds., *Germans for a Free Missouri: Translations from the St. Louis Radical Press, 1857–1862* (Columbia: University of Missouri Press, 1983), 202–3; Mahin, *Blessed Place of Freedom*, 11; Martin W. Öfele, *German-Speaking Officers in the U.S. Colored Troops, 1863–1867* (Gainesville: University Press of Florida, 2004), 10–15; McMorrow, "Nineteenth Century German Political Immigrant and the Construction of American Culture and Thought," 28–94; Frederick C. Leubke, "German Immigrants and American Politics: Problems of Leadership, Parties, and Issues," in Miller, *Germans in America*, 57–74.

25. Burton, *Melting Pot Soldiers*, 1–9; Wittke, *Refugees of Revolution*, 224–25; Hans L. Trefousse, "Abraham Lincoln and Carl Schurz," in *The German Forty-Eighters in the United States*, ed. Charlotte L. Brancaforte (New York: Peter Lang, 1989), 179–201; Hans L. Trefousse, *Carl Schurz: A Biography* (Knoxville: University of Tennessee Press, 1982), 58–95; see also Veit Valentin, *1848: Chapters of German History*, trans. Ethel T. Schaffauer (Hamden, CT: Archon, 1965); and Theodore Huebener, *The Germans in America* (Philadelphia: Chilton, 1962); Lonn, *Foreigners in the Union Army and Navy*, 174. Wilhelm Kaufmann, *Die Deutschen im amerikanischen Bürgerkriege* (Munich: R. Oldenbourg, 1911), 61–69, also appeared in 1999, published as a translated work by Steven Rowan under the same title, *The Germans in the American Civil War* (Carlisle, PA: John Kallmann, 1999); for purposes of this essay this work will be hereinafter cited as Kaufmann, *Germans in the American Civil War*. Because some 500,000 Germans came to America between 1847 and 1854, it is difficult to discern the precise number of those Germans who came because of political persecution and those who came for purely economic reasons.

26. Kamphoefner and Helbich, *Germans in the Civil War*, 297–303.

27. Daniels, *Coming to America*, 151; Carl Wittke, "Ohio's Germans, 1840–1875," *Ohio Historical Quarterly* 62 (1957): 339–54.

28. Daniels, *Coming to America*, 151.

29. Ibid.

30. Keller, *Chancellorsville and the Germans*, 30–35.

31. U.S. Bureau of the Census, *Eighth Census, 1860: The Statistics of the Population of the United States* (Washington, DC: Government Printing Office, 1864–66), xxii, xxix, xxxi, 29, 32, 299–300; Lonn, *Foreigners in the Union Army and Navy*, 1–13. Albert B. Faust, *The German Element in the United States* (New York, 1909; reprint, New York: Steuben Society of America, 1927), vol. 1, 522–24; Kaufmann, *Germans in the American Civil War*, 70–79; Frederick C. Phisterer, *Statistical Record of the Armies of the United States* (New York: Scribner's, 1883), 1–10; Levine, *Spirit of 1848*, 58–59; James S. Lapham, "The German-Americans of New York City, 1860–1890" (Ph.D. diss., St. John's University, 1977), 201. Massachusetts senator Henry Wilson expressed with great satisfaction that 907 Germans from his state had mustered into four regiments; *Congressional Globe*, 38th Cong., 2nd sess., 607; *New York Times*, October 24, 1864.

32. Kamphoefner and Helbich, *Germans in the Civil War*, 7. These authors identify James M. McPherson as the historian claiming that German Protestants entered the Union army in larger numbers than German Catholics; see *Ordeal by Fire: The Civil War and Reconstruction* (New York: Knopf, 1982), 358.

33. Kamphoefner and Helbich, *Germans in the Civil War*, 3–9; Burton, *Melting Pot Soldiers*, 48–50, 205–6; U.S. Bureau of the Census, *Eighth Census, 1860*, xxii, xxix, xxxi, 29–32, 299–300; Lonn, *Foreigners in the Union Army and Navy*, 1–13; Kaufmann, *Germans in the American Civil War*, 61–69.

34. *Providence Daily Journal*, April 24, 1861.

35. Kamphoefner and Helbich, *Germans in the Civil War*, 114–15.

36. Lonn, *Foreigners in the Union Army and Navy*, 114, 162, 658–59; Stephen D. Engle, "A Raised Consciousness: Franz Sigel and German Ethnic Identity in the Civil War," *Yearbook of German Studies* 34 (1999): 1–17.

37. James S. Pula, *The Sigel Regiment: A History of the 26th Wisconsin Volunteer Infantry, 1862–1865* (Campbell, CA: Savas, 1998); James S. Pula, "The Sigel Regiment," *German-American Studies* 8 (1974): 27–52; U.S. Bureau of the Census, *Eighth Census, 1860*, 29, 32, 299–300; Lonn, *Foreigners in the Union Army and Navy*, 114, 162, 658–59; Burton, *Melting Pot Soldiers*, 48–50, 205–6.

38. Kaufmann, *Germans in the American Civil War*, 61–69; see also Brancaforte, *The German Forty-Eighters in the United States*, passim.

39. Kaufmann, *Germans in the American Civil War*, 61–69; Öfele, *German-Speaking Officers in the U.S. Colored Troops*, 3–10; Wittke, *Refugees of Revolution*, passim; the best modern study of the German Forty-Eighters is the edited collection of essays by Brancaforte, *The German Forty-Eighters in the United States*; Adolf E. Zucker, ed., *The Forty-Eighters: Political Refugees of the German Revolution of 1848* (New York: Columbia University Press, 1960); see also Hans L. Trefousse, *Germany and America: Essays on Problems of International Relations and Immigration* (New York: Brooklyn College Press, 1980); Lonn, *Foreigners in the Union Army and Navy*, 7, 44. For an

excellent analysis of the activism of the Forty-Eighters, see Levine, *Spirit of 1848*, 213–56.

40. Mahin, *Blessed Place of Freedom*, 15; Lonn, *Foreigners in the Union Army and Navy*, 156; Kaufmann, *Germans in the American Civil War*, 70–79.

41. Ella Lonn published her classic work *Foreigners in the Union Army and Navy* in 1951 (see pp. 94–115 for estimates). Although numerous historians have criticized Lonn for the inaccuracies in her calculations of German soldiers fighting in Union armies and navies, surprisingly, no one has taken on the formidable task of updating or even supplanting her work.

Some modern historians have tackled Germans and ethnicity in the Civil War and have provided more estimates of German participants. William Burton has produced by far the most scholarly study of the Union's ethnic regiments.

42. Ibid.

43. Numerous scholars have studied the Germans in the Union army and attempted to provide an accurate number for their participation in the Union armies and navies. Benjamin A. Gould was among the first to examine the number of actual Germans fighting in the Union armies in his seminal work, *Investigations in the Military and Anthropological Statistics of the American Soldier* (New York: Hurd and Houghton, 1869). In 1886, Joseph G. Rosengarten's book *The German Soldier in the Wars of the United States* (Philadelphia: Lippincott) appeared. In 1911, Kaufmann's work *The Germans in the American Civil War*, appeared (see pp. 102–8 for estimates); see also Lonn, *Foreigners in the Union Army and Navy*, 94–115. Most recently published are Dean Mahin, *Blessed Place of Freedom*, and Tim Engelhart *Zu den Waffen: Deutsche Emigraten in New Yorker Unionsregimenten während des Amerikanischen Bügerkrieges, 1861–1865* (Zella-Mehlis, Germany: Heinrich-Jung Society, 2000), as well as Wolfgang Hochbruck, Ulrich Bachteler, and Henning Zimmerman, eds., *Achtundvierziger/Forty-Eighters: Die deutschen Revolutionen von 1848/49, die Vereingten Staaten und der amerikanische Bürgerkrieg* (Münster: Westfaelisches Dampfboot, 2000), have all provided estimations of Germans fighting in the Civil War. Wolfgang Hochbruck has also investigated the number of German Forty-Eighters who fought for the Union; see, for example, http://freepages.genealogy.rootsweb.ancestry.com/~dettweiler/genweb/e006.htm (accessed April 2010), and also Hochbruck, Bachteler, and Zimmermann, *Achtundvierziger/Forty-Eighters*.

44. Kamphoefner and Helbich, *Germans in the Civil War*, 8–10.

45. Ibid.

46. Kaufmann, *Germans in the American Civil War*, 96–106; Burton, *Melting Pot Soldiers*, 72–89; see also Reinhart, *August Willich's Gallant Dutchman*.

47. Dicey, *Six Months in the Federal States*, vol. 2, 21; Burton, *Melting Pot Soldiers*, 84–89.

48. *St. Paul Pioneer and Democrat*, February 25, 1862; see also Michael Burlingame, ed., *Lincoln's Journalist: John Hay's Anonymous Writings for the Press, 1860–*

1864 (Carbondale: Southern Illinois University Press, 1998), 241; Burton, *Melting Pot Soldiers*, 84–89.

49. *St. Paul Pioneer and Democrat*, February 25, 1862.

50. Kaufmann, *Germans in the American Civil War*, 96–106; Burton, *Melting Pot Soldiers*, 72–89; Miller, "The Contribution of German Immigrants to the Union Cause," 466–69; Lonn, *Foreigners in the Union Army and Navy*, 94–105; Wittke, *Refugees of Revolution*, 234; Russell H. Beatie, *Army of the Potomac: McClellan Takes Command, September 1861–February 1862* (Cambridge, MA: Da Capo Press, 2004), 215–17; Bodger, "The Immigrant Press and the Union Army," 126–27, 132–33; Carl Schurz, *The Reminiscences of Carl Schurz* (New York: McClure, 1907), vol. 2, 235. Schurz referred to Blenker as a "perfect stage general." See also Constantine Grebner, *We Were the Ninth*, trans. Frederic Trautmann (1897; reprint, Kent, OH: Kent State University Press, 1987).

51. Reinhart, *August Willich's Gallant Dutchman*; Burton, *Melting Pot Soldiers*, 72–89; Stephen D. Engle, *Yankee Dutchman: The Life of Franz Sigel* (Fayetteville: University of Arkansas Press, 1993), 49–58; Trefousse, *Carl Schurz*; Kaufmann, *Germans in the American Civil War*, 106; Wittke, *Refugees of Revolution*, 223.

52. Lonn, *Foreigners in the Union Army and Navy*, 594–95; Thornbrough, *Indiana in the Civil War Era*, 126; Mahin, *Blessed Place of Freedom*, 15–18, 228–33.

53. Mark H. Dunkelman, "Hardtack and Sauerkraut Stew: Ethnic Tensions in the 154th New York Volunteers, Eleventh Corps, during the Civil War," *Yearbook of German-American Studies* 36 (2001): 69–90. See also Mark Dunkelman, *Brothers One and All: Esprit de Corps in a Civil War Regiment* (Baton Rouge: Louisiana State University Press, 2004); see also Eric Benjaminson, "A Regiment of Immigrants: The 82nd Illinois Volunteer Infantry and the Letters of Captain Rudolph Mueller," *Journal of the Illinois State Historical Society* 94 (Summer 2001): 137–80.

54. Dunkelman, "Hardtack and Sauerkraut Stew," 69–90; Adolph von Steinwehr to Abraham Lincoln, April 5, 1863, and Carl Schurz to Lincoln, April 6, 1863, both in Abraham Lincoln Papers, Library of Congress, Washington, D.C. All the citations to the Lincoln Papers are taken from the online Abraham Lincoln Papers of the American Memory Project Web site at the Library of Congress.

55. Adolph von Steinwehr to Abraham Lincoln, April 5, 1863, and Carl Schurz to Lincoln, April 6, 1863, both in Lincoln Papers, Library of Congress

56. Keller, *Chancellorsville and the Germans*, 2–4. Several midwestern newspapers, including the *Indianapolis State Journal*, condemned the New York press for throwing the blame for the loss at Chancellorsville squarely upon the Germans of the 11th Corps. The editor published a rebuttal claiming that the New York papers were merely revealing their prejudices against the Germans in blaming them; he countered by arguing that the 11th Corps was only partially composed of Germans in any case and laid out in detail for their readers the exact composition of the corps.

57. Ibid.

58. Keller, "Germans in Civil War–Era Pennsylvania," 180; see also Keller, *Chancellorsville and the Germans*, 2–12; Dunkelman, "Hardtack and Sauerkraut Stew," 80.

59. Mahin, *Blessed Place of Freedom*, 16.

60. Joseph R. Reinhart, ed. and trans., *Two Germans in the Civil War: The Diary of John Daeuble and the Letters of Gottfried Rentschler, 6th Kentucky Volunteer Infantry* (Knoxville: University of Tennessee Press, 2004), 67–68; see also David Gould and James B. Kennedy, eds., *Memoirs of a Dutch Mudsill: The "War Memories" of John Henry Otto, Captain, Company D, 21st Regiment Wisconsin Volunteer Infantry* (Kent, OH: Kent State University Press, 2004); Lonn, *Foreigners in the Union Army and Navy*, 648–49.

61. Kamphoefner and Helbich, *Germans in the Civil War*, 141

62. Hubbard's quote taken from Leo M. Kaiser, ed., "Letters from the Front," *Illinois State Historical Journal* 56 (Summer 1963): 152; Burton, *Melting Pot Soldiers*, 202–12;

63. Reinhart, *Two Germans in the Civil War*, 67–68; Gould and Kennedy, *Memoirs of a Dutch Mudsill*, xvi; Kevin J. Weddle, "Ethnic Discrimination in Minnesota Volunteer Regiments during the Civil War," *Civil War History* 35 (September 1989): 239–59. For an excellent regimental history that provides a window into the relations of Americans with and perceptions of Germans see Dunkelman, *Brothers One and All*, 186–88, 189, 235; see also Reinhart, *August Willich's Gallant Dutchman*, 54–55. See the March 4, 1862, issue of the *Cincinnati Volksfreund* in which Willich writes with indignation that his 32nd Indiana Regiment was selected to guard the country road and the railroad while other, less experienced troops marched ahead, expecting to fight. According to Willich, because of the unit's previous success at Rowlett's Station, Kentucky, in January 1862, the Americans were afraid that the Germans might "snatch the laurels" earlier gained by the Germans and that they wanted to "push the Germans out of their place of honor."

64. Keller, "Germans in Civil War–Era Pennsylvania," 52, 143–66; Keller, *Chancellorsville and the Germans*, 136–37, 165–67.

65. Kamphoefner and Helbich, *Germans in the Civil War*, 161.

66. Öfele, *German-Speaking Officers in the U.S. Colored Troops*, x. For an overview of American reactions to Germans in the Civil War, see, for example, Fred Tangwell, "Immigrants in the Civil War: Some American Reactions" (Ph.D. diss., University of Chicago, 1962). For an excellent analysis of the illegal recruitment of Germans for the Union army, see Andrea Mehrländer, "'Ist dass nicht reiner sclavenhandel?' Die illegale rekrutierung deutcher auswanderer für die unionsarmee im amerikanischen bürgerkrieg" ["Is that not pure slave trading?" The Illegal recruitment of German emigrants for the Union Army during the American Civil War], *Amerikastudien* 44 (1999): 65–93.

67. Reinhart, *Two Germans in the Civil War*, 67–68; Kaufmann, *Germans in the American Civil War*, 98–99, 106–16; Karen Jean DeBres, "From Germans to Ameri-

cans: The Creation and Destruction of Three Ethnic Communities" (Ph.D. diss., Columbia University, 1986), 118; Bodger, "The Immigrant Press and the Union Army," 158–60; see also Louis Gerteis, *Civil War St. Louis* (Lawrence: University Press of Kansas, 2001), 73–76, 90–92; Thomas L. Snead, *The Fight for Missouri from the Election of Lincoln to the Death of Lyon* (New York: Scribner's, 1888), 148–49. For an excellent analysis of the German attitude during the early days of the war in a border state, see Rowan, *Germans for a Free Missouri*, 16–45.

68. Adolf E. Schroeder, *The German Contribution to the Building of the Americas* (Worcester, MA: Clark University Press, 1977), 291; DeBres, "From Germans to Americans," 118.

69. Levine, *Spirit of 1848*, 257.

70. Wittke, *Refugees of Revolution*, 233; Kaufmann, *Germans in the American Civil War*, 99–102.

71. *St. Paul Pioneer and Democrat*, February 25, 1862; Burton, *Melting Pot Soldiers*, 85–88; Lonn, *Foreigners in the Union Army and Navy*, 174; Kaufmann, *Germans in the American Civil War*, 98–99.

72. Earl J. Hess, "Osterhaus in Missouri: A Study in German-American Loyalty," *Missouri Historical Review* 77 (1984): 144–67; Lonn, *Foreigners in the Union Army and Navy*, 174, 180–84, 189–90, 280–83, 434 (Lonn argues that during the war, some German officers were imported from Germany); Kaufmann, *Germans in the American Civil War*, 102; Engle, "Raised Consciousness," 1–17; and Engle, *Yankee Dutchman*; see also Trefousse, *Carl Schurz*, 98–149; Öfele, *German-Speaking Officers in the U.S. Colored Troops*; Wittke, *Refugees of Revolution*, 235–39.

73. James M. Bergquist, "The Transformation of the German-American Newspaper Press, 1848–1860," in *The German-American Press*, ed. Henry Geitz (Madison: WI: Max Kade Institute for German-American Studies, 1992), 216–23; Lapham, "The German-Americans of New York City," 206–7; Bodger, "The Immigrant Press and the Union Army," 15–16, 114–23, 128–32; Harmut Keil, "A Profile of Editors of the German-American Radical Press, 1850–1910," in *The German-American Radical Press: The Shaping of Left Political Culture, 1850–1940*, ed. Elliott Shore, Ken Fones-Wolf, and James Danky (Urbana: University of Illinois Press, 1992), 15–28.

74. Reinhart, *August Willich's Gallant Dutchman*.

75. Lapham, "The German Americans of New York City," 205–8; Levine, *Spirit of 1848*, 257–63; Engle, "Raised Consciousness," 1–17; Wittke, *Refugees of Revolution*, 180–84, 280–84, 286–88; Burton, *Melting Pot Soldiers*, 207–11; Keller, "Germans in Civil War–Era Pennsylvania," 60; Keller, *Chancellorsville and the Germans*, 21–23, 108–9; see also Reinhart, *August Willich's Gallant Dutchman*, 2–3.

76. Frederick Rauchtuss to Lincoln, March 24, 1864, Lincoln Papers, Library of Congress; *Hartford Daily Times*, November 1, 1862.

77. Caspar Butz quote taken from Mahin, *Blessed Place of Freedom*, 187–202; Öfele, *German-Speaking Officers in the U.S. Colored Troops*, 3–15; Faust, *German Element in the United States*, vol., 2, 127; Lonn, *Foreigners in the Union Army and Navy*,

48–49, 658–59; Levine, *Spirit of 1848*, 256–71; Paludan, *"A People's Contest,"* 182–83, 195–96; Jörg Nagler, "The Lincoln-Fremont Debate and the Forty-Eighters," in Brancaforte, *The German Forty-Eighters in the United States*, 158–74; Kamphoefner and Helbich, *Germans in the Civil War*, 4–8, 13; *Chicago Tribune*, May 26, 1864.

78. Mahin, *Blessed Place of Freedom*, 202; Gustav Körner, *The Memoirs of Gustav Koerner, 1809–1896*, ed. Thomas I. McCormack (Cedar Rapids, IA: Torch Press, 1909), vol. 2, 410, 432; see also Paul Jagode et al. to John G. Nicolay, March 31, 1864, and Gustave Körner to Lincoln, September 22, 1864, both in Lincoln Papers, Library of Congress. *Chicago Tribune*, November 25, 1861, provides a good example of the problems the radical Germans created for all Germans in protesting Fremont's removal; see also *Chicago Tribune*, May 26, 1864. The best treatment of the German reaction to Fremont's removal is Jörg Nagler, "The Lincoln-Fremont Debate and the Forty-Eighters," 157–74.

79. Bergquist, "Germans and the Cities," 37–56; Kathleen Neils Conzen, "The Paradox of German-American Assimilation," *Yearbook of German-American Studies* 16 (1981): 153–60. See also Kathleen Neils Conzen, David A. Gerber, Ewa Morawska, George E. Pozzetta, and Rudolph J. Vecoli, "The Invention of Ethnicity: A Perspective from the U.S.A.," *Journal of American Ethnic History* 12 (Fall 1992): 3–41; Kathleen Neils Conzen, "German-Americans and the Invention of Ethnicity," in *America and the Germans: An Assessment of a Three-Hundred-Year History*, ed. Frank Trommler and Frank McVeigh (Philadelphia: University of Pennsylvania Press, 1985), 132–47.

80. Öfele, *German-Speaking Officers in the U.S. Colored Troops*, x.

81. Lonn, *Foreigners in the Union Army and Navy*, 658–59; Nagler, "The Lincoln-Fremont Debate and the Forty-Eighters," 157–65; Daniels, *Coming to America*, 159–64; Engle, "Raised Consciousness," 2–4; David Steven Cohen, "Reflections on American Ethnicity," *New York History* 72 (July 1991): 319–36; Conzen, "Germans Americans and the Invention of Ethnicity," 132–47; see also Keller, "Germans in Civil War–Era Pennsylvania," 1–15; Keller, *Chancellorsville and the Germans*, 2–12.

82. Reinhart, *August Willich's Gallant Dutchman*, 141–44. See the May 20, 1863, letter in the *Cincinnati Wöchentlich Volksfreund*.

83. Lonn, *Foreigners in the Union Army and Navy*, 658–59; Nagler, "The Lincoln Fremont Debate and the Forty-Eighters," 157–74; Keller, *Chancellorsville and the Germans*, 15–17.

84. Engle, "Raised Consciousness," 2–3; see also Engle, *Yankee Dutchman*, 94–99, 129–30, 151–70. Keller argues this in his work "Germans in Civil War–Era Pennsylvania," 52–54, 95–100; Keller, *Chancellorsville and the Germans*, 2–23.

85. John S. Carlisle to Salmon P. Chase, August 18, 1861, Lincoln Papers, Library of Congress. Carlisle was a representative from that portion of Virginia that was attempting to become West Virginia.

86. Charles Sumner to Lincoln, September–October 1861, Lincoln Papers, Library of Congress. Prior to the war, Sigel gave a speech at a Pennsylvania Teachers'

Association in Reading in which he confessed that he had lived among Americans for almost a decade and in that time had "struggled hard to gain a knowledge of the American people and their institutions," but that he loved the United States, wanted to continue to live in America, and wanted to die in America. The editor commented at the time that Sigel was unique in his desire to want to gain knowledge of America and that other Germans would be well served to follow his example, for if they did there would "far less antagonism" directed against them. See the *St. Louis Missouri Republican*, August 12, 1863.

87. Engle, "Raised Consciousness," 2–4; Levine, *Spirit of 1848*, 257–63; McMorrow, "Nineteenth Century German Political Immigrant and the Construction of American Culture and Thought," 105–23; Murray M. Horowitz, "Ethnicity and Command: The Civil War Experience," *Military Affairs* 42 (December 1978): 185; Franz Sigel, "The American Republic," *Atlas Essays*, no. 3 (1878): 61–77; for Sigel's views, see Western Reserve Historical Society, Sigel Papers, Miscellaneous Journals and Diaries; New York Historical Society, Sigel Papers, Miscellaneous Journals and Diaries; and Conzen et al., "Invention of Ethnicity," 4–17; Bodger, "The Immigrant Press and the Union Army," 58–59.

88. Trefousse, *Carl Schurz*, 124; Earl J. Hess, "Sigel's Resignation: A Study in German Americans and the Civil War," *Civil War History* 26 (1980): 5–17; Engle, "Raised Consciousness," 4.

89. Earl J. Hess, ed., *A German Yankee in the Fatherland: The Civil War Letters of Henry A. Kircher* (Kent, OH: Kent State University Press, 1983), 14–15; *Wisconsin State Journal*, August 15, 1861; *New York World*, July 27, 1861; see also C. F. E. Blaich to Simon Cameron, August 4, and G. Bajenks [sp] to Cameron, September 18, 1861, both in RG 107, Letters Received "Irregular Series," National Archives and Records Administration, Washington, D.C. These correspondents wanted to fight with Sigel, and Bajenks [sp] requested permission to use German in artillery drills, although the men were fluent in English.

90. *St. Paul Pioneer and Democrat*, December 7, 1861; see also Burlingame, *Lincoln's Journalist*, 287–88. In his travels back and forth between Washington and the western cities during the war, John Hay came to appreciate the value of Sigel. In late July 1862, he characterized the commander as the "bold, generous, confident, fortunate 'Flying Dutchman'—who can't be caught and who won't stay whipped, no matter what the odds against him may be, or how well the enemy may fight; who compels coy victory to his sturdy wooing in her own despite, and snatches glory from the dreadful front of defeat. Happy the man whose name is found on the list of Sigel's corps. For him the cup shall foam—the harp shall twang. The world will some day learn the proverb that the Springfield fight made common in St. Louis: 'You fights mit Sigel—you drinks mit me.'"

91. Howell's quote comes from Keller, *Chancellorsville and the Germans*, 47; *St. Louis Daily Missouri Democrat*, January 11, 1862; Engle, "Raised Consciousness," 4; Bodger, "The Immigrant Press and the Union Army," 171; Lonn, *Foreigners in the*

Union Army and Navy, 180; Kaufmann, *Germans in the American Civil War*, 451–66; see also *St. Paul Pioneer and Democrat*, December 7, 1861; September 23, 1861.

92. *Chicago Tribune*, November 21, 1861; *New York Times*, January 17, 1862; March 2, 1862; Sacramento *Daily Union*, March 25, 1863; *St. Paul Pioneer*, March 25, 1863; Rowan, *Germans for a Free Missouri*, 310–11; Wilhelm Kaufmann, "Sigel und Halleck," *Deutsch-Amerikanische Geschichtsblätter* 10 (October 1910): 210–16; Kaufmann, *Germans in the American Civil War*, 145–48.

93. Michael Burlingame, ed., *Lincoln Observed: Civil War Dispatches of Noah Brooks* (Baltimore: Johns Hopkins University Press, 1998), 44; Hess, "Sigel's Resignation," 5–17; Engle, "Raised Consciousness," 4–6; Wittke, *Refugees of Revolution*, 238–41; U.S. Government, *War of Rebellion: A Compilation of the Official Records of the Union and Confederate Armies* (Washington, DC: Government Printing Office, 1880–1900), ser. 1, vol. 7, 937; vol. 8, 502, 828–29; vol. 25, pt. 2, 71; vol. 27, pt. 3, 563 (hereafter *OR*); Basler, *Collected Works of Lincoln*, vol. 3, 303; vol. 5, 101; vol. 6, 93; see also Pula, "Sigel Regiment," 36–37. In a letter to Governor John Andrew of Massachusetts, on September 2, 1862, J. A. [Wetherly], a former Bay State resident, wrote from Iowa City that he wanted Andrew and other loyal governors to use their influence on behalf of Sigel. Arguing that Sigel was mistreated by Halleck and other West Pointers, he claimed that Sigel deserved a chance to prove "what a "military *genius* can do." J. A. [Wetherly] to John Andrew, September 2, 1862, John Andrew Papers, Massachusetts Historical Society, Boston, Massachusetts; *Indianapolis State Journal*, October 1, 1862. Even Northern governors who had raised troops for Sigel's command pressed the Lincoln administration to carry out the promises it had made to the Germans wanting to fight with Sigel. The *Chicago Tribune*, February 6, 1862, provides a wonderfully detailed description of how the press treated the affair between Halleck and Sigel, which was taken and translated from the *New Yorker Demokrat*. The February 17, 1862, issue of the *Tribune* published Sigel's public letter in response to Halleck and referred to his handling of the affair like a "tricky attorney and not like a soldier." "The affair must go on to its complete development," declared Sigel; "these gentlemen now have the opportunity to show whether they are disposed to let justice be done to us, or would like to trifle with us." "I say '*us*,'" he declared, "because my affair has become the affair of the Germans, at large." See also the issues of October 1 and 2, 1862, for the Sigel affair.

94. As quoted in Dunkelman, "Hardtack and Sauerkraut Stew," 79. Quoting from the *Chicago Journal*, the editor of the *St. Paul Pioneer and Democrat*, October 9, 1862, highlighted the importance of the press and Sigel. The editor argued that some German papers believed that Sigel himself really did not feel aggrieved as alleged, and that even if he did, he was "too faithful a soldier to go about among the newspaper reporters to get them to validate his grievances. The coinage of the Sigel story is but part and parcel of the tricks and intrigues of certain political and manful business of sowing the seeds of jealousy and division in the army of the Union. They selected Sigel to make an imaginary martyr of, in order to influence the Germans of the

North into an opposition to the Administration, and to make political capital for a seditious faction, but the contemptible trick will fail."

95. Adam Klippet to Lyman Trumbull, January 13, 1862, Lyman Trumbull Papers, Library of Congress, Washington, DC; see, for example, *Louisville Daily Journal*, January 16, 1862; *Cincinnati Daily Enquirer*, January 12, 1862; January 15, 1862; *New York Daily Tribune*, January 18, 1862; January 20, 1862; January, 28, 1862.

96. *Delaware Republican*, January 9, 1862; *Providence Daily Journal*, October 16, 1862; *St. Paul Pioneer and Democrat*, February 8, 1862.

97. P. A. Ladue to Francis P. Blair Jr., January 6, 1862, Lincoln Papers, Library of Congress. Ladue went on to observe that "if he [Sigel] did not possess the rare qualities with which, as a soldier, he is endowed, it would be policy to keep him in position and to elevate him. In Mo. you know our party needs to foster every element of strength. We must prepare to win future elections as well as battles. Sigel can serve us in both, and is worthy of our highest confidence." Ladue concluded that while he had no personal interest in Sigel, he had an "abiding interest in the success of our cause," both "in the field & at the polls; and I believe that Sigel can do *us* much more good in the one & in the other than can Granny Curtis." See also *Chicago Tribune*, August 4, 1862; August 5, 1862.

98. *Anzeiger des Westens*, January 13, 1862; Rowan, *Germans for a Free Missouri*, 298–99; Francis P. Blair to Lincoln, January 6, 1862, Lincoln Papers, Library of Congress; Nagler, "The Lincoln-Fremont Debate and the Forty-Eighters," 164.

99. *St. Louis Westliche Post*, January 15, 1862; *Louisville Daily Journal*, January 9, 1862; January 16, 1862; *New York Times*, January 27, 1862; March 2, 1863; *St. Louis Missouri Daily Democrat*, January 11, 1862; *Chicago Tribune*, January 11, 1862; *Missouri Republican*, January 14, 1862; *Indianapolis Daily Journal*, January 8, 1862; Hess, "Sigel's Resignation," 10–11; Wittke, *Refugees of Revolution*, 238–39; Bodger, "The Immigrant Press and the Union Army," 54–57. See also *St. Paul Pioneer*, October 5, 1862, which argued that Sigel's problem was he "suffered from what has been the ruin of many a man before him—too many friends." The editor added that all this restlessness and discontent about his resignation was attributed to the "goadings of indiscreet friends actuated by feelings springing out of nationality." See also the *St. Paul Pioneer and Democrat*, February 21, 1862, which talked about a *New York Times* article that translated a letter Sigel had written for the *New Yorker Demokrat* describing the same sentiment about Sigel's friends and his reactions.

100. Joseph Medill to Lincoln, February 17, 1864, Lincoln Papers, Library of Congress; Isaac Arnold to George Schneider, January 16, 1862, George Schneider Papers, Chicago Historical Society, Chicago, Illinois.

101. M. A. Jacobi to Lincoln, September 9, 1864, Lincoln Papers, Library of Congress. Jacobi's lengthy letter included a plea to allow Sigel a court of inquiry in order that he be exonerated from the "blame that has been attached to his conduct," and would restore him to command. "I know that an action like this, by your excellency, will secure us thousands of votes at the ensuing election."

102. Carl Schurz to Lincoln, February 29, 1864, Lincoln Papers, Library of Congress; Adam Klippet to Lyman Trumbull, January 13, 1862, Lyman Trumbull Papers, Library of Congress; Hess, "Sigel's Resignation," 5–17; Engle, "Raised Consciousness," 7–8.

103. Ben Field to Lincoln, October 20, 1862, Lincoln Papers, Library of Congress; see also Basler, *Collected Works of Lincoln*, 5, 472. Lincoln denied Field's request.

104. Keller, *Chancellorsville and the Germans*, 20; Lonn, *Foreigners in the Union Army and Navy*, 548, 551–53, 557.

105. La Vern J. Rippley, *The German-Americans* (Boston: Twayne, 1976), 70; Lonn, *Foreigners in the Union Army and Navy*, 548, 551–53, 557; Conzen, "German-Americans and the Invention of Ethnicity," 139–41; Keller, "Germans in Civil War–Era Pennsylvania," 320–24; Keller, *Chancellorsville and the Germans*, 137–67.

ᴄᴀ 2 ᴄᴀ

"WITH MORE FREEDOM AND INDEPENDENCE THAN THE YANKEES"

The Germans of Richmond, Charleston, and New Orleans during the American Civil War

Andrea Mehrländer

D ue to an extremely difficult source situation, a monographic discussion of the position of Germans or German Americans in the Confederacy is still the largest and most serious research gap in the field of American studies of the Civil War era.[1]

By 1850, no fewer than 44.3% of all foreigners who had emigrated to the antebellum South lived in the eight largest Southern cities and represented together more than 39% of the free white population of these cities. The Germans dominated especially in New Orleans (12.9%) and Charleston (9.1%), followed by Memphis (5.5%) and Richmond (5.0%).[2] Highly urbanized, single, and male, there were 71,962 native Germans living in the eleven states of the subsequent Confederacy in 1860, constituting only 1.3% of the entire free population in that area. In the social order of the antebellum South, the city was the synapse where the interests of the planter aristocracy came together with the interests of those in trade and finance; the diverse branches of trade and finance were the two professional options that attracted German immigrants most. By 1860, the Germans constituted between 6.2% in Richmond, 8.3% in Charleston, and almost 14% of the free white population in New Orleans.

Summarizing antebellum German life in Richmond, Charleston, and New Orleans, it becomes clear that by the end of 1860 the ethnic German minorities of all three cities had very similar characteristics: each city had one or two daily German-language newspapers, had a number of German societies, including the athletic and shooting associations, and supported at least one German theater. In addition, there was at least one Protestant, Catholic, and

Jewish congregation in each city and a colonization project furthered more or less actively by the Germans.

Among the German immigrants in either one of these three Southern cities, religious distinctions—surprisingly enough—had no cultural or social implications for their sense of community: longing for religious freedom so long suppressed in the homeland, the Germans of Charleston, Richmond, and New Orleans established Lutheran and Catholic churches that were independent units, many of which did not affiliate with a synod or a diocese for years. A body of representatives from the membership, which reported to the congregation, administered their affairs. They were empowered to hire and fire pastors, buy property, and direct the financial structure of the church. This independence explains why so many German immigrant congregations formed and disbanded over the years prior to 1865, resulting in a lack of religious ethnic leadership.[3] Especially for German Jews, economic survival was the paramount concern. Those who needed to work on Saturday just to keep a job could not afford to follow the commandment to keep the Sabbath—thus, only about 10% of all newly arrived German Jews within New Orleans officially belonged to a synagogue prior to the Civil War.[4] The German antebellum communities of Richmond and Charleston were too small to sustain more than one or two congregations of either denomination; to them, it was more important to worship in their native tongue than to argue about matters of liturgy or theological creeds, and sometimes German Lutherans, German Catholics, and even German Jews could be found sitting next to each other harmoniously in the same pew—something unheard of in the German fatherland.[5] How visible, then, was such a small ethnic minority that not only worshiped together in antebellum times but fought in the same military companies during the war?

When the War between the States broke out, the Confederacy required and used German expertise and craftsmanship almost from day one. It was the twenty-nine-year-old Carl H. Schwecke from Hannover, a member of the German Artillery of Charleston, who fired the so-called secession gun as a salute in front of the *Charleston Mercury* building in honor of South Carolina's secession from the Union on December 20, 1860.[6] Bavarian-born William Flegenheimer's penmanship can still be admired in Virginia's Ordinance of Secession.[7] As far as Virginia maps were concerned, General Robert E. Lee used the topographical works of Louis von Buchholtz throughout the entire war. Von Buchholtz, a retired officer and engineer, was a native of Wurttemberg.[8] Twenty-five-year-old Julius Baumgarten of Hannover not only designed the great seal of the Confederacy but also the Confederate Medals of Honor.[9] Philip P. Werlein, who was born in Bavaria in 1812, printed the unofficial national anthem of the Confederacy, "Dixie," for the first time in 1860.[10]

President Jefferson Davis surrounded himself with a number of Germans: on February 21, 1861, Davis appointed German-born Christopher G. Memminger of the city of Mergentheim as the first Confederate secretary of the Treasury.[11] The Hannoverian horticulturist E. G. Eggeling cared for the gardens of Davis's residence, the "White House of the Confederacy." Heinrich Georg Müller, a native of Lauterbach/Hesse, served as bodyguard for the president until 1864. Finally, Westphalia-born pastor Karl Minnigerode became famous as Jefferson Davis's personal confessor and as an ardent supporter of the institution of slavery. No fewer than sixteen times did Minnigerode say the benediction prayers at the Confederate House of Representatives.[12]

Though correct, this short sketch of a German-Confederate symbiosis would be misleading and distorts historical facts. However, the German minority of the South—largely represented in this study through the interests and perceptions of their ethnic spokesmen[13]—was all but insignificant politically, militarily, and economically during the American Civil War.

Richmond, Virginia (1860)—"More German names than any other appear over the doors in some parts of it"[14]

In no other city of the Confederacy was it more difficult for German-born citizens to maintain a pro-Confederate attitude than in Richmond, Virginia. The reasons for this are fivefold, beginning with the fact that unlike many other urban centers of the Confederacy, Richmond was located only 107 miles south of Washington, D.C., and thus was conveniently situated for those who no longer wanted to put up with home front hardships but preferred to take the easy way out by crossing the lines into Union territory.[15] The German exodus began in 1861 and continued throughout the war, widely noticed and highly disapproved of by the non-German citizens of Richmond and the Confederate government.

Also, during antebellum times, Richmond's Germans had maintained very close ties to their fellow citizens residing in Northern cities like Baltimore,

Washington, and Philadelphia. Public native suspicion, due to this traditional behavior, allowed the provost marshal to focus on the Germans as a main target group suspected of disloyalty, espionage, and treason while Richmond was under martial law.

In addition, beginning with John Herbig's medical support for wounded Union soldiers of German descent in 1861, Richmond's Germans showed an alarming closeness to the "enemy" and thus became the victims of a decidedly antiforeign, anti-Jewish, and anti-German Confederate propaganda.

Fourth, due to Richmond's status as the Confederate capital, the city's Germans were under a lot more public pressure than their fellow citizens in Charleston or New Orleans. Because Richmond was the Confederate seat of government, officials there were more concerned about safety control and, thus, supervised civilian aliens more intensely and with much more suspicion than anywhere farther south. Finally, the absence of ethnic spokesmen in Richmond's German community, usually stemming from the officers' ranks of German antebellum militia companies, divided German pro-Confederate patriotism and loyalty along economic lines. Those who could afford to live through wartime hardships, had families in Richmond, and were eager to protect as much as possible of their antebellum fortunes and businesses showed an unwavering support of the Confederacy. Poorer Germans, not yet established, mostly male and single, opted for the easy way out: they either went west in pursuit of economic success or north to escape military service and to join friends and family.

Richmond's Germans, who came mainly from Hesse and Saxony and were mostly craftsmen, may have had ambivalent feelings about the war, but in the spring of 1861, they were convinced that secession was the correct political move. Not only did 6.45% of the Richmond Germans own a total of eighty-one slaves and were thus owners of 0.8% of all the slaves in the city,[16] but as adopted citizens, they offered loyalty and patriotism to the newborn Confederacy: quickly they assembled the Virginia Rifles under Captain Florence Miller and the Marion Rifles" under Captain August Lybrock to join the 1st Virginia Infantry and the 15th Virginia Infantry as Company K, respectively. In Richmond, 24.6% of all Germans in the city were in ethnic German units. Because of the separation of West Virginia, it is difficult to estimate the size of the contingent of ethnic German soldiers that Virginia contributed to the Confederacy; one can assume approximately 10%.

Civilian Germans, however, were unwilling to let go of old traditions—such as their close private relationships to German-born family members and friends up north.

By the summer of 1861, therefore, German civilians started leaving the city—to go either back home to Germany or, worse, up north. This behavior was untimely, appeared highly opportunistic, and was not at all in line with the patriotism shown by the Germans who had just been mustered into military service. Burghardt Hassel, the editor of the German gazette *Richmonder Anzeiger*, who passionately defended slavery and secession, disapproved of this exodus and voiced his opinion strongly. The escape of Erhard Richter, a well-known German brewery owner, made the local headlines. His two sons, seventeen and eighteen years of age, joined the 5th New York Artillery and were killed in battle.[17]

Now that German loyalty appeared to be of questionable character, those patriotic Germans who were left behind had to take care of the families of their fellow soldiers themselves. In May 1861, the *Richmonder Anzeiger* called for the establishment of an aid society to support the families of those serving with the Marion Rifles and the Virginia Rifles.[18] When the German singing society known as "Virginia" announced plans in June 1861 to "support the families of the fighting German soldiers for the entire duration of the war," it triggered the formation of a general German aid committee, which was set up on June 11, 1861.[19]

At this time—in June 1861—countless wounded from either side poured into the city of Richmond. Hospitals emerged on every corner. Adequate apothecaries were needed: Hannoverian-born August Bodeker, who had served as first captain of the Virginia Rifles from 1850 to 1853, and his brother, Henry, were well respected in the field ever since they had founded the Bodeker and Company Apothecary in 1846. In 1860, the apothecary was worth $40,000. When the war broke out, August and Henry were exempt from military service and were free to devote all their energy to delivering drugs and medication to Confederate hospitals. Special contacts existed between the Bodeker brothers and Sally Tompkins's hospital: "Never once did [urgent calls for drugs] go unheeded if the Bodekers had the drugs."[20] The Bodekers were guided by sheer pragmatism: August was married to an American woman, and he owned slaves. His professional well-being was closely interrelated with that of the Confederacy.[21]

By August 1861, the first trials for treason against Germans were announced. At this time, Richmond was filled with innumerable wounded and prisoners of war, the latter being fairly often of German descent. Their very presence and close proximity made life extremely uncomfortable for Richmond's Germans and contributed to dangerous feelings of distrust and suspicion among Richmond's native population.[22] Despite this atmosphere, and parallel to the trials for treason, Bavarian-born grocer and fruit dealer John Herbig started his campaign to nurse fifty badly wounded Union soldiers of German descent, who had been brought into the Richmond Poor House. For his project, he placed an ad in the paper and asked his fellow citizens to donate old shirts and cotton cloth. Herbig had been denied his request to raise his own Confederate Infirmary Company; instead, he concentrated on wounded German Yankees.[23]

With martial law in effect since March 1, 1862, a wave of arrests washed over Richmond's German community, also concerning other foreign nationals, as a result of an unfortunate coincidence: the discharge of the twelve-month-volunteers from the Virginia Rifles and the Marion Rifles on May 16, 1862, became effective one month after the Confederacy had passed its first conscription law, ordering all males between the ages of eighteen and thirty-five to serve in the military. German veterans, who had served for a year and now felt cheated by the government, sought the protection of Consul Edward Wilhelm DeVoss.[24] DeVoss, who had been appointed consul of the city of Bremen for Richmond, Petersburg, and Norfolk in 1833, not only represented fellow citizens from thirty different German states but also headed a minority group that had no ethnic spokesmen, as did Charleston or New Orleans. Men like August Bodeker, former militia captain John Hartz, Captain Albert Lybrock of the Marion Rifles, and staff officer Louis v. Buchholtz moved mainly in American circles and kept their distance from German traditions; their interest seldom went beyond support in organizing German festivals. Thus, DeVoss issued a total of 1,378 certificates of nationality until the end of 1862.[25]

Between 1862 and 1863, no fewer than 385 German civilians—almost a quarter of Richmond's entire ethnic German community—were arrested for alleged disloyalty.[26] Well-known saloon proprietor and slave owner Valentin Hechler was jailed for treason, as were prominent Turner Hermann L. Wiegand and the former speaker of the Social Democratic Turners Association,

Carl Kenne. Almost 20% of the men arrested turned out to be veterans of the 1st or 15th Virginia Infantry and the 19th Virginia Militia Regiment.[27] Provost marshal officers forced their way into German homes in the middle of the night, arrested the men out of bed, or tracked them down on their way to work—only consular papers could save them from jail. All of them were freed upon the intervention of Consul DeVoss. Naturally, most of these men were traumatized by their experiences and felt that they had been treated as criminals.

Parallel to the wave of arrests, though, the Confederate government tried hard to single out German businesses that were wealthy enough to stand surety for the Confederacy in Europe. The prosperous tobacco merchants Daniel von Gröning and Emil Nölting signed up, whereas Consul DeVoss refused.[28] Besides Philip Rahm's Eagle Machine Works, Richmond was home to a number of smaller German businesses that had engaged in the production of war goods out of a mixture of loyalty and opportunism. These included Thomas Westermann's boot factory; the iron, steel, and brass production firm of Gerhard and Morgenstern; Koch's military hat company; the button factory of Wildt and Linnemann; F. Polster's drum-making company; and John Hartz's tailor shop for military textiles.[29] The printing company of Hoyer and Ludwig, which had produced Confederate five-cent stamps since October 1861 and engraved seventeen Confederate war bonds as well as paper money, even gained national fame but was confiscated by November 1865.[30]

In 1862, thousands of Union prisoners of war flooded into a war-torn city that was already filled beyond capacity. Due to the ignorance of non-German Confederate officers about the ethnic backgrounds of their soldiers, the secret illegal business of providing "German Yankees" with food through German-born Confederate guards increased in 1863 and 1864. During those years, the men of the 19th Virginia Militia Regiment were detailed as guards in Libby prison. Companies H and M happened to be composed exclusively of Germans—in many cases, blood indeed proved to be thicker than water.[31]

In July 1863, the situation in Richmond turned dramatic. The *Richmond Enquirer* wrote: "Foreigners of every age and sex crowded the office of the provost-marshal in Richmond, anxious to get passports to go North by way of the blockade. The Jew, whose ample pockets were stuffed with confederate money; the Germans, with hands on pockets tightly pressed."[32] By the summer of 1864, alleged "secret police" broke into Mr. Schwarz's home in

Rocketts; a day later the same happened to the home of Mrs. Schwägerly—in search of counterfeit passports.[33] Literally any kind of crime or offense in Richmond was attributed to Germans. In February 1864, the *New York Herald* reported that "the government has been in possession of facts that hinted, beyond a doubt, to the existence of a secret organization of disloyal men, having for its object the forcible release of the prisoners held at Libby and on Belle Isle, the assassination of President Davis, and the destruction of the government buildings and workshops. A German, named Heinz, was arrested as the ringleader of the plot."[34]

German civilian morale finally broke in the winter of 1864 and brought a new dimension to German-Confederate relations in Richmond: a commercialized form of illegal border crossing, including espionage.[35] After several Germans had been caught in the summers of 1863 and 1864 trying to cross borders without permission, Germans now had organized a professional "underground railroad" and used it frequently. In 1864, one of the organizers, Friedrich W. E. Lohmann, former first lieutenant of the Virginia Rifles, befriended Elizabeth Van Lew and Samuel Ruth and turned an ardent Unionist spy. In April 1865, as a reward for his services, Lohmann was well paid and hired as a detective for the U.S. provost marshal in Richmond.[36] Patriotic Germans, like the lager beer saloon owner John Gottfried Lange, despised him for this act of treason and shunned him in public.[37]

It was because of greedy and opportunistic "Unionist turncoats" like Lohmann that Richmond's German civilians had been caught in a vicious cycle of distrust and suspicion, becoming Provost Marshal Winder's main target group in 1864 and 1865. With every German who left for the North, the situation grew worse for those remaining in the Confederate capital; patriotic actions were overlooked and hardly mattered. By 1865, even the most pro-Confederate German felt humiliated and unable to keep up devotion for a cause that had long excluded Richmond's ethnic German community. The majority of the Germans, who had passed the war in Germany or up North, however, came back to Richmond in 1865–66, returning to a city that had rejected them in times of need, ready to rebuild their looted homes from scratch.

In 1866, August Bodeker joined the city government of Richmond as the first ethnic German councillor.[38] In 1866–67, George A. Peple, who had taught at the Confederate Naval School and had briefly edited the *Richmonder*

Anzeiger, became the spokesman for the Germans leaning toward the Democrats. The smaller group of Republicans among the Germans gathered around Hermann L. Wiegand, a merchant from Saxony and formerly a Turner.[39] The ethnic German minority, under Peple's chairmanship, held a mass meeting in Dueringer's Park on June 5, 1868, and passed a joint resolution against military occupation and the preferential treatment of the black population: "We are proud to be of German descent and we reject with indignation as an insult to be placed on equal political and social footing with the negroes just extracted from the mire of slavery. We consider it as sacrificing the nation, to force the white population of the South under the rule of a half-civilized and inferior race."[40]

In 1869, the German minority was able to elect two Democratic candidates, William Lovenstein[41] and August Bodeker, to the Virginia legislature. Lovenstein, who later became president of the Senate of Virginia, held the highest political office ever attained by a Jew in Virginia in the nineteenth century. In the same year, the Democrats succeeded in electing Gilbert C. Walker as governor of Virginia. By 1870, with political turmoil coming to an end, 1,650 Germans resided in the city of Richmond again.[42]

Charleston, South Carolina (1860)—"In 1860, the Germans of Charleston were comfortable and highly respected . . . and were just in general happy and optimistic"[43]

Between 1850 and 1860—while the ethnic German community of Richmond grew by 114% and that of New Orleans by 71%—the ethnic German minority of Charleston was almost stagnant, with an increase of only 7%. Because there was so little fluctuation in the personal structure of the ethnic German community of Charleston, an immigrant community could arise here that was extraordinarily homogeneous in a number of areas. More than 73% of the Germans in Charleston were Protestants who came from the northwestern German states of Hannover, Oldenburg, and Holstein; in many cases the immigrants were related to each other or had at least known each other in the homeland. This kind of selective immigration was supported by the direct shipping route that had existed between Bremerhaven and Charleston since 1832, as well as by Captain Heinrich Wieting from Bremen, who transported more than three-quarters of all Charleston Germans across the Atlantic on his ships between 1839 and 1860.[44] Occupationally, the Charleston Germans were small traders and retail businessmen. On the eve of the Civil War, no fewer than 81% of all the groceries in the city were in German hands.

The Germans of Charleston approved and supported the institution of slavery and swore absolute loyalty to their adopted home; studies from 1850 have shown that 18.52% of Charleston's Germans owned a total of 583 slaves.[45] Thus Germans owned almost 3% of the slaves living in Charleston. By the outbreak of the Civil War, the numbers decreased in Charleston, as was the general trend: in 1860 only 8.9% of the Germans owned a total of 325 slaves— in the case of secession, this clearly meant a decision in favor of leaving the Union. In the *Charleston Daily Courier* from November 11, 1860, German ethnic spokesmen Johann A. Wagener and editor Franz Melchers, together with other German compatriots, called for a convention "for the purpose of dissolving connection with the Federal Union." Wagener's name appeared in the paper at the beginning of December 1860 as the "immediate secession" candidate for the election to the Secession Convention of December 6. Due to the strong presence of the pro-Confederate German ethnic spokesmen, the German community of Charleston can be judged as a leader in pronouncing itself decidedly pro-secessionist and supportive of slavery.[46]

In Charleston, the group of ethnic German spokesmen came from the officers' ranks of the voluntary militia. Ethnic militias were a means of self-definition in the martially oriented culture of the South and, on the basis of their societal structures, took on buffering functions similar to those of the Little Germanies sprouting up all over the North. Because ethnic militias did not belong to the regular militia, but rather to the voluntary militia of a state, and were founded on the private initiative of individual persons, their founding alone was a statement of the desire to participate in the military and political culture of the adopted country. In 1860 Charleston's German minority not only had the oldest German militia unit in the United States—the Charleston German Fusiliers of 1775—but also could support six active militia companies, of which five were formed between 1842 and 1859, including the only ethnic German cavalry militia of the South.

The social life of Charleston's German minority was almost completely in the hands of these twenty-four militia officers who, through a complex network of clubs, nepotistic connections, and their business contacts as merchants, had created a watertight structure of mutual interests that allowed

TABLE 2.1

Hampton's Legion	German Volunteers	Capt. Bachman
1st Regiment of Artillery	German Artillery, Co. A	Capt. Harms
	German Artillery, Co. B	Capt. Werner
1st Regiment of Rifles	German Riflemen	Capt. Small
	Palmetto Riflemen	Capt. Melchers
17th Regiment Infantry	German Fusiliers	Capt. Lord
Mounted Troops	German Hussars	Capt. Cordes

them to reach nearly every aspect of community life. The German officers of the antebellum militias of Charleston were democratically oriented, loyal adoptive citizens of South Carolina, and more than one-third of them belonged to the group of slaveholders. Because of their publicly declared acceptance of the Southern way of life, there existed a symbiosis based on mutual respect between the natives and the German immigrants.

By New Year's Day 1862, the *Charleston Mercury* reported that the city of Charleston had mobilized forty-eight militia companies with more than 3,000 soldiers. Among these were seven German companies, as shown in Table 2.1. Charleston's numbers for military service among Germans are especially notable when compared with those for either Richmond or New Orleans: 395 men, or 20.3% of all the Germans of Charleston—are known to have served in ethnic German army units, excluding the militia. If one assumes that South Carolina as a state contributed about 500 ethnic German soldiers, this meant that almost 17% of all the Germans fought for the Confederacy, as opposed to 14.6% of native soldiers.[47] Considering that 61% of the Confederacy's able-bodied men served in the military—as opposed to only 35% within the Union—it seems rather natural that German military participation shows somewhat higher percentages.

But Charleston's Germans also participated in other Confederate undertakings: on April 19, 1861, President Lincoln announced the establishment of a blockade of the ports of all seceded states from South Carolina to Texas,[48] the largest blockade in history at that time. The immediate consequence was the development of a new wartime professional—blockade-runners: "When the war broke out and ports were blockaded, every old barge or river flatboat was picked up and made seaworthy to run the blockade. Foreign-born were usually prime movers in this enterprise."[49] A total of eighty-eight ships registered in the ports of New Orleans and Charleston by the summer of 1861 belonged to German owners or partners.[50] However, probably only a small fraction of these were involved in the business of blockade-running because fifty-three of these ships were registered in the port of New Orleans, which fell into Union hands in April 1862.

Because of the often phenomenal profits, many men were ready to assume the enormous risks of running the blockade. If a blockade-running ship was captured by the Union, foreign sailors, according to international law, had to fear only a two- to three-week arrest, whereas Confederate citizens automatically became prisoners of war, and in the worst cases remained so until the end of the war. It soon became an open secret that Confederate captains liked to equip their ships with foreign sailors. The helpful contributions of Marcus W. Price listing blockade captains and pilots assume a number of about forty-five German captains who ran the blockade professionally for the Confederacy between 1861 and 1865.[51]

By far the best-known German captains' families in Charleston were the Habenicht brothers and the Tecklenburg brothers. Georg F. and August Habenicht, brothers from Osterholtz near Hannover, were trained seamen; the third brother, John F. L. Habenicht, with whom they lived on Elliott Street, ran a grocery store. At the ages of twenty-six and twenty-eight, respectively, Georg and August had come a long way. August Habenicht was the sole owner of the schooners *Mary* and *Acorn*. As captain, he ran the blockade on the *Acorn* three times himself in 1861–62; he delivered sand to Castle Pinckney on the *Mary* but lost the ship on the way to Nassau on December 3, 1864. Habenicht owned half of the schooner *Sarah*; the ship returned home successfully nine times before it went up in flames on June 19, 1862. The *Jasper*, however, one-third of which belonged to August Habenicht, had only one successful voyage. All the ships' owners, Habenicht's partners, were natives of Charleston. Habenicht sailed only between Charleston and Nassau.

His brother Georg F. Habenicht was originally the sole owner of the *Julia Anne* but later sold half of the ship to Messrs. Bee and Jervey of W. C. Bee and Company. He commanded the *Anne Deas*, the steamship *Celt*, and the schooner *Petrel*. As captain of the *Petrel* in the spring of 1864, on the way to Nassau, alerted by floating cotton bales, he found the pieces of the wreck of the blockade-runner *Juno* and rescued the two survivors.[52] The younger of the two Habenichts ran the blockade on the *Petrel* four times before the ship was destroyed in December 1864. It is not known what happened to the brothers after the war.[53]

The Tecklenburg family followed a different pattern. Peter and John Tecklenburg,[54] both born in St. Margarethen, in Holstein, not only were captains but also had invested in other ships. In this way they made a double profit. Peter Tecklenburg sailed as captain on the *Flora* and the *Laura* between Wilmington and Nassau; he also sailed between Charleston and Nassau on the *Victoria* and the *James R. Pringle*. Except for the *Victoria*, whose owner was John Campsen, all the other ships belonged to natives. As captain, John Tecklenburg commanded the *Experiment* before it was renamed *Laura* and given to his brother.[55] John Tecklenburg was captured in December 1864 and was held as a prisoner of war in Fort Warren, near Boston.[56] As the war came to an end shortly thereafter, Tecklenburg returned unharmed to Charleston. Both brothers traveled first-class[57] with their families to Bremen in October 1867; they probably set up business connections there with their profits. Three years later, Peter Tecklenburg no longer went to sea but established himself in a grocery business in Charleston in 1870, with a financial volume of under $2,000 and a moderate line of credit.[58]

The motives of the Habenicht and Tecklenburg brothers are clear: the blockade situation fit in with their occupational activities and was independent of patriotism and war enthusiasm; for a brief time, they were part of a needed and admired occupational group that, considering the risk, was well paid. But patriotism also mattered—especially among Charleston's German women, as the following incident attests: inspired by the activities of the ladies of New Orleans to finance a cannon boat through donations, a similar project was started in Charleston in the spring of 1862 with the significant support of the *Charleston Courier*. One Miss Gelzer donated five dollars, and thus began South Carolina's legendary Ladies' Gunboat Fund; a wave of donations poured in from women throughout the state, resulting in the financing of the gunboat *Palmetto State*. The list of donors, which is extant only for 1862 and discreetly names no sums, names eleven German women from Walhalla,[59] including the wife of the publisher of the *Deutsche Zeitung*, Franz Melchers, who was there at the time. In Walhalla, a rural community that served as a summer refuge for Charleston's Germans, the German ladies were removed from the critical eye of the Charleston society and were thus under no public pressure to contribute patriotic donations. They did so in spite of this, because they all had at least one male family member in the ranks of the Confederate army.

Civilian Germans, especially those who were exempt from military service, were eager to support the Confederacy in other ways: the Importing and Exporting Company, established by William C. Bee,[60] was the first of a total of five trading companies that were incorporated in South Carolina in 1862–63 for the purpose of running the blockade.[61] On May 27, 1863, the *Charleston Mercury* announced that company shares had been sold for a value of $1 million. The stockholders' list of Bee and Company was a who's who of Charleston society, especially because at the beginning of 1863 only a minority of the city's inhabitants could afford the minimum amount of $1,000 to participate in risky speculations.

Among the 245 Bee stockholders of the Importing and Exporting Company were twenty-six German businesses,[62] amounting to 10.6% of all shareholders; they were thus overrepresented in relation to their population percentage in Charleston.[63] They had purchased shares valued at $79,000. No fewer than 42.3% of the participating German businesses were groceries; 19.2% dealt in dry goods or sold spirits.

The German businessmen were of course conscious of the risks of running the blockade. They trusted William Bee because his company, as opposed to Fraser, Trenholm and Company, employed Germans at the decisive contact points: among the first captains who sailed for Bee was Georg F. Habenicht, the commander of the *Julia Anne*.[64] Bee's bookkeeper was C. G. Mueller,[65] who accompanied Theodore D. Jervey, Bee's most trusted director, to Cuba and Europe to buy three new ships for Bee in April and May 1863.

In order to replace the absent Mueller, August Conrad took over. Born in Hannover, he had just come to Charleston in 1859 at the age of seventeen, boarding at the Carolina House Hotel, where he made friends with C. G. Mueller. Conrad's tasks included issuing share notes, "which were to be signed by the president and treasurer and which had to be reissued every time there was a change of ownership."[66] Conrad was thus well informed about every shareholder. In the fall of 1863, he became the procurator and deputy head of the Bee Company in Wilmington, North Carolina:

I grew increasingly into my position . . . and in the trust of my superiors, and when Mr. Jervey resigned his office of treasurer and secretary of the company,[67] this was offered to me. I thus had achieved a responsible and respected position, with full powers over the means of the company and also power of attorney for W. C. Bee & Co. in connection with its private business. I was now partially responsible for this extensive company and . . . can say without exaggeration that I enjoyed great respect among the people of Charleston, because everyone was delighted with the Bee Company and everything connected with it; besides politics the company was the main object of interest. Yes, I felt happy with all my work.[68]

August Conrad's right hand and inspector of cargo brought into Wilmington by ship was a certain Mr. Kittel, presumably a German of Wilmington, North Carolina, while Mueller, the former bookkeeper, headed up the intermediary office of the company in Nassau.[69] Mueller paid off the captains arriving in Nassau and oversaw the forwarding of the cargo stored there on its way to or from Europe.

German shareholders could thus acquire information about the liquid assets of the company at any time from their compatriots Conrad and Mueller. William C. Bee and August Conrad trusted and respected each other highly.[70] Young Conrad was tireless in advertising the newly founded stock company: in 1863, he was able to win over H. W. Kuhtmann, the retired former business partner of Conrad's original boss, as a shareholder; Kuhtmann bought ten shares.[71] Conrad was also able to sell two shares to the Italian merchant A. Canale,[72] who traded in foreign fruit and had served as a private in Theodor Cordes's German Hussars until 1862. Conrad knew Canale because both of them lived in the Carolina Hotel. Conrad was also able to sell one share for $1,000 to the Clasius and Witte Company; in this case as well, Conrad had met Clemens and Felix Clacius in the Carolina Hotel in 1860. In addition, the twenty-year-old Clacius and his twenty-four-year-old partner, Armin F. Witte, had served with Conrad in Chicester's Charleston Zouave Cadets in 1861–62.[73]

In 1864, August Conrad took over the consulate of Hannover in Charleston from his older brother, which he directed until the end of the war and which brought him into contact with almost all the Germans living in Charleston. Investing funds in blockade-running was a two-sided affair for the participants: the ships chartered by Bee delivered urgently needed weapons and ammunition for the Confederate army. Cotton, in return, which had collected in great quantities in the port of Charleston and was to bring profit in Europe, was exported. Until the end of the war this aspect of blockade-running was publicly considered highly patriotic.

The importation of all luxury articles and natural goods, for which there was a need especially among the civilian population of the South, was a different story. These items were not essential for the war, but they were much more lucrative for the investors because they could be sold for the highest prices. A ton of salt could be purchased in Nassau for $6.50 and sold in the South for $1,700 in Confederate currency. The purchase price in Nassau of a ton of coffee was $249; in the starving South it could be sold for $5,500 or twenty-two times the purchase price.

In the face of this enormous profit opportunity, it must be mentioned that some German Bee investors were also active on their own: For example, John Campsen, owner of Campsen's Flour Mills, was the sole owner of the blockade-runner *Victoria*, on which his friend Peter Tecklenburg served as captain.[74] There are no documents to show how successful the *Victoria*'s voyages were. It is known, however, that John Campsen owned a plantation outside of Charleston in November 1865, which he had purchased during the war.

For August Conrad, who had neither family nor property in Charleston and did not have to demonstrate loyalty to principles, the situation in 1863 was very simple: "I have already mentioned that, as a good German, I was less enthusiastic about the interests of the South and put my own interests before those of the Confederate States."[75] Thus he speculated with cotton and jewels in 1863 and 1864, made a profit ten times over, and received "a nice little sum."[76]

Who were the Germans who had invested in Bee, and why had they done so? Of the thirty-one German businessmen listed individually by name, twenty-six (83.9%) could prove their approximate arrival in Charleston: two of them had been born in Charleston and ran their fathers' businesses; one immigrated in the 1820s, nine in the 1840s, and fourteen in the 1850s.[77] As the taxed fortunes of 1859 show, all were established in the Charleston business world at the outbreak of war; they had acquired property, and some had started families. The Germans listed were certainly interested in financial profits and had not bought the shares solely for patriotic reasons, even if J. C. H. Claussen, slave owner and head of Claussen's Steam Bakery, recommended the products of his bakery only to those customers who stood up with a pure heart for "Southern Rights and Southern Interests,"[78] and if John Campsen announced his leanings in November 1860, by putting up a dark blue Palmetto flag with the motto "Now or Never" over the business entrance of his grain store.[79]

For these men there was never a question if they would have a future in the South after the war. Charleston had become their home; they had invested every cent in their new existence in it and refused to let a war destroy their achievements. On the contrary, they wanted to increase their property and, at the same time, do something good for the Confederacy.

Financial figures for 1859–60 are available for twenty-two (84.6%) of the twenty-six German companies that had invested in the Importing and Exporting Company. According to these figures, these companies possessed private and business fortunes amounting to $481,510, as well as eighty-nine slaves, and were thus quite wealthy before the outbreak of war.[80] Much of this was invested in property and bound the men locally to Charleston or the state of South Carolina. The profit in shares (not counting the sale of shares) earned by blockade-running increased the companies' prewar total fortunes by 147.6% to $711,000. Sixteen companies (61.5%) were run by war veterans, and four companies (15.4%) had one or more partners or brothers in the army. Almost 77% of the businessmen had thus served in the military for the South.

German Bee investors were mainly men who had belonged to the economic elite of Charleston even before the war and had established themselves professionally. These men had much to lose from the war and had every reason to protect their life's work with careful investments.[81] It is also clear that the investors were not war profiteers who fled the country in April 1865, at the latest, but rather men who, after serving in the war and in spite of difficult conditions, chose to remain in the new country. Eight of them became involved in local politics in Charleston and the German minority there after 1865 and used their economic power to finance the postwar immigration programs for German compatriots. By December 1901, Charleston was able to boast the South Carolina Interstate and West Indian Exposition, financed almost exclusively by Friedrich Wilhelm Wagener, an ex-officer of the Confederate army and Johann A. Wagener's brother.[82]

Moreover, their economic power allowed the Germans of Charleston to nominate Johann A. Wagener, their spokesman for decades, as the independent candidate of the Conservative Party in Charleston's mayoral election of 1871.[83] Wagener won by a majority of 777 votes against Gilbert Pillsbury, becoming Charleston's third German-born mayor after Mintzing and Schnierle. Wagener, who had been appointed as brigadier general of the 4th Militia Brigade of South Carolina by Governor Orr in 1866, was fifty-five years old at the time. He had lived through the end of the war on his farm in Walhalla and had experienced what "Yankee rule" meant.[84]

The native population of Charleston knew about Wagener's almost four decades of absolute loyalty to the South, remembered the "hero of Port Royal," and approved of his business and social efforts for the good of Charleston.[85] Northern carpetbaggers and scalawags saw in Wagener first and foremost a German, who presumably, like his compatriots in the rest of the country, sympathized with the Union and besides had never owned slaves. He thus was an ideal candidate. What the carpetbaggers among the Republicans, especially those new to town, did not know was that Wagener saw slavery as the only reasonable institution for the coexistence of both races and was hardly a friend of emancipation. As he wrote to his former teacher in 1840, "The Negro must be ruled by force," if necessary "with the help of the whip."[86] A decided "Negro enmity" could also be felt in Wagener's new newspapers, the *Charlestoner Zeitung*[87] and the *Südlicher Correspondent.*[88] The *New York Herald* described Wagener as the "old rebel element," not an incorrect estimate. The local press, however, was jubilant: "This triumph cannot be overestimated. It is the victory of law, order, and peace."[89]

New Orleans, Louisiana (1860)—
"There are many Germans here, also many Negroes and slaves.
These are treated better than servants are in Germany"[90]

Of the eleven states that formed the Confederate States of America in 1861, Louisiana had by far the largest number of German immigrants within its borders: by 1860, a total of 24,614 Germans had settled there, of whom no fewer than 19,752 (80.23%) lived in the port city of New Orleans.[91] The geographic location of the city was practically the sole reason for the increased settlement of Germans there, since Louisiana itself offered few economic prospects to German immigrants in the antebellum period. The immigrant who wanted to make his fortune in Louisiana could do this only in the single large city of the state, New Orleans: only here did German small traders, craftsmen, and laborers have the possibility of working for profit and a real chance of competing with cheaper slave labor.[92] New Orleans, therefore, was inhabited by immigrants from all the German states and had more German laborers, skilled and unskilled, than any other Southern city. Here, too, the subnational divisions among the ethnic German community were most noticeable.

The "Queen of the South," as New Orleans was affectionately known, was the only city in the Confederate South in which a distinctive and visible German quarter developed that was comparable to the many Little Germanies in the North. Between 1820 and 1850, 53,909 German immigrants landed in the port of New Orleans,[93] of whom the majority of the earlier immigrants (up to 1830) were so-called redemptionists.[94]

In 1860, there were 6,367 more Germans than slaves in the city; this was unique in the South and was one of the factors that made New Orleans attractive to Germans. Because slaves constituted only 8% of the city's population, there was less competition in the labor market. The atmosphere of the city, dominated less by blacks than by a mixture of nationalities, was not as strange to Germans as was, for example, that of Charleston. In New Orleans, Germans could feel more quickly at home.

Because of its population of almost 170,000, large for a Southern city, New Orleans was the first city of the Confederacy for which food procurement became a problem. It was also the city in which the poorest Germans within the Confederacy could be found. Here, more than elsewhere, German men joined the Confederate army to keep themselves and their families alive. Not one of the German soldiers researched owned slaves.

In New Orleans, 376 ethnic German soldiers are known to have fought in the five German companies of the 20th Louisiana Infantry Regiment; this figure represented about 2% of all the Germans in New Orleans. If one includes the companies that cannot be called ethnic German,[95] but that consisted partially of ethnic German soldiers, one arrives at the number of about 4,000 ethnic German soldiers given by the *Tägliche Deutsche Zeitung* on June 15, 1861. This number indicates that about 16.3% of all the Germans of Louisiana fought for the Confederacy, a higher percentage than that of the natives; Louisiana contributed about 56,000 soldiers to the Confederacy, which was only 14.9% of the state's white population.[96]

The Germans of New Orleans were mostly laborers and craftsmen who were organized into more than fifty associations to help alleviate misery in times of peace. These structures did not function during the war. Many of the Germans, therefore, were among the persons fed by the Free Market. On the other hand, Germans were among its most generous donors—after all, New Orleans was also the city in which the German consuls were among the richest citizens of all. New Orleans was the Confederate city with the largest number of German consuls in 1861: ten consuls representing fourteen German states:[97]

Pro-Southern support can be proved for practically every German consul in Richmond and Charleston, but only in New Orleans did the pronouncement of loyalty to the South go so far that Augustus Reichard, the Prussian consul, resigned from his office in order to go to war as a colonel in the 20th Louisiana Infantry Regiment.

The German consuls of New Orleans were an unswerving group, closely involved with each other in business matters;[98] of the ten consular offices, six were located close to each other on Carondelet Street. The founding of the influential Deutsche Gesellschaft von New Orleans was their idea; eight of the ten consuls were founding members in 1847; five of them held various offices over the years. The Deutsche Gesellschaft was their political and cultural platform; without the explicit support and practical involvement of the consuls, who almost always presented themselves in total agreement, nothing could be moved within the German minority. Their argumentative compatriots, on the other hand, often disagreed along mini-state lines. All ten men enjoyed a high degree of respect in New Orleans society; five of them had married into the highest circles and had been citizens for many years.

All ten men were merchants and directed, as was customary with consuls, financially strong trading houses. Cotton and tobacco trade were equally important; coffee and sugar exportation were less significant. As consuls, these men were bound by the instructions of the German states they represented; on the other hand, they also clearly followed private interests and were thus forced by the secession of Louisiana to set priorities based on their family obligations, if they did not want to lose everything that they had achieved in decades of work: financial riches, landed property, and slaves.

The German consuls of New Orleans were an exception in the South because of their open display of pro-Southern leanings. Most conspicuous was Augustus Reichard, who, voluntarily and completely against the instructions of his sending state, served as a Confederate officer in the war, followed by Charles Kock and Wilhelm Prehn, who heavily supported the establishment of the Hansa Guards Battalion and the Florance Guards. All three consuls exercised close influence on the treatment and equipment of their units through their clerks who headed these ethnic companies in the rank of captain. Friedrich R. Rodewald, Augustus Reichard, and John Kruttschnitt invested in the Committee of Public Safety and thus in the defense of the city of New Orleans, their home, while Friedrich Wilhelm Freudenthal founded and managed the fund to support the families of active German soldiers. The ships of Kirchhoff and Eimer ran the Union blockade in June 1861, and Charles Kock regularly contributed food to the Free Market.

The city fathers of New Orleans had managed to overlook the poverty, need, and hunger of the inhabitants during the antebellum period,[99] and the war aggravated the situation, because many companies specialized in armament production rather than food production.[100] In no other city in the South was German participation in Confederate food distribution across ethnic boundaries as extensive as in New Orleans, where it also corresponded to the actual need of the German population

On August 16, 1861, less than seven months after Louisiana's secession from the Union and the official beginning of the blockade, the Free Market of New Orleans was opened, "where the families of those who had taken up arms of defense against Northern aggression might receive supplies."[101] On the opening day of the market, 762 families were fed. The distribution of food was organized at first through coupons given by the individual district managers to families on the basis of need; in December 1861, this procedure had to be stopped because too many needy people were already dependent on the Free Market. According to the report issued by the executive committee at the end of December 1861, on only 137 days, food valued at more than $22,000 was handed out. The highest number of dependent families in the period of the report received aid on November 1, 1861, when 1,893 families were given food from the Free Market.[102]

The executive committee consisted of thirty persons under the leadership of Thomas Murray, a sawmill owner;[103] E. F. Schmidt, a pharmacist,[104] represented the German minority. In antebellum New Orleans, there were no independent charity organizations of German women on whose talents for feeding military dependents the New Orleans Germans could depend. Almost every one of the approximately fifty German clubs or societies in existence in the city in the 1850s, however, had a "sick person's committee" and a fund for "widows and orphans."[105] In times of peace, needy Germans could be adequately cared for with the resources from these charitable institutions. The care and support of a family, however, depended on the father's membership in an association; thus, each society could care for only a small number of persons, and due to the fifty organizations, some of which competed with others, there was too much division to allow for an all-encompassing relief program for the German minority. The means of the Deutsche Gesellschaft and the Asyl für mittellose genesende Deutsche were far from adequate given the immense need.

As early as April 1861, the *Tägliche Deutsche Zeitung* found it necessary to call on the German ladies of the city to organize charitable events whose proceeds could help the families of the soldiers.[106] This project was supported by a letter to the paper signed by "J. W.," which requested the founding of a German women's organization for the purpose of "Charpiezupfen."[107]

The organization of a German festival was immediately set in motion:

> It is even more necessary that we Germans show how closely the affairs of the South are tied up with our situation and that we will not lag behind other nations in bringing a sacrifice and that we will defend our home and our rights, which the fanatical North tries to attack and destroy, with our goods and blood in order to maintain our institutions. This festival offers Germans an opportunity to eradicate a certain suspicion that has awakened against us and that could easily spoil things for us.[108]

The German festival, held on May 3, 1861, raised almost $7,500 for the benefit of the Free Market. The German theater, led by Hausmann, also put on regular concerts and events for the benefit of the same,[109] so that the German minority supported the Free Market more than proportionately but also frequented it in great numbers.[110]

At the suggestion of Major Hellwig from the German Battalion, the Fonds zur Unterstützung der Familien der abwesenden deutschen Soldaten (Fund for the Support of the Families of Absent German Soldiers) was founded on May 31, 1861. Consul Freudenthal became president; his assistants were F. W. Schönfeld, J. M. Wagner, and Edward Strohmeyer. In each of the eleven city districts, five men were to collect a weekly sum of at least ten cents per family.[111] According to the *Louisiana Staats-Zeitung*, Freudenthal was able to send $300 to the New Orleans Free Market on September 26, 1861:

May we point out with pride that patriotism is a virtue that Germans are born with, and, although it is sometimes sleeping, it always tries to come to the fore. The practical patriotism of the German shows itself not only in the fact that our young people who are able to fight are devoting themselves to serving the fatherland against the armies threatening to conquer us, but also in the readiness to accept other material sacrifices on the part of those who are prevented from carrying weapons in the field.[112]

In February 1862, the committee, which at the time was financially supporting forty-four wives of active German soldiers, received a donation of $250.[113] The money came from the disbanding of the Thalia Club and was presented by the liquidators to Consul Freudenthal.[114]

In spite of these attempts by the German community to lessen the economic need of their compatriots through aid within the community, the Free Market fed a great number of German citizens in New Orleans. Many active soldiers' needy wives collected cash support in front of the aid office of T. D. Sully at 90 Gravier Street on July 1, 1861.[115] In order to prevent the feared disadvantaging of German women during the money distribution by Mr. Sully, Karl Potthoff was sent to oversee the action. He found no irregularities:

There were young women with and without children and others expecting to give birth very soon, all waiting fearfully for the moment when they would receive the dollars they wanted so much. . . . It was a particularly pleasing fact during this distribution that all of our compatriots without exception were able to sign their names, whereas among the other countries at the most ten out of one-hundred were in a position to hold the pen and write their names.[116]

One month later, on August 1, 1861, the situation on Gravier Street escalated into a hunger riot. The wives of the German soldiers from Captain Roemer's German Guard were among the approximately 300 desperate women who took part in the melee. Roemer had been court-martialed in July because he had ordered sixty food rations for his company's twenty-two men for several days, so that they could thus provide sustenance for their families.

This first complete collapse of aid distribution finally led to the "official" founding of the Free Market on August 16, 1861. On October 3, 1861, the Deutsche Gesellschaft through its president, Wilhelm DelaRue,[117] was able to donate the remarkable sum of $1,000 to the Free Market; the *True Delta* commented on the donation as follows: "Such acts as these are calculated to cover a multitude of sins."[118]

The rage that arose that same afternoon among Germans in response to this comment could only be calmed with great effort and only after the insult was corrected in the press.[119] After two further donations by Swiss organizations to the Free Market totaling $120 and the gift of $100 from the Deutsche Brüderschaft under President Dirmeyer, the *Louisiana Staats-Zeitung* wrote as follows: "At this point we appeal to our German brothers. There are so many organizations with treasuries that would allow a small gesture of support for the wives and children of our good men in the field. Forget all objections whether the constitution allows this or not; if the heart allows it, the mouth cannot say no."[120]

Within the four months covered by the executive committee report, there were 1,120 donations by companies, plantation owners, and private citizens to the Free Market. German donors, especially Consul Charles Kock, could be found on the lists.[121] Considering the lack of money in the South, these contributions take on an even greater significance, since they allowed the purchase of scarce articles that could not be produced locally.

In 1847, J. F. Behnke, the first secretary of the Deutsche Gesellschaft, gave $10, Charles T. Buddecke and Company contributed $50,[122] Reichard and Company a total of $30, and Sturzenegger and Company, $50. In addition, the contributions of German-Jewish organizations totaled almost $1,100.[123]

On the evening of February 8, 1862, the Magnolia Guard, Company B, under Captain Frank Roder,[124] organized a large military ball in the Odd Fellows' Hall. Although the company consisted mainly of laborers,[125] Engsminger, Ohmstedt, and Staiger, prosperous businessmen, were also members.[126] The proceeds from the event went to the Free Market.[127]

The motives for this German involvement were clear; New Orleans was their home. When Louisiana seceded from the Union, the German consuls and German leading businessmen went with it and paid a high price for their actions: Consul Kirchhoff died in faraway Bremen during the war; Kock, Reichard, and Kruttschnitt were dispossessed and lost their company empires; the firms of Rodewald and Freudenthal no longer existed after the war; Prehn, Thiele, and Honold tried to return to tobacco and cotton trading during Reconstruction but never managed to reach their prewar balances.

None of the consuls ever received any compensation for their losses, from either the German or the American side.

In 1873, there were only three German consulates left in New Orleans: the consulate of the North German Federation under Kruttschnitt, the consulate of Bavaria and Baden under A. Eimer Bader, and that of Württemberg under H. H. Klumpp.

Conclusion

The Germans of Charleston, Richmond, and New Orleans had adjusted to the specific needs of their chosen adopted homeland between 1850 and 1870. In general, the Germans had been able to improve themselves economically during the war because the underdeveloped industry of the South demanded the skills they had brought from Europe. Burghardt Hassel, editor of the *Richmonder Anzeiger*, wrote:

> When this country cut itself off from all sources of aid by seceding from the Union and when it stood there helplessly, it was Germans who helped first, a German who established the war laboratory,[128] a German who supplied the powder for the percussion caps. Germans, who called forth a thousand-armed industry all at once; Germans showed how leather is made; Germans made buttons, poured cannons and finished artistic instruments. . . . Every [person] . . . must admit that the Confederacy, in spite of the well-known courage of its natives, in spite of the warmth and patriotism of so many, would not have gotten far without its citizens who speak foreign languages.[129]

Many German companies did business with the Confederate government, and these contracts had of course a basically hybrid character: on the one hand, financial profit stood in the foreground; on the other hand, personal patriotism could be expressed in this way.

The postwar immigrant recruitment efforts of the Germans of South Carolina and Virginia was led by Civil War veterans, true to their antebellum structures: in Charleston by Wagener, Melchers, and Claussen, and in Virginia by German-Confederate ex-officers Frank Schaller, Gaspard Tochman, and Albert Lybrock. Only New Orleans was not able to find noted Civil War veterans for immigrant recruitment; Lieutenant Colonel Leon von Zinken dedicated himself to social responsibilities, and the deposed Consul Reichard was out of the country.

All three ethnic German communities were, in structure and profile, a microcosm of the example given them by the majority society of their adopted cities. This is particularly true for the war experience of the ethnic German minority.[130]

The adaptation to the dominant culture by the ethnic German minority of the antebellum South, the adoption of "southern distinctiveness"[131] in social and cultural aspects, and the unconditional acceptance of slavery—even if only as a controlling function—were basic and elementary preconditions for successful survival as an ethnic German-Confederate minority in a system that to its roots was xenophobic.

NOTES

1. For the most comprehensive survey of available publications, see Andrea Mehrländer, "'Gott gebe uns bald bessere Zeiten...': Die Deutschen von Charleston, Richmond und New Orleans im Amerikanischen Bürgerkrieg, 1861–1865" (Ph.D. diss., Ruhr-Universität Bochum, 1998), 5-13; Wolfgang Helbich and Walter D. Kamphoefner, eds., *Deutsche im Amerikanischen Bürgerkrieg: Briefe von Front und Farm 1861–1865* (Paderborn: Ferdinand Schöningh, 2002), 36–48. As late as 1994, James M. McPherson noted that "foreign born-soldiers are decidedly underrepresented" in Civil War studies, especially referring to non-English-speaking participants—a statement enthusiastically supported by Joseph R. Reinhart: *Two Germans in the Civil War: The Diary of John Daeuble and the Letters of Gottfried Rentschler, 6th Kentucky Volunteer Infantry*, ed. and trans. Joseph R. Reinhart (Knoxville: University of Tennessee Press, 2004), xx–xxii; James M. McPherson, *What They Fought for 1861–1865* (Baton Rouge: Louisiana State University Press, 1994), 14. The difficulties in mastering the primary-source situation for non-English-speaking ethnic participation is most obvious in Dean B. Mahin's book *The Blessed Place of Freedom: Europeans in Civil War America* (Washington, DC: Brassey's, 2002), 255–56.

2. Herbert Weaver, "Foreigners in Ante-Bellum Southern Towns of the Lower South," *Journal of Southern History* 13, no. 1 (1947): 67.

3. Of the twenty-seven Protestant and Catholic churches and two Jewish synagogues established in New Orleans between 1818 and 1859, seven congregations disbanded or merged prior to 1865, and six disbanded after 1865: Ellen C. Merrill, *Germans of Louisiana* (Gretna, LA: Pelican, 2005), 214–17. Charleston's St. Paul's German Catholic Church was founded in October 1860 and merged with St. Matthew's German Lutheran church in 1863, due to lack of membership.

4. Bobbie Malone, "New Orleans Uptown Jewish Immigrants: The Community of Congregation Gates of Prayer, 1850–1860," *Louisiana History* 32 (1991): 249.

5. As early as 1846, Rabbi Maximilian Michelbacher (1810–79) of Richmond even established a Christian-Jewish school, serving the children of members of both Beth Ahabah Synagogue and St. John's Evangelical German Church.

6. *Charleston Mercury*, January 21, 1861.

7. *Richmond Whig*, May 28 and June 24, 1861.

8. "Map of the State of Virginia: Containing the counties, principal towns, railroads, rivers and all other internal improvements" (Richmond, VA: Ritchie and Dunnavant, 1858); "A Map of the State of Virginia, reduced from the nine sheet map of the state in conformity to law by Herman Böye, 1828, corrected by order of the executive by L. v. Buchholtz, 1859," Virginia State Library and Archives, Richmond.

9. Michael P. Musick, "The Mystery of the Missing Confederate Medals of Honor," *Military Collector and Historian* 23, no. 3 (Fall 1971): 74–78.

10. *New Orleans Times-Picayune*, January 25, 1937.

11. Helene M. Kastinger Riley, "Deutsche Einwanderer in South Carolina vor, während und nach dem amerikanischen Bürgerkrieg: Ein Beitrag zur deutschamerikanischen Kulturgeschichte," in *Die Auswanderung nach Nordamerika aus den Regionen des heutigen Rheinland-Pfalz*, ed. Werner Kremp and Roland Paul (Trier: WVT Wissenschaftlicher Verlag, 2002), 9–11.

12. See sessions from December 1863, as well as from February, May, November, and December 1864: *Journal of the Congress of the Confederate States of America, 1861–1865* (Washington, DC: Government Printing Office, 1904–5), vols. 6 and 7.

13. I follow Willi P. Adams's definition of ethnic spokesmen: they support the material interests of their ethnic group, promote the reputation and status of the group, defend the lifestyle of their group, and present the public expression of the relationship of the group and the South to the homeland. See Willi Paul Adams, "Ethnische Führungsrollen und die Deutschamerikaner," in *Amerika und die Deutschen: Bestandsaufnahme einer 300jährigen Geschichte*, ed. Frank Trommler (Opladen: Westdeutscher Verlag, 1986), 173.

14. Samuel Mordecai, *Virginia, Especially Richmond in By-Gone Days*, 2nd ed. (Richmond, VA: West and Johnston, 1860), 246.

15. By 1863, so many German-born refugees had settled in nearby Alexandria, Virginia, which had been occupied by the Union early on, that the city could afford to run a German-language weekly (*Alexandria Beobachter*) from June 1863 onward: Karl J. R. Arndt and May E. Olson, *The German Language Press of the Americas / Die deutschsprachige Presse der Amerikas*, 3rd ed. (Munich: Verlag Dokumentation, 1976), vol. 1, 638.

16. Michael E. Bell, "Germany upon the James: German Immigrants in Antebellum Richmond, 1848–1852" (M.A. thesis, University of Richmond, 1990), 39ff.

17. *Richmonder Anzeiger*, September 14, 1861. Richter left Richmond on June 23, 1861.

18. *Richmonder Anzeiger*, May 27, 1861; May 31, 1861; June 1, 1861; June 6, 1861.

19. *Richmonder Anzeiger*, June 5, 1861. The board of the singing society consisted of B. Brauer, Wm. Pfeiffer, Th. Ganter, and G. Kann. The board of the German aid committee was made up of W. Albert Spott (president), Th. Ganter (secretary) and S. Hirsch (treasurer). Further members were F. Holle, Hattorf, Seiberling, and Honnegger; see *Richmonder Anzeiger*, June 11, 1861.

20. *A Century of Service: Bodeker Drug Company*, comp. Bodeker Drug Comp. (Richmond, VA: Dietz, 1946), 12. Sally L. Tompkins (1833–1916) headed the privately run Robertson Hospital in Richmond and by 1865 had nursed approximately 1,333 Confederate soldiers, of whom only 75 died from their wounds.

21. August Bodeker left his German hometown of Hannover in 1836 at age seventeen, taking four younger brothers with him to Richmond; in May 1843 he and Charles Bodeker were among the fifty founding members of the Evangelical Lutheran St. John's Church: *65.Jubiläum der Deutschen Evang. St. Johannes-Gemeinde zu Richmond, Va.* (Richmond: Dietz, 1908). Members of the Bodeker family who served the Confederacy were William Bodeker, August's younger brother (Company K, 2nd Virginia Cavalry, "Radford's Rangers" [RG 109, M 382, roll 5]), and Henry Bodeker's son George H. Bodeker (Company B., 1st Virginia Infantry, "William's Rifles" [RG 109, M 382, roll 5]), National Archives, Washington, D.C. For the orders the drug company shipped, see the receipts from December 1863 to November 1864: RG 109, "Confederate Papers Relating to Citizens or Business Firms" (M 346, roll 76), National Archives.

22. *Richmonder Anzeiger*, June 23, 1861; August 4, 1861; August 11, 1861; *Richmond Daily Examiner*, July 27, 1861; July 30, 1861; *Richmond Dispatch*, March 19, 1861; September 11, 1861; *Virginische Zeitung: Wochen- und Sonntagsblatt des Täglichen Anzeigers*, June 9, 1861. Wounded German prisoners of war trickled in from the 1861 Virginia battlefields of Arlington Heights (May 24), Phillippi (June 3), Big Bethel (June 10), Rich Mountain (July 11) and, finally, First Manassas (July 21).

23. *Richmonder Anzeiger*, August 12, 1861. In March 1862, every German household was asked to take in one wounded soldier—the Battle of Yorktown was in full swing: *Richmonder Anzeiger*, March 19, 1862.

24. For DeVoss, see Franz Josef Pitsch, *Die wirtschaftlichen Beziehungen Bremens zu den Vereinigten Staaten von Amerika bis zur Mitte des 19. Jahrhunderts* (Bremen: Selbstverlag des Staatsarchivs der Freien Hansestadt Bremen, 1974), 85, 201–2. By mid-April 1862, a total of 711 people had been interned in Richmond prisons: 435 Union prisoners of war; 232 disloyal citizens, 9 Yankees, 25 deserters, and 10 Negroes: *Richmonder Anzeiger*, April 12, 1862.

25. Roster by Consul DeVoss, Richmond, addressed to Rösing, dated January 7, 1863: approximately 85% of the certificates (1,167) were issued for Prussians (446), Bavarians (204), Hessians (197), Hannoverians (109), citizens of Baden (106), Wurttembergians (105); StA Hamburg, 132-5/9, B6: Hanseatische Gesandtschaft

Washington: Schriftwechsel mit dem bremischen Konsulat in Richmond, insbesondere während des Sezessionskrieges.

26. RG 109, chap. IX, vol. 244, "Secretary of War, Register of Arrests, Provost Marshal Generals Office Richmond, VA, 1862–1864," National Archives. Among the 1,168 foreigners interned in Richmond between 1862 and 1864, a total of 385 were Germans (almost 33% of all prisoners). Because Germans constituted about 33% of all foreigners in Richmond, this percentage corresponds to the actual demographic proportions in the city.

27. In 1862, a total of 62 Germans were interned; 13 Germans were arrested in 1863. With those 75 men, 23% of the Germans belonging to Companies H and M, 19th Virginia Militia Regiment, 19.3% of the Germans belonging to Company K, 15th Virginia Infantry Regiment, and 9.3% of the Germans belonging to Company K, 1st Virginia Infantry Regiment were in jail: Mehrländer, "'Gott gebe uns bald bessere Zeiten . . . ,'" 400–403.

28. Frank L. Owsley, *King Cotton Diplomacy: Foreign Relations in the Confederate States of America*, 2nd ed. (Chicago: University of Chicago Press, 1959), 384; letter of Major J. B. Ferguson, Richmond, to Geo. W. Randolph, Richmond, August 2, 1862, RG 109, "Letters Received by the Confederate Secretary of War" (303-F-1862), National Archives.

29. *Richmonder Anzeiger*, January 22, 1861; June 5, 1861; August 7, 1861; September 21, 1861; October 5, 1861.

30. *Daily Examiner*, Richmond, October 16, 1861; "The New Postage Stamps," *Daily Dispatch*, Richmond, October 17, 1861; August Dietz, *The Postal Service of the Confederate States of America* (Richmond, VA: Dietz, 1929), 96; Klaus Wust, "German Immigrants and Nativism in Virginia 1840–1860," *Society for the History of the Germans in Maryland* 29 (1956): 48; *Republic* (Richmond), November 20, 1865; Grover Criswell, *Confederate War Bonds* (Salt Springs, FL: Criswell's, 1992), 4–8, 12–13, 25–26, 38–39, 47, 51, 69.

31. *Richmonder Anzeiger*, August 1, 1864; Gary Thomas and Richard Andrew, "Houses of Misery and Hope," *Civil War* 59 (December 1996): 16; Lee A. Wallace Jr., *A Guide to Virginia Military Organizations 1861–1865*, 2nd ed. (Lynchburg: H. E. Howard, 1986), 260. For similar cases among German Unionists and German Confederates, see Bernhard Domschke, *Twenty Months in Captivity: Memoirs of a Union Officer in Confederate Prisons*, ed. Frederic Trautman (Rutherford, NJ: Fairleigh Dickinson University Press, 1987), 79–80; Louis F. Kakuske, *A Civil War Drama: The Adventures of a Union Soldier in Southern Imprisonment*, ed. Herbert P. Kakuske (New York: Carlton Press, 1970); Frederick Emil Schmitt, "Prisoner of War: Experiences in Southern Prisons," ed. John P. Hunter, *Wisconsin Magazine of History* 42 (Winter 1958–59): 83–93.

32. *Richmond Enquirer*, July 15, 1863.

33. *Richmonder Anzeiger*, June 30, 1864; July 1, 1864; *Richmond Dispatch*, June 29, 1864.

34. "The Situation," *New York Herald*, February 10, 1864. The alleged "Mr. Heinz" was never identified.

35. Meriwether Stuart, "Dr. Lugo: An Austro-Venetian Adventurer in Union Espionage," *Virginia Magazine of History and Biography* 90 (July 1982): 341–58; *Richmonder Anzeiger*, August 10, 1864; August 31, 1864.

36. Edwin C. Fishel, *The Secret War for the Union: The Untold Story of Military Intelligence in the Civil War* (Boston: Houghton Mifflin, 1996), 147–48, 552–55; *A Yankee Spy in Richmond: The Civil War Diary of "Crazy Beth" Van Lew*, ed. David D. Ryan (Mechanicsburg, PA: Stackpole Books, 1996), 68–74; Meriwether Stuart, "Samuel Ruth and General R. E. Lee: Disloyalty and the Line of Supply to Fredericksburg, 1862–1863," *Virginia Magazine of History and Biography* 71, no. 1 (January 1963): 35–109.

37. J. Gottfried Lange, "Der Veränderte Nahme oder Der Schuster In der alten und Neuen Welt - Dreisich Jahre in Europa und Dreisich Jahre in Amerika von J. Gottfried Lange," Virginia Historical Society, Richmond (MSS 5.1 L 2605:1), p. 291 in the German original, pp. 226–27 in the English translation by Ida S. Windmueller (1991).

38. *Richmonder Anzeiger*, April 14, 1866.

39. In his study about "Richmond scalawags," Michael B. Chesson concludes that one-sixth of the 130 "scalawags" that he identifies were born in Germany and that 103 of the identified Republicans were "of unknown origin." I consider it exaggerated to assume from this that the majority of the Germans in Richmond supported the Republican Party. It should also be noted that between 1865 and 1870, sides were switched often: Michael B. Chesson, *Richmond after the War, 1865–1890* (Richmond: Virginia State Library, 1981), 107, 229n50.

40. Copy of the resolution in Herrmann Schuricht, *The German Element in Virginia* (Baltimore, 1900), vol. 2, 137.

41. William Lovenstein was a "second-generation German," born in Richmond on October 8, 1840, the son of Sal Lovenstein, a Jew. During the war he served in the Richmond Light Infantry Blues and married Dora Wasserman in 1863: Robert N. Rosen, *The Jewish Confederates* (Columbia: University of South Carolina Press, 2000), 169.

42. *Richmonder Anzeiger*, March 31, 1866; June 30, 1866.

43. Johann A. Wagener, "Die Deutschen von Süd-Carolina: Die Stadt am Meer," *Der Deutsche Pionier* 3 (1871): 214.

44. Andrea Mehrländer "' . . . überall hiest man fahnen': Bremens Einwanderer während des amerikanischen Bürgerkriegs in den Konföderierten Staaten— Ausgewählte Fallbeispiele," in *Genealogie und Auswanderung: Über Bremen in die Welt*, ed. Die Maus, Gesellschaft für Familienforschung, e. V. (Clausthal-Zellerfeld: Papierflieger, 2002), 137–39, 148. For a close study of Captain Wieting's career and nineteenth-century German immigration into Charleston, South Carolina, see my forthcoming book, *Mit Kurs auf Charleston, S.C.: Kapitän Heinrich Wieting und*

die deutsche Auswanderung nach Süd Carolina im 19. Jahrhundert (Bremen: H. M. Hauschild, 2010).

45. Michael E. Bell, "'Hurrah für dies süsse, dies sonnige Leben': The Anomaly of Charleston, South Carolina's Antebellum German-Americans" (Ph.D. diss., University of South Carolina, Columbia, 1996), 97.

46. Andrea Mehrländer, "' . . . To Strive for Loyalty': German-Confederate Newspapers, the Issue of Slavery, and German Ideological Commitment," *American Studies Journal* 48 (Winter 2001): 44–51.

47. "What Charleston Is Doing for the War," *Charleston Mercury*, January 1, 1862. South Carolina contributed about 44,000 volunteers. After the end of the war, the state claimed a contingent of 71,000 soldiers (23.6% of the white population) for the Confederacy; this included all "over and under age" recruits: R. H. Woody, "Some Aspects of the Economic Condition of South Carolina after the Civil War," *North Carolina Historical Review* 7 (1930): 353.

48. Gunter Schomaekers, *Der Bürgerkrieg in Nordamerika* (Wels/Munich: Verlag Welsermühl, 1977), 20.

49. Ella Lonn, *Foreigners in the Confederacy* (Chapel Hill: University of North Carolina Press, 1940), 309.

50. Of these, thirty-five ships came from Charleston and fifty-three from New Orleans. Of these Charleston ships, twelve were registered for foreign trade, twenty-two for domestic trade, and one for coastal fishing. In New Orleans thirty-three ships were registered for foreign trade and twenty for domestic trade. There are no documents in existence for Richmond for the years between 1860 and 1865 (RG 41, National Archives); RG 41: "Records of the Bureau of Marine Inspection and Navigation, Customhouse Copies of Vessel Documentation": (a) DOMESTIC TRADE: Charleston Customhouse, Certificates of Enrollment, vols. 307 A, 308 A, 309 A, 311 A, 428 A: 03/06/1853–12/08/1869; New Orleans Customhouse, Certificates of Enrollment, vols. 7771, 7990, 7917, 7919: 02/26/1859–11/09/1865; (b) FOREIGN TRADE: Charleston Customhouse, Certificates of Registration, vols. 63 A, 400 A, 401 A, 402 A, 403 A, 4926: 02/14/1853–06/17/1876; New Orleans Customhouse, Certificates of Registration, vols. 7914, 7918, 7940, 7986, 7991: 01/02/1854–1862 and 05/04/1864–04/08/1869; (c) DOMESTIC FISHING/ COASTAL TRADE: Charleston Customhouse, Licenses, vols. 2 A, 348 A, 350 A: 06/01/1853–07/27/1861 and 08/14/1865–12/30/1869; New Orleans Customhouse, Licenses, vols. 7775, 7677: 07/02/1862–12/10/1862 and 07/05/1865–06/30/1866, National Archives.

51. In Price's lists there are obviously German family names; because he does not indicate the nationality, however, it can only be an assumption. Most of these men are hard to find in census lists because they did not have a permanent residence and were only listed according to the routes on which they sailed (e.g., Charleston-Nassau or Mobile-Havana). Nonetheless, a captain of the Mobile-Havana line could live in Wilmington, North Carolina. Although there were a number of foreign captains, here too the opinion was prevalent that native captains, for patriotic reasons, were

prepared to take on greater risks in getting the cargo through than were "foreign mercenaries": P. C. Coker, *Charleston's Maritime Heritage 1670–1865* (Charleston, SC: Cokes Craft Press, 1987), 273; Lonn, *Foreigners in the Confederacy,* 304–5, 309; "South Carolina History, Civil War, ships and boats which took part in the war," no. 30-11-6E, South Carolina Historical Society, Charleston.

52. "Loss of the Confederate Steamer *Juno,*" *Charleston Mercury,* April 14, 1864. The *Juno* had broken apart during a storm, and most of the surprised crew had drowned. See letter of Cornelius L. Burckmyer to his wife, Summersville, S.C., April 8, 1864, in *The Burckmyer Letters, March 1863–June 1865,* ed. Charlotte R. Holmes (Columbia: State Company, 1926), 308–9.

53. For information about the individual ships, see RG 109, "Papers Pertaining to Vessels of or Involved with the Confederate States of America ('Vessel File')," National Archives: M 909, no. 20: *Mary* (M 12), pp. 695–706; M 909, no. 53: *Jasper* (J 53), pp. 569–81; M 909, no. 28: *Sarah* (S 26), pp. 612–30; M 909, no. 2: *Acorn* (A 51), pp. 1017–22; M 909, no. 17: *Julia Ann* (J 55), pp. 596–98, and *Juliane* (J 46), pp. 170–77; and "South Carolina History, Civil War, ships and boats which took part in the war," no. 30-11-6E, South Carolina Historical Society, Charleston, M 653, no. 1216, S. 197.

54. According to the historian Thomas Begerow of Bremen, there is no likely connection between the Tecklenburgs from St. Margarethen and the shipping companies of Franz Tecklenborg (Bremen) and J. C. Tecklenborg (Bremerhaven). In 1864 the latter owned four immigrant ships, including the barque *Helvetia* under Captain J. B. H. Wieting: "Verzeichnis der Bremer Seeschiffe für das Jahr 1864," 132-5/9: Hanseatische Gesandtschaft Washington B5, Schriftwechsel mit Bremer Konsulaten u. Bremer Konsulatsangelegenheiten 1862–1867, StA Hamburg; Uwe Schnall, *Auswanderung Bremen - USA,* hg. Deutsches Schiffahrtsmuseum (Bremerhaven: Deutsches Schiffahrtsmuseum, 1976), 36.

55. For information about the individual ships, see RG 109, "Papers Pertaining to Vessels of or Involved with the Confederate States of America ('Vessel File')," National Archives: M 909, no. 10: *Experiment* '(E 42), pp. 1055–62; M 909, no. 20: *Laura* (L 43), pp. 40–48; M 909, no. 30: *Victoria* (V 12), pp. 939–40.

56. In a letter from the Prussian envoy Baron von Gerolt to Secretary of State Seward on December 15, 1864, the former requested Tecklenburg's release with the comment that the prisoner was willing "to enter into any obligations with the United States": RG 59, "Notes from the Legations of the German States and Germany in the United States to the Department of State: Jan. 2nd–Dec. 31st, 1864" (M 58, T 4), National Archives.

57. Passenger list of the *Gauss,* Captain Heinrich Wieting, from Charleston to Bremen on October 5, 1867. In Thode Family Papers (1845–1935), South Caroliniana Library, University of South Carolina at Columbia.

58. After 1915, the family of Peter Tecklenburg donated the monumental entrance gate, unique in its dimensions for Charleston cemeteries, of the German Bethany

Cemetery (today: 10 Cunnigton Street, North Charleston, SC 29405): "IN MEM-
ORY OF CAPT. PETER TECKLENBURG (1836–1915) THROUGH WHOSE
GENEROSITY THIS STRUCTURE WAS ERECTED" and acquired a tremen-
dous tomb right next to the entrance, next to that of Captain Wieting. Tecklenburg
died on April 22, 1915, at the age of seventy-eight.

59. The ladies came from the Ostendorff, Bahntge, Wendelken, Ahrens, Mehrtens,
Michaelis, Riecke, and Schroeder families. The chairman of the commission that
had been appointed by the state of South Carolina to have gunboats and armored
ships built was J. K. Sass, whose ancestor Jacob Sass had come to Charleston from
Gutenberg, in Hesse, at the end of the eighteenth century: Maxwell Clayton Orvin,
In South Carolina Waters 1861–1865 (Charleston: Nelson's Southern Printing and
Publishing, 1961), 95, 185; "St. John's Births and Deaths 1700's and 1800's," I/7,
Robert Scott Small Library, College of Charleston, Charleston, South Carolina.

60. William Cattell Bee (1809–81), son of John S. Bee and Charlotte A. Ladson
Bee, was the cousin of the subsequent CSA brigadier general Barnard E. Bee and,
until 1852, a partner in the rice business of James H. Ladson & Co.; with the help of
his partner, Theodore D. Jervey, Bee went into business for himself under the name
of William C. Bee & Co. Bee's sons did not participate in blockade-running; they
were killed in the war in 1863 and 1864: BEE-CHISHOLM FAMILY, Correspondence 1865, no. 23-302A-4/Genealogy no. 23-302B-1, South Carolina Historical
Society, Charleston.

61. Lynda Worley Skelton, "The Importing and Exporting Company of South
Carolina," *South Carolina Historical Magazine* 75 (1974): 24–32. President of the
business was William C. Bee; the four directors were Theodore D. Jervey, William
P. Ravenel, C. T. Mitchell, and Benjamin Mordecai: "An Act to Incorporate the
Importing and Exporting Company of South Carolina," no. 4651, December 18,
1862, in *Statutes at Large of South Carolina* 13 (1861–66), (Columbia: Republican
Printing Co. State Printers, 1875), 141–42. The other companies, besides Bee's I. &
E. Co., were J. A. Enslow (a partner of Mordecai & Co.), the Steamship Charleston
Company, the Palmetto Exporting and Importing Company (whose stock value rose
by 800% in 1864), the Chicora Importing and Exporting Company, and the Atlantic
Steam Packet Company of the Confederate States: Coker, *Charleston's Maritime
Heritage*, 278–79.

62. An alphabetical, difficult-to-read, handwritten shareholders' list can be found
in William C. Bee & Co., no. 23/301/11 (accounts and business papers 1865),
South Carolina Historical Society, Charleston. This is probably the only extant shareholders' list of a Southern blockade company; it was most likely reconstructed after
the war by Theodore Jervey.

63. There were three mixed companies: Klinck, Wickenberg & Co. consisted of
John Klinck Sr. (1797–1888), John Klinck Jr. (1831–64), Germans, and Fabian
Reinhold Wickenberg (1813–75), a Swede; see a picture of the stock certificate
in Charles Wickenberg Jr., *Kith and Kin: Wickenberg and Klinck* (Lexington, SC:

Palmetto Bookworks, 2000), 92; half of E. H. Rodgers & Co. (after 1866, Pelzer, Rodgers & Co.) belonged to Francis J. Pelzer, born in Charleston in 1826, the son of Anthony (Anton) A. Pelzer, who had immigrated from Aachen. Francis J. Pelzer was educated in German circles and served in the German Hussars. Hermann Leiding was born in Hannover in 1828 and was in business with his American partner, E. L. Kerrison, under the name of Kerrison & Leiding: "St. John's Births and Deaths 1700's and 1800's," I/7, Robert Scott Small Library, College of Charleston, Charleston, South Carolina.

64. Georg F. Habenicht and Messrs. Bee and Jervey were each 50% owners of the schooner *Julia Anne* (built in 1848 in Washington, D.C.). The ship ran the blockade at least once: *Julia Anne* (J 46), pp. 170–77 and (J 55), pp. 596–98, in RG 109, "Papers Pertaining to Vessels of or Involved with the Confederate States of America ('Vessel File')," National Archives: M 909, no. 17.

65. C. G. Mueller, a bookkeeper, owned two shares of the Bee Co., lived before June 1860 in the Carolina House Hotel belonging to Mrs. R. C. Finney, 54 Broad Street, then moved to D. Mixer's Charleston Hotel, at Meeting and Hayne streets, and in 1863 went as an agent of the company to Nassau: *Directory of the City of Charleston 1860*, 65, 103. Mueller is registered as C. A. Miller.

66. After his arrival in 1859, August Conrad worked first for the consul of Hannover, G. C. Baurmeister, served as a private in Captain Chichester's Charleston Zouaves Cadets until April 1862, and joined Bee & Co. in the summer of 1862 as a bookkeeper, recommended by Mueller, who lived in the same hotel. In 1865, he returned to Hannover and published his memoirs: August Conrad, *Schatten und Lichtblicke aus dem Amerikanischen Leben während des Secessions-Krieges* (Hannover: Th. Schulze's Buchhandlung, 1879), 72–73.

67. At the age of fifty-four, Theodore D. Jervey volunteered as a private in Captain F. T. Miles's company of the Charleston Battalion in the winter of 1863 and only returned at the end of April 1865: A. S. Salley Jr. "The Jervey Family of South Carolina," *South Carolina Historical and Genealogical Magazine* 7 (1906): 43–44.

68. Conrad, *Schatten und Lichtblicke aus dem Amerikanischen Leben während des Secessions-Krieges*, 76.

69. Nassau (Bahamas) and St. George's (Bermuda) were the preferred intermediary locations, where cargo coming from Europe was transferred to smaller ships and smuggled into the blockaded ports: Patricia L. Faust, ed., *Historical Times: Illustrated Encyclopedia of the Civil War*, 2nd ed. (New York: HarperPerennial, 1991), 67. A very good description of these two ports as reloading points can be found in Theodore D. Jervey, "Charleston during the War," *Annual Report of the American Historical Association* 1 (1913): 167–76.

70. As late as 1879, Bee, then seventy years old, and Conrad, thirty-seven, were corresponding. Conrad wrote to his former boss "after a long time, from a distance but with the greatest devotion, respect, and gratefulness": Conrad, *Schatten und Lichtblicke aus dem Amerikanischen Leben während des Secessions-Krieges*, 71.

71. H. W. Kuhtmann withdrew from the business in January 1855 and transferred the direction of the trading house to his twenty-six-year-old partner, G. C. Baurmeister. In 1860 Kuhtmann resided in Pickens County and had property managed for him in Charleston: *1860 South Carolina Census Index*, vol. 1, comp. Bryan Lee Dilts (Salt Lake City, UT: Index Publishing, 1985), 560.

72. A. Canale, born in Genoa in 1815, immigrated to Charleston in 1838 at the age of twenty-three, accumulated an impressive fortune of $60,000 and three slaves by the outbreak of war, and in 1861 volunteered at the age of forty-six for the German Hussars (twelve months). In 1883, Canale and his business were the oldest fruit traders in Charleston; he had ten employees, and his yearly turnover amounted to more than $100,000: *Charleston: Her Trade, Commerce and Industries, 1883–1884*, comp. John E. Land (Charleston, SC: John E. Land, 1884), 76.

73. "Roll of the Charleston Zouave Cadets at Castle Pinckney," September 20, 1861, in Anthony W. Riecke, Scrapbook vol. III, pp. 213, no. 34-390, South Carolina Historical Society, Charleston; and "Compiled Service Records: Capt. C. E. Chichester's Co., 1st Regt. Rifles, Branch's Rifle Regiment, S. C. Militia," RG 109, M 267, roll 153, National Archives.

74. See *Victoria* (V 12), in RG 109, "Papers Pertaining to Vessels of or Involved with the Confederate States of America ('Vessel File')," National Archives: M 909, no. 30, p. 0939. The ship's ownership is dated on June 6, 1862. Campsen probably owned the *Victoria* even earlier. On March 19, 1862, Judah P. Benjamin, in a letter to Senator R. W. Johnson, regretted that the *Victoria* had no weapons on board, with which General Pike's army could be equipped: RG 109, "Letters Sent by the Confederate Secretary of War," 03-19-1862 (National Archives: M 522), p. 178.

75. Conrad, *Schatten und Lichtblicke aus dem Amerikanischen Leben während des Secessions-Krieges*, 82.

76. Ibid., 75, 82, 94.

77. E. L. Kerrison and E. H. Rodgers (Americans) and Fabian Wickenberg (a Swede) are, as non-Germans, not considered here. The years given indicate either the acquisition of American citizenship or else the notice of intention or the earliest date on which the person could be proved to have been in Charleston; this information was found in the following source: *1860 Manuscript Census*, M 653, roll 1216.

78. Advertising for the South Carolina Steam Bakery, *Daily Courier*, Charleston, S.C., November 20, 1860.

79. "More Flags," *Charleston Mercury*, November 16, 1860. The paper commented: "The whole is very neat, and is the production of Mr. Kock."

80. Here we will cite again Loren Schweninger's opinion that persons with property valued at $2,000 in 1850 belonged to the richest 13% of the population of the entire United States and, in 1870, because of inflation, etc., to the richest 20% of the country: Schweninger, "Prosperous Blacks in the South, 1790–1880," *American Historical Review* 95 (1990): 34. In the Confederate States in 1860, only 31% of all whites (385,000 slaveholders) possessed slaves. Of these, almost 50% had fewer

than five slaves each. Of the twenty-six companies, six companies had more than five slaves; two had exactly five slaves; thus eight of the German companies (30.8%) belonged to the 38% of slaveholders in the entire South who possessed between five and twenty slaves: Charles Joyner, *Down by the Riverside: A South Carolina Slave Community* (Urbana: University of Illinois Press, 1984), 34; Peter J. Parish, *Slavery: History and Historians* (New York: Harper and Row, 1989), 26–28.

81. Property was confiscated in 1864 from the Claussen company and from Klinck, Wickenberg & Co.; thus there could be no upswing in 1870: "Records of the Confederate States, the Judiciary, District Courts: South Carolina, RG 109: Material relating to the sequestration of alien-enemy property in South Carolina, minute book (Sept. 9th, 1861–Dec. 16th, 1864)," chap. X, vol. 210, pp. 407, 471, National Archives (Southeast Region), East Point, Georgia.

82. Anthony Chibarro, *The Charleston Exposition* (Charleston, SC: Arcadia Publishing, 2001), 128; Judy Lorraine Larson, "Three Southern World's Fairs: Cotton States and International Exposition, Atlanta, 1895, Tennessee Centennial, Nashville, 1897, South Carolina Inter-State and West Indian Exposition, Charleston, 1901–1902: Creating Regional Self-Portraits" (Ph.D. diss., Emory University, 1999); and *South Carolina Inter-State and West Indian Exposition Pass Book Photographs* (Charleston, 1902), Public Library, Charleston, South Carolina.

83. As opposed to the total estimated ethnic German fortune of $6 million in 1870, the city of Charleston had bank capital of only $1.9 million: Woody, "Some Aspects of the Economic Condition of South Carolina after the Civil War," 362–65.

84. Heinrich A. Rattermann, *General Johann Andreas Wagener: Eine biographische Skizze* (Cincinnati: Mecklenborg and Rosenthal, 1877), 22.

85. In the battle of Port Royal on November 7, 1861, Major Wagener commanded 220 men of the German Artillery who armed 15 cannons at Fort Walker (Hilton Head). For five long hours, the German Artillery heroically fought off eighteen Union warships with 4,000 cannons on board, before they had to abandon the fort. News about this gallant fight spread quickly and earned Wagener his nickname, "Hero of Port Royal."

86. A twenty-one-page letter from J. A. Wagener from Charleston to his Sievern schoolteacher, Johann Heinrich Böckmann (1784–1874), on November 8, 1840. Wagener was at the time twenty-four years old and had been in South Carolina for seven years. Printed in Artur Burmeister, *John-Wagener-Haus: Niedersächsisches Bauernhaus von 1850–Auswanderer-Erinnerungsstätte* (Langen-Debstedt: Selbstverlag, 1994), 27–42.

87. See Wagener's thoughts about the new year 1867–68 in *Charlestoner Zeitung,* January 1, 1868: "In this respect the German should never forget that he stands at the top of the white race and must remain loyal to his blood. This is our advice. And our wish."

88. "Die Feier des Unabhängigkeitsfestes am 4. Juli in Charleston," *Südlicher Correspondent,* July 8, 1869, 2.

89. *Daily Courier*, August 4, 1871. The *Daily Courier* printed overwhelmingly positive press reports from the South: *Savannah Republican, Augusta Chronicle and Sentinel, Selma Times, Augusta Constitutionalist, Columbia Phoenix, Savannah Advertizer, Wilmington Journal, Washington Patriot*; there was much disappointment in Republican circles: *Washington Chronicle, Orangeburg News, New York World*.

90. Letter from Joseph Eder from New Orleans, January 16, 1854, to his friends in Teisendorf, Bavaria: "A Bavarian's Journey to New Orleans and Nagodoches in 1853–1854," ed. Karl J. R. Arndt, *Louisiana Historical Quarterly* 23 (1940): 494.

91. The remaining 4,862 Germans settled mainly in Germantown and Baton Rouge. The demographic dominance of New Orleans meant that between 1810 and 1910 Louisiana had the highest percentage of urbanization of the entire South; in 1860, 26.1% of the population of Louisiana was urbanized, whereas the entire country had a rate of only 19.8% and the South as a whole of only 7.2%: Lewis M. Killian, *White Southerners* (New York: Random House, 1970), 161.

92. In Germany the publications of Charles Sealsfield, Vincent Nolte, Friedrich Gerstäcker, and Ludwig v. Reizenstein had helped to focus "attention . . . on Louisiana": *Louisiana's German Heritage: Louis Voss' Introductory History*, ed. Don Heinrich Tolzmann (Bowie, MD: Heritage Books, 1994), xii.

93. John Hanno Deiler, *Geschichte der Deutschen Gesellschaft von New Orleans* (New Orleans: by the author, 1897), 39–40.

94. In the seventeenth century and early eighteenth century, a "redemption agreement" allowed European immigrants to travel to America without paying their fares, but when they got there, the shipowner had the right to sell the immigrants at journey's end for a term of years, to trade them off for their debt. For New Orleans's most spectacular German redemptionist, see John Bailey, *The Lost German Slave Girl: The Extraordinary True Story of Sally Miller and Her Fight for Freedom in Old New Orleans* (New York: Atlantic Monthly Press, 2003)..

95. According to my definition, an ethnic German unit had to have consisted originally of 90% ethnic German soldiers to qualify for the description "German." Louisiana was the only state that had a number of companies with a high ethnic German share, but always less than 90%.

96. Ted Tunnell, *Crucible of Reconstruction: War, Radicalism, and Race in Louisiana 1862–1877* (Baton Rouge: Louisiana State University Press, 1984), 9.

97. See *Gardner's New Orleans Directory for 1861*, "Consuls." Kirchhoff was not listed as a consul, although he held this office until 1863.

98. Consuls Eimer and Freudenthal were business partners, as were Consuls Reichard and Kruttschnitt or Thiele and Kirchhoff; the Kock and Kruttschnitt families were related by marriage after 1882.

99. Gilles Vandal, "The Nineteenth-Century Municipal Responses to the Problem of Poverty: New Orleans Free Lodgers, 1850–1880, as a Case Study," *Journal of Urban History* 19, no. 1 (1992): 39–40. During the war an average of 3% of the

inhabitants of New Orleans were homeless, many of them single, unskilled, or foreign-born.

100. Larger German companies were the saber factory of A. Himmel; the Crecent Woll-Manufaktur of F. Gueble and H. Oertling; Philip Hoelzel's Louisiana Flour und Korn-Mühle; Bastian's Southern Schnallen-Manufaktur; and Kloppenburg's rope factory: *Tägliche Deutsche Zeitung* (New Orleans), June 6, 1861; July 20, 1861; March 30, 1862; April 15, 1862.

101. *Report of the Committee of the Free Market of New Orleans Established for the Benefit of the Families of Our Absent Volunteers, Together with the List of Contributions, Number of Markets, and Families Supplied, from 16th August to 31st December, 1861, Inclusive* (New Orleans: Bulletin Book and Job Office, 1862), iii.

102. If one assumes an average family size of a mother with three children, this means 7,552 persons (5.2% of the white population of New Orleans). Massey doubts that the market would have been able to sustain this level of aid for long if New Orleans had not been taken by the Union in April 1862: Massey, *Ersatz in the Confederacy*, 164.

103. Murray was the owner of Hunts' Mills in Florida in 1861 and ran Murray & Co., which supplied Pensacola Lumber. His business partners were Joseph C. Pooley, Wm. L. Criglar, and G. F. C. Batchelder: *Gardner's New Orleans Directory for 1861*, comp. Charles Gardner (New Orleans: Gardner, 1861).

104. Clark describes the Free Market, referring to the *Tägliche Deutsche Zeitung* of October 4, 1861, and October 9, 1861, as "largely under German supervision"; this is definitely a subjective estimation of the newspaper publisher. The role of Schmidt is also not clear, because in 1860 there were two men with this name in New Orleans—a pharmacist and a bookseller, of whom one was a Swede and owned two slaves: Robert T. Clark Jr., "The New Orleans German Colony in the Civil War," *Louisiana Historical Quarterly* 20 (1937): 1000.

105. *Tägliche Deutsche Zeitung* (New Orleans), December 6, 1859: for 1859, 20,000 Germans were registered in almost fifty German societies, associations, and clubs; the majority belonged to the "laboring class." The purpose of these groups was "almost exclusively charitable." The drayman's club (Louisiana Draymanns-Verein), for example, had 250 to 280 members.

106. "An unsere Frauen und Jungfrauen," *Tägliche Deutsche Zeitung* (New Orleans), April 28, 1861.

107. "Aufruf an deutsche Frauen!" *Tägliche Deutsche Zeitung* (New Orleans), April 28, 1861.

108. *Tägliche Deutsche Zeitung* (New Orleans), April 28, 1861.

109. About the planning of the festival: *Tägliche Deutsche Zeitung* (New Orleans), April 28, 1861; about the proceeds: *New Orleans Crescent*, July 19, 1861; donation of $242.50 from Madame Ruhl's concert on November 19, 1861: *Report of the Committee of the Free Market of New Orleans*, 61.

110. Clark, "The New Orleans German Colony in the Civil War," 1000.

111. The "Collectors of the Committee to Support Needy Families of Our Active Soldiers" were W. von Königslöw (First District), B. Bahndorf (Second District), J. F. Mayer (Third District), John Kimmk (Fourth District), Christian Schopp (Jefferson City): "An die Deutschen in N. Orleans," *Louisiana Staats-Zeitung* (New Orleans), October 15, 1861.

112. "Patriotismus," *Louisiana Staats-Zeitung* (New Orleans), October 1, 1861.

113. *Louisiana Staats-Zeitung* (New Orleans), February 15, 1862.

114. The liquidators were H. H. Riemann, Conrad Streeder, and Carl Schäfer: *Louisiana Staats-Zeitung* (New Orleans), April 20, 1862.

115. The admittedly subjective estimate of the *Tägliche Deutsche Zeitung* on June 15, 1861, revealed that of the approximately 14,000 soldiers sent by Louisiana (up to June 1861) to the Confederacy no fewer than 4,000 were Germans. This seems realistic according to my research to date, but there were most probably more than 4,000 soldiers. An examination of all nominal rolls with information about place of birth in the Manuscript Division of Tulane University resulted in the following numbers: 1st La Inf., Co. D: 18% German soldiers; 5th La Inf., Co. G: 28% German soldiers; 6th La Inf., Co. G: 53% German soldiers; 8th La Inf., Co. B: 23% German soldiers; 14th La Inf., Co. C, D, F, and K: 19%, 14%, 9%, and 39% German soldiers: 55-V, Record Rolls, Louisiana Volunteers, Army of Northern Virginia, Manuscript Division, Tulane University, New Orleans. The 10th Louisiana Infantry Regiment included a total of 9% Germans; the German share in Companies F and G was 30% and 14%: Thomas W. Brooks and Michael D. Jones, *Lee's Foreign Legion: A History of the 10th Louisiana Infantry* (Gravenhurst, Ontario: Watts Printing, 1995), 81.

116. "Unterstützung der Familien unserer abwesenden Soldaten," *Tägliche Deutsche Zeitung* (New Orleans), July 2, 1861.

117. Wilhelm DelaRue, born in Erlangen, Bavaria, in 1800, immigrated to the United States in 1822, served as an officer in the Mexican War, and finally settled down as a merchant in New Orleans. In 1861, DelaRue & Sloan was disbanded because DelaRue, who was hard of hearing, retired; his condition worsened, and he became deaf. He was the secretary of the Deutsche Gesellschaft from 1851 to 1861 and was president from 1861 to 1873: Louis Voss, *History of the German Society of New Orleans* (New Orleans: Sendker Printing Service, 1927), 90.

118. "Generous Contribution," *True Delta*, New Orleans, October 4, 1861. Among all the donations of money for which the Free Market wrote receipts, only three amounted to $1,000 or more; besides the Deutsche Gesellschaft, the city council contributed $2,500 in partial payments, and the Confederate Regiment gave $1,707.07. The payments of the city council were made on October 30, 1861, and on November 28, 1861; the Confederate Regiment paid on December 23, 1861: *Report of the Committee of the Free Market of New Orleans*, 63; *Louisiana Staats-Zeitung* (New Orleans), October 4, 1861.

119. *Louisiana Staats-Zeitung* (New Orleans), October 6, 1861.

120. *Louisiana Staats-Zeitung* (New Orleans), October 9, 1861.

121. See Kock's contributions on 08/02/1861, 10/18/1861, 10/23/1861, 11/08/1861, 11/26/1861, and 12/31/1861; the goods came on the *Music*, the *Laurel Hill*, and the *Mary T.*: *Report of the Committee of the Free Market of New Orleans*.

122. Charles T. Buddecke & Co. (up to the beginning of 1861, his business partner was Emile Maier) were agents of Hazard Powder Co. and Carpenter's White Lead, Shot, Percussion Caps and Safety Fuse, on 21 Common Street: *Gardner's New Orleans Directory for 1861*, 83.

123. *Report of the Committee of the Free Market of New Orleans*, 57–63.

124. Frank Roder came to New Orleans with his parents in 1832 at the age of one year; in the 1850s he opened a rice and spirits shop, Frank Roder & Co. with his partner, Georg Jürgens. His social climb began with his election as president of the New Orleans Manufacturing and Building Co. in June 1867: *Tägliche Deutsche Zeitung* (New Orleans), June 4, 1867; *Progressive New Orleans: Young Men's Business League*, comp. Wm. E. Myers (New Orleans, 1895), 30; and *New Orleans and Her Relations in the New South*, comp. Andrew Morrison (New Orleans: L. Graham and Son, 1888), 83.

125. In April 1861, the "members of a German Odd Fellows' lodge" had announced that they wanted to organize themselves militarily (*Tägliche Deutsche Zeitung* [New Orleans], April 28, 1861); the Magnolia Guard developed from this group. Members of the Independent Order of Odd Fellows, whose ideology was related to Freemasonry, belonged mainly to the laboring class; this group supported an occupational sickness insurance scheme, in order to assure every member a minimal existence in case of illness: Jürgen Holttorf, *Die Logen der Freimaurer* (Hamburg: Nikol Verlagsgesellschaft, 1991), 158–59.

126. Undated nominal roll for the Magnolia Guards, Continental Regiment, Book 148, Jackson Barracks, New Orleans. A. Engsminger, who had lived in New Orleans since 1848, opened the Crescent Trunk Factory in 1852, the first luggage factory in the South; in 1888 he exported to Mississippi, Texas, and Arkansas; Staiger, a flour merchant in business for himself, also donated a ton of flour to the Free Market on September 16, 1861; John Ohmstedt was the owner of the spirits company, Ohmstedt & Schultze, which was taken over by Lochte & Cordes in 1872: *New Orleans and Her Relations*, 107.

127. *Louisiana Staats-Zeitung* (New Orleans), February 8, 1862.

128. Hassel seems to refer here to Charles Theodor Mohr, a chemist and Forty-Eighter from Württemberg, who carried out his research in Mobile and produced a number of antibiotics for the Confederacy: Lonn, *Foreigners in the Confederacy*, 272–73.

129. "Die Conföderation und die Deutschen," *Richmonder Anzeiger*, February 5, 1865.

130. Due to my socioeconomic focus, the battle history of the German companies mentioned in this essay has been almost completely neglected. A sound description of their military impact is provided in my forthcoming book *"In Dixieland I'll Take*

My Stand": The Germans of Charleston, Richmond, and New Orleans during the American Civil War, 1861–1865 (Columbia: University Press of South Carolina, 2010).

131. Even in 1995, Tindall described people from the Southern states as "homegrown outsiders in the nation": George Brown Tindall, *Natives and Newcomers: Ethnic Southerners and Southern Ethnics* (Athens: University of Georgia Press, 1976), 23.

☙ 3 ☙

"YE SONS OF GREEN ERIN ASSEMBLE"

Northern Irish American Catholics and the Union War Effort, 1861–1865

Susannah J. Ural

Surrounded by rain-soaked roads and the brisk chill of a Minnesota March, Christopher Byrne struggled to understand the events whirling about him. It was early spring in 1863, a date that marked his tenth year in America and his six-month anniversary with the U.S. Army. Encamped along the Blue Earth River, Byrne composed a letter to his brother in Ireland, trying to explain to his sibling the causes of America's Civil War, his personal involvement in the conflict, and what he hoped for his new home land and himself. Byrne's letter offers a powerful example of how Irish American Catholics understood the war and their role in it, and how their personal and familial views evolved as the Northern war effort came to include emancipation, a federal draft, and increasingly high casualties. Byrne, like many Northern Irish American Catholics, contemplated the war as both an Irishman and an American, and the decisions he made regarding this conflict were shaped by these dual loyalties to his natural and adopted homelands. To understand Irish Americans' actions and motivations during the Civil War era, historians must examine these shared and sometimes competing loyalties.

"I am a soldier in the so called Union Army," Christopher Byrne explained, "not from a conviction of Being fighting in a Just-cause but [from] the excitement of the time and the misrule of the administration." These events "forced me and thousands like me into [the army] who never sympathized with the war[.] [T]rue I was not Drafted. I went voluntary, but the country got into such a wild state of excitement that a young man would be looked on as a traitor if he did not go." Byrne believed the United States had "the best government that ever the sun shone on," yet he feared he was witnessing its destruction. He bemoaned America's "commerce ruined, her finance[s] crippled, a depreciated currency forced on the people, No specie in circulation, gold at a premium of from fifty to eighty percent and numberless hordes of officers monopolizing and consuming the wealth of the country whilst the Chickahominy, the Potomac, and the Mississippi Rivers are drinking the blood of her best citizens and still no signs of Peace." Byrne blamed the Republicans, a party he saw dominated by abolitionists, for most of these problems. These "Hordes of Fanatics . . . regardless of the Constitution . . . used the most arbitrary means that ever was used by freemen to cause the people in general to come down to their views."[1]

Byrne's letter pours forth a frustration commonly seen in the letters and diaries of Irish Catholic volunteers in the Union army in 1863. That year had already brought the implementation of the Emancipation Proclamation, war weariness, and the passage of a federal draft. Within months Irish Catholics like Byrne would give violent demonstration to their anger in the worst riots in American history. When many of them enlisted, however, especially those who joined the army in the first year of the war, most Northern Irish Americans maintained a tremendous faith in the Union cause; indeed, it is what often inspired their service. These soldiers proudly proclaimed their decisions to enlist free from social pressure and cited a conscious choice to defend the interests of Ireland and America, as they understood these terms. This chapter will investigate the initial motivations behind Irish American Catholics' enlistments in the early years of the war, how their views of the conflict, as well as the opinions of their communities, changed as the war evolved, and how this influenced the memory of Irish American volunteerism during the Civil War.

Nearly 150,000 Irish Americans served in the Union army during the Civil War. Many served in nonethnic units, but the most well known include James Mulligan's Irish Brigade (officially known as the 23rd Illinois Volunteer Infantry) and General Michael Corcoran's Legion, which was composed of the 155th New York, 164th New York, 170th New York, and 182nd New York Volunteer Infantry Regiments. The most famous of all, though, was General Thomas Francis Meagher's Irish Brigade. Meagher's men served in the 63rd, 88th, and 69th New York Volunteer Infantry Regiments, the 28th and, for a time, the 29th Massachusetts, and the 116th Pennsylvania Volunteer Infantry Regiments. They participated in all the major eastern battles of the war, including First Manassas, the Seven Days' Battles, Antietam, Fredericksburg, Chancellorsville, and Gettysburg. Their service, and that of tens of thousands of Irish Americans in the Civil War, is well recorded. The question of why they fought and why some members of their communities refused to fight, however, remains debated. The answer is both complex and simple.

As historians William Burton and Lawrence Frederick Kohl have demonstrated, Irish Americans volunteered for a number of reasons. Some were members of the Irish nationalist organization the Irish American Brotherhood, better known as the Fenians, and joined the Union army to gain military experience that they could apply to a future war of independence from Great Britain. Other Irish Americans volunteered to preserve America as a refuge for Irish immigrants like themselves. Some Irish men cited a sense of debt to America when they enlisted and hoped to prove their loyalty through dedicated service. This motivation, however, is rarely found in material written during the war. It is seen more frequently in postwar writings by Irish veterans hoping to demonstrate Irish sacrifices for American union, frustrated by continuing postwar prejudices. Finally, Irish Americans volunteered to secure a steady income, especially when local, state, and federal enlistment bounties totaled several hundred dollars.

While there are differences between these commonly cited motivations, one thread runs through them. Irish volunteers, regardless of geography, had dual loyalties to Ireland and the United States, and it was this shared devotion to both countries that inspired their service. These ties first called them to war and helped them and their communities explain and comprehend the decision to volunteer. These intense and competing loyalties would also help Irish volunteers and their families to defend their increasing dissatisfaction with the war and the Lincoln administration in late 1862 through the end of the fighting in 1865.

A classic example of these motivations appeared in Chicago, Illinois, in 1861 as songs, newspaper announcements, and broadsides called Chicago's Irish community to war. Advertisements in the *Chicago Tribune* challenged Irish men to join the Union army with reminders of past and present loyalties, crying: "For the honor of the Old Land, rally; Rally for the defense of the new."[2] Similarly, the popular new "Camp Song of the Irish Brigade" cited obligations to the "Goddess of Liberty," who sighed with disappointment at the "treason" in America and trusted Irish men to "defend her in season, and bring back the joy of her eyes." Like the announcement in the *Tribune*, this song cited ties to Ireland that inspired action in America, calling, "Ye sons of green Erin, assemble":

> Old "Grann" now looks over the ocean
> And hears the fierce bugle of Mars
> And the strength of her heart's high devotion
> Is rous'd for the stripes and the stars;
> And she raises her voice loud as thunder,
> That voice which was always obey'd,
> Saying Boys cut the rebels asunder
> With the swords of the Irish Brigade

On the evening of April 20, 1861, hundreds of Irish Americans responded to these calls with a meeting at North Market Hall to consider raising an Irish regiment to challenge the Confederate attack at Fort Sumter. Irish American attorney and nationalist James A. Mulligan led the rally and held his audience's attention through the entire evening. A total of 325 men enlisted within an hour of Mulligan's speech. Within days, Irish militia companies from Chicago, Waukegan, and surrounding communities offered their services "to sustain the Government of the United States in and through the present war." Illinois, however, had already filled its quota of volunteers to suppress the Southern rebellion. The men refused to disband, however, and sent Mulligan to Washington, D.C., to argue their case. As convincing before the Lincoln administration as he was that April night on North Market Street, Mulligan helped create the 23rd Illinois Infantry, which would become more famously known as Mulligan's Irish Brigade.[3]

Throughout 1861, Irish American neighborhoods witnessed frequent outbursts of pro-war activity like that seen in Chicago. Although tepid in their support for the Lincoln administration, most Irish American Catholics remained loyal to the Democratic Party, which had been far more welcoming to immigrants in general than the old Federalists and Whigs who preceded the Republicans.

In the six months following Lincoln's election, seven Southern states seceded from the Union, formed the Confederacy, and launched an attack on Fort Sumter, South Carolina. Irish Americans, like most foreign and native-born Northerners, reevaluated their position. The editors of Boston's *Pilot* explained that Irish Catholics faced a "kingdom divided in itself" and must, considering this desperate situation, "stand by the Union; fight for the Union; die by the Union."[4] Even so, Boston's Irish Catholic leaders worried about putting such bold statements into practice. Two weeks later they appeared to reverse course and asked, "Why do not the people say 'we shall stack our rifles and not an inch shall we move when you command us to march to a fratricidal war!'"[5] They were torn between their deep-seated suspicion of American's historic prejudice against them and their genuine loyalty to the country.

New York's Irish American community remained similarly troubled. Referring to the nativist prejudice Irish immigrants frequently faced, the *Irish-American* insisted, "We deprecate the idea of Irish-Americans—who have themselves suffered so much for opinions' sake not only at home but *here even*—volunteering to coerce those with whom they have no direct connection."[6]

While Irish American leaders across the North hesitated to fully support President Lincoln, they eventually agreed to support the Union. When President Lincoln called for 75,000 volunteers to suppress the rebellion on April 15, 1861, most northern Irish Americans rallied to the Union cause. The Irish-born Thomas Francis Meagher represents a classic example of this transition. Meagher was already famous for his role in the failed Irish uprising of 1848 and his subsequent escape to the United States from British imprisonment on Van Diemen's Land. By the spring of 1861 he was a leading figure in New York's Irish Catholic community and a member of the local Irish 69th New York State Militia. Meagher, however, was torn in his sympathies for any cause against federal tyranny and his love for the United States and American government. As he struggled to resolve this conflict of conscience, Meagher came to believe the causes of Union and Irish independence were linked. He explained:

> Duty and patriotism prompt me to [support the Union]. The Republic, that gave us an asylum and an honorable career,—that is the mainstay of human freedom, the world over—is threatened with disruption. It is the duty of every liberty-loving citizen to prevent such a calamity at all hazards. Above all is it the duty of us Irish citizens, who aspire to establish a similar form of government in our native land. It is not only our duty to America,

but also to Ireland. We could not hope to succeed in our effort to make Ireland a Republic without the moral and material aid of the liberty-loving citizens of these United States. That aid we might rely upon receiving at the proper time. But *now*, when all the thoughts, energies, and resources of this noble people are needed to preserve their own institutions from destruction—they cannot spare . . . sympathy, arms, or men, for any other cause.[7]

Irish Americans in Boston reached similar conclusions. Daniel George MacNamara, the Boston-born son of Irish immigrant parents, took pride in his service and that of his brothers and friends in the Irish 9th Massachusetts Volunteer Infantry Regiment. After the war he wrote a history of the "Irish 9th" to remind "the world how well the Irish men, exiled from their native land by the ruthless system of English law practiced in Ireland, . . . [served] their adopted country in the day of her trial."[8]

Here again was an Irish American who understood his Civil War military service in terms of both Ireland and America. MacNamara seized an opportunity to portray Irish military service in a manner calculated to improve native-born whites' perceptions of Irish Americans. Rather than seeing them as lazy and downtrodden, MacNamara hoped to show the reader how "Irish soldiers turn the 'horrors of war' into the most enjoyable of festivities." For instance, MacNamara recalled that many Irish soldiers drew inspiration from old memories of Ireland's "Wild Geese," warriors who fled English rule in Ireland to serve in foreign armies, always hoping to return and liberate their homeland. This included the historic Irish Brigade of France that "won so much glory and shed so much blood."[9] Finally, MacNamara explained that a love of Erin did not dim the affinity of Irish soldiers for their new homeland. "They could fight for it as bravely," he argued, "and shed their blood for it as freely, as any 'to the manor born.'"[10] While reinforcing some anti-Irish stereotypes, MacNamara's work offers excellent documentation of what Irish Americans hoped to gain from military service in the war.

Irish Catholic immigrant James McKay Rorty fought for a combination of these reasons and others. Like MacNamara, Rorty served in the 69th New York State Militia and would reenlist in the fall of 1861 and later die at Gettysburg, leaving behind parents and siblings who had just arrived in America and were almost totally dependent upon him for support. In 1861, though, Rorty listed for his father several motivators behind his decision to volunteer, including his tremendous "attachment to, and veneration for the Constitution, which urged me to defend it at all risks." He also linked his service in America to a future cause in Ireland, noting "that the military knowledge or skill which I may acquire [in the American Civil War] might thereafter be turned to account in the sacred cause of my native land." Rorty, like Meagher and thousands of other Irish Americans, saw this link between the United States and Ireland. He believed that the Union must be preserved or a permanently divided America "would close forever the wide portals through which the pilgrims of liberty from every European clime have sought and found it. Why? Because at the North the prejudices springing from the hateful and dominant spirit of Puritanism, and at the South, the haughty exclusiveness of an Oligarchy would be equally repulsive, intolerant and despotic." For Rorty the answer was simple: "Our only guarantee is the Constitution, our only safety is the Union, one and indivisible."[11] For men like Meagher, MacNamara, and Rorty, dual loyalties to America and Ireland shaped their decision to serve and informed their explanations to their families at home.

Not all Irish Catholic volunteers in 1861 were Fenians. But even these non-Fenians drew links between Ireland and the United States to explain and understand their service. The predominantly Irish St. Patrick's Church of Philadelphia linked religious duty with American patriotic duty. In November 1861, it hosted a lecture by a Dr. Moriarty titled "The Flag of the Nation and the Cross of the Church." Years later a church historian would note with pride that "many a brave fellow of St. Patrick's congregation watered the battle-fields of the Civil War with his blood."[12]

Similarly, the parish of St. John the Baptist in Manayunk, Pennsylvania, took pride in the rapid enlistment of a local militia company that sprang largely from members of its community. The Jackson Rifles entered the U.S. Army as Company A, 21st Regiment, Pennsylvania Infantry, less than three weeks after the Confederate attack on Fort Sumter. While this unit mustered out of service after the men's ninety-day enlistments expired, many of them reenlisted for three years service in Company A of the 98th Pennsylvania Volunteers in the fall of 1861. The parish of St. John the Baptist boasted that these men "saw considerable service and engaged in most of the principal battles of the Civil War," and the parish historian carefully listed each member of Company A, 98th Pennsylvania, noting every casualty the unit suffered through the end of the war. These Philadelphian religious leaders linked their Catholic identities, even more so than their parishes' ties to Ireland, with their support for the Union cause.[13] Irish Catholics in New York City heard a similar message from Archbishop John Hughes, who spoke to them in a cathedral over which flew an American flag. Hughes instructed them to "be patriotic, to do for the country what the country needs," and he promised that "the blessing of God will recompense those who discharge their duty."[14]

Similar sentiments in Irish Catholic communities across America inspired Irish men to join the Union army through 1861 and 1862. These men and their families noted Irish sacrifices for the Union in battles at Manassas, Virginia, and Lexington, Missouri, during the Peninsula Campaign through the summer of 1862 and into Maryland later that fall. As the fighting continued, however, Irish soldiers became increasingly concerned by the high casualty rates. Meagher's Irish Brigade suffered nearly 500 casualties during the Seven Days' Battles of the Peninsula Campaign in Virginia from June 25 through July 1, 1862.[15]

The Irish 9th Massachusetts likewise suffered intensive casualties during the Peninsula Campaign, fighting off three separate assaults that day and losing 231 men, killed, wounded, and missing. Several days later, at Malvern Hill, Colonel Thomas Cass, the regimental commander, died amid heavy losses.[16] The 69th Pennsylvania, composed primarily of Philadelphia Irish, gained acclaim for its service at the Battle of Glendale on June 30, 1862. The *Pilot* went so far as to overlook the 69th's local Boston fighters and claim that there was "no better fighting material in the army than this regiment," citing in particular the leadership of its commander, Colonel Joshua T. Owen.[17] The division commander, General Joseph Hooker, made similar references to Owen and the 69th Pennsylvania's bravery, congratulating them on Owen's heroism and the regiment's "reckless daring."[18]

While the Irish Americans of the eastern regiments earned fame in the early summer battles of 1862, similar praise fell on midwestern Irish men. It is significant to note that these reports appeared in native papers hardly known for their support of Irish Catholic immigrants. In May 1862 the *Detroit Free Press* noted the heroism of Captain Thomas G. Fitzgibbon, commander of the all-Irish Company B of the 14th Michigan Infantry at the Battle of Farmington, Mississippi.[19] In Illinois, native and Irish papers reported that Mulligan's Irish Brigade was preparing for duty and looking forward to making similar contributions to the war. At the battle of Lexington, Missouri, in September

1861, the unit suffered a severe defeat, and Confederate forces captured most of the men of the Irish Brigade. When they were finally released in a prisoner exchange, the Irish men may have found their next assignment ironic: they were to guard Confederate prisoners at Camp Douglas, Illinois. Finally, in June 1862, Mulligan's Irish Brigade received orders more to its liking and headed eastward to join the fighting in Virginia and what would become West Virginia.[20]

Despite the positive native press coverage of the service of Irish soldiers, nativist complaints, focused particularly on Irish Catholics, did surface in the spring of 1862. Charges appeared across the Midwest that relatively few Irish men were volunteering compared with their numbers in the population. In Indiana, a recruiter reported that the few Irish units he could muster refused to serve under native officers.[21] At a town meeting in Quincy, Illinois, in July 1862, similar proclamations were made that "the Irish have not done their duty, in the way of volunteering during the present war."[22]

Irish American communities strongly denied these charges. They noted that nativists "had no objection to the Irish enlisting and fighting, but [non-Irish] did not want to lose the chance of putting their services to the credit of the 'descendents of the Puritans.'"[23] Reprints of the article ran in several eastern papers, including Boston's *Pilot*, in an attempt to challenge similar claims in local communities. Meanwhile, other native presses, including the *Philadelphia Evening Journal* and the *Baltimore Mirror*, published reports that Massachusetts governor John Andrew opposed the idea of raising additional Irish regiments, that he refused to commission additional Irish field officers, and that Irish men were turning away from recruiting stations as a result of this news. The *Pilot* published the governor's rebuttal to these reports, declaring such statements completely false, but the rumors continued.[24]

As the controversy grew, Irish American leaders countered with the common complaint that Americans did not appreciate Irish military service: "Some of our contemporaries regret the appearance and valor of the Irish in the national army—out of an effeminate horror for blood,—and we can point the finger at correspondents who deplore the fact, seemingly from the same principle, but in reality from Secession motives." Even so, the *Pilot* argued that Irish Americans should continue to serve out of a sense of duty and honor. They had a responsibility to help save the Union because it had offered Irish men so much in their hour of need. "The Irish are citizens of the

United States," the *Pilot* insisted. "By fair contract they owe the country their lives. To their honor let it be said that they have freely and gloriously paid the debt." The editors quickly added that Irish Americans would continue to fight because they knew their kinsmen across the Atlantic were watching. Irish Americans' "native country—of which the Irishman never loses sight—will honor them forever for their splendid support of the best government that ever existed."[25] Here again Irish American leaders motivated their communities by linking the causes of Ireland and America.

Amid this turmoil, General Thomas Francis Meagher journeyed home to New York in July 1862 to recruit replacements for his dwindling Irish Brigade. His reception echoed the mood expressed by the *Pilot*. In some ways the Irish remained true to their pledge to defend American freedom and preserve a united country for future Irish emigrants. The Fenians were happy with the military experience they had gained, and other Irish soldiers were grateful to be earning a steady income. Some of these men and their families at home, however, were concerned that the cost of this service might be too great for their communities to handle.

On July 25, Meagher hosted a recruitment rally at the 7th Regiment Armory in New York City, once again invoking his skills as an orator for the causes of Irish freedom and American union. He presented his audience with a brief glowing synopsis of the tremendous sacrifices Irish American volunteers had made for their adopted country. The 69th New York had entered the Battle of Fair Oaks that June with 750 men but reported only 295 survivors. The 88th New York left its winter encampment that spring with nearly 600 men and now had fewer than 400. Although relatively unscathed, the 63rd New York had likewise dwindled to 500 men. Meagher informed the Irish Catholics gathered around him that he needed 2,000 recruits to keep the Irish Brigade together as a distinct unit dedicated to serving Irish honor, preserving America as a refuge for future Irish immigrants, and demonstrating Irish Americans' gratitude toward the United States. Meagher insisted, "It should be the vehement desire and the intense ambition of every Irishman, who has one chord within him that vibrates to the traditions of that old lyric and martial land of his, not to permit its flag, so vividly emblematic of the verdure of its soil and the immortality of its faith, to be compromised in any just struggle in which it is displayed." Cheers from the audience rang through the armory and poured out into the streets.

Despite this tremendous response, some Irish men in attendance were feeling neither grateful toward Anglo-Americans nor eager to reenlist. After Meagher explained the Irish Brigade's losses and his need for recruits, one member of the audience suggested, "Take the Black Republicans," referring to the Republican abolitionists so many Irish Americans disliked. Other members of the audience wondered why the Irish Brigade had lost so many men that spring. They suggested that perhaps nativists were at work to make sure their own troops received better equipment, food, and supplies than the Irish soldiers. The losses, Meagher insisted, were not due to "insufficient food, or clothing, or undue labor, or neglect of any kind, or sickness, but hard fighting of the enemy that had thinned the ranks—fighting that was the glory and pride of Irishmen." Remember, Meagher told his audience, the debt Irish men owed America and their families in Ireland. We must preserve this nation for ourselves and future Irish men, he said, and asked his countrymen for "one more effort, magnanimous and chivalrous for the Republic, which to the thousands and thousands of you, has been a tower of impregnable security, a pedestal of renown and a palace of prosperity, after the worrying, the scandals, and the shipwreck that, for the most part, have been for many generations the implacable destiny of our race."[26] The Irish audience responded once more with deafening applause and appeared ready to fill the ranks of the Irish Brigade as it had when the war began, turning out in such large numbers that recruiters had to turn Irish men away.

Native-born Americans were similarly impressed with Meagher's call for Irish service. After covering the entire evening's events and Meagher's speech in detail, the *New York Times* correspondent reflected, "The meeting . . . adjourned amid the most earnest enthusiasm, evince[ed] as determined patriotism and unswerving loyalty as ever was displayed in a public gathering, and practically demonstrate[ed] that the hearts of Irishmen throb with as pure devotion to our flag as ever animated the hearts of a free and noble people."[27] These demonstrations of loyalty pleased the *Times*, particularly because they came from an immigrant population that native-born Americans had not always trusted for such sentiments.

Sometime during the night, though, much of the Irish American support faded. The *Times* estimated that perhaps 10,000 people attended Meagher's speech. Even assuming that number was slightly inflated and recognizing that not all participants were eligible for military service, the 120 recruits who actually pledged service to the Union were many fewer than Meagher and the *Times* expected.[28] Despite inspiration from Meagher's speech, Irish Americans reconsidered their service to a cause about which they were receiving mixed messages. This was due to a variety of reasons, but one of them lay in reports from Irish American soldiers to their families that painted a very different picture of life in the Irish Brigade.

Irish-born Captain James B. Turner, an aide to Meagher in the 88th New York, offered an excellent example of these discouraging reports. After receiving a letter that mentioned his father's idea of joining the Union army for financial reasons, Turner insisted that his father abandon such plans. Turner warned:

> As to any idea you may have of joining the Army give it up at once. Unless a man occupies a position among the very highest, the amount of vulgarity, profanity and utter tyranny that exist is to a man of any regiment and religious training such as you are, a perfect hell. Then when I see young strong men about me, who hold commissions, sinking daily and fast under the mingled fatigue, exposure and want of proper nourishment it makes one wish that never a friend of his should be placed in like predicament. Then what must it be in the ranks or even non-commissioned [officers]. It's not like garrison duty. Think of lying, eating, and daily life in a small tent with from seven to ten men none of them the cleanest or with any pretense to education or refinement, then being cursed and cuffed about by some vulgar wretch in authority. . . . No. [The idea of] soldiering in any capacity you must give up.[29]

Turner's descriptions of the rigors of camp life contradicted those Meagher offered at his recruiting speech four nights earlier. Also, they came from a man who served on Meagher's staff and admired the general. Thus his statements are all the more powerful considering that they come from such a strong advocate of Meagher and Irish America. The statement is even more powerful when combined with the fact that the senior Turner had been unemployed for more than a year and could earn significant money through local and state bounties and military pay.

The same month James Turner conveyed his concerns to his family, Matilda Sproul expressed similar unease over her son. She could barely believe the news that he had joined the 16th Ohio Infantry Regiment. "Please, Fanny," she asked her daughter-in-law, in Fredericksburg, Ohio, "let me now if he was compelled or not. . . . If he could [have] stayed at home I think he was wrong for going as he was not too stout."[30] Sproul asked repeatedly for clarification in the letter, baffled as to why her son would have joined, unless he was drafted into the army, and disappointed that he had not explained his decision in his recent letters. James Turner and Matilda Sproul were not alone in their sentiments, which could have discouraged enlistments by an Irish American population that was hearing one portrayal of war from leaders like Meagher but receiving different stories from their loved ones in camp and advice against service from family in America and Ireland.

In Laporte, Indiana, Irish American Catholic Hugh Harlin noted similar concerns about the local draft. "There were about twenty-five men going to leave this town for Canada, Ireland, and Germany so as to avoid the [state] draft," Harlin observed in August 1862. He knew that men had more options if they volunteered, with the opportunity to join a unit of their choice rather then be assigned to a particular regiment, and worried that he might now be drafted and forced to serve among men with whom he had little in common, particularly his Catholic faith. "What a terrible fate it would be," he told his brother, "to die on the battle field and be thrown into a hole like a dog, no priest perhaps, no friends." He was "sorry now [that] I did not go when I was offered the commission." Harlin had refused the opportunity early that year to serve with fellow Irish Catholics, even as an officer, in an effort to avoid military service, and it appeared that he might now enter the army against his will.[31] His experiences, along with those of fellow Irish Catholics like James Turner, indicate that Northern Irish American concerns about military service and the mistreatment of Irish Catholics within the army influenced recruiting efforts in the summer of 1862. Even among pro-war Irish Protestants, families like the Greenleeses indicated a desire to avoid military service.

It was also during this tumultuous summer that Christopher Byrne enlisted in the Union army with similar reservations in mind. Byrne noted that "the country got into such a wild state of excitement that a young man would be looked on as a traitor if he did not go." The young Irish Catholic immigrant insisted that he was not alone in succumbing to these pressures. Nor was this a common problem by the summer and fall of 1862 as Northern state governments resorted to drafts to fill their federal military quotas.[32]

Despite the economic problems referenced by Turner, Greenlees, and Byrne, some areas of the North experienced economic growth from mid-1862 to 1865. Overall economic improvements made the twenty-dollar recruiting bonuses offered by Meagher and the fifty-dollar state enlistment bonuses less attractive than they had once been to unemployed laborers. Combined with this and the discouragement from family at home and in camp were the growing casualty lists in local papers. Heroic Irish exploits appeared on the pages of the *Pilot* and the *Irish-American*, but these were accompanied by detailed descriptions of the cost of such bravery. Lengthy columns continued for pages with curt reports of "Sergeant Conlin, Co. I, wounded by a fragment of a shell; Sergt. Daniel J. Reagan, Co. G, mortally wounded, since dead," and such grim reminders took a toll on Irish America.[33] As news came in that their sons and husbands were ill supplied or, worse yet, had been killed or maimed in battle, many Irish wondered if any of this would really improve their condition in America, whether there would be any soldiers left for the liberation of Ireland, and if they were sacrificing too much for union.

The lengthy casualty lists and continued nativist prejudice reinforced these fears. One member of the Irish 9th Massachusetts complained that the *New York Herald's* coverage of the Battle of Hanover Court House, fought in Virginia in May 1862, purposefully omitted any reference to Irish heroism in that struggle. "I had, it appears, erroneously labored under the impression, that the age of narrowmindedness, bigotry and intolerance had passed away," the soldier wrote. "I had thought that the heroic valor and bravery of the Irish soldiers had sufficiently manifested itself during the war, to disarm those prejudices that were so long entertained against us, and insure for us that even-handed justice which even those against whom we are combating are forced to accord." Other Irish Americans at home complained of still being targeted for their support of Catholic parochial schooling. In Lowell, Massachusetts, Irish community leaders reported that "bigotry and injustice still [exists] in New England," citing the city government's refusal to charter a Catholic college or to recognize the local Catholic schools, which would grant Irish students the same privileges in the community as those enjoyed by children in the public schools.[34]

Similar outrage surfaced in Chicago, Illinois, where Irish Americans accused nativist reporters of recognizing "the bravery and daring of the descendents of Puritans" for acts performed by Irish Americans. Irish men from Chicago challenged nativists' claims that the 9th Massachusetts casualty lists were an example of "the blood of old Massachusetts watering the soil of Virginia." The city's Irish leaders reminded readers that Irish or Irish American volunteers dominated that unit, and it was they and their families who were making these sacrifices. Colonel Cass, the commander of the Irish 9th, "had great difficulty in obtaining permission to fill his regiment with exclusively Irish troops," the *Chicago Post* explained, due to nativists' fears of arming the Irish men of Massachusetts. When it came time, however, to recognize dedicated military service, the editors complained that native-born Protestants gave Irish sacrifices "to the credit of the 'descendents of the Puritans.'"[35]

The growing sense among Irish Americans that they were being asked to sacrifice too much for American union contributed to their diminishing support for the war. As Meagher witnessed this in the summer of 1862, he argued that it was the result of "treachery or treason here among us." By July 29, four days after his celebrated recruiting speech at the 7th Regiment Armory, Meagher had still had so little success that he requested and received an extension on his leave to continue his recruiting efforts. He complained that his difficulties were "numerous, and most vexatious and embarrassing. The Army of the Potomac has to fight desperate open enemies in front," but he was fighting an equally difficult struggle against "an army of implacable conspirators in the rear." Meagher believed his problems were the result of two factors. First, Irish laborers knew that a draft was coming and that they would earn more money as substitutes than volunteers. Second, most Irish American Catholics and Democrats opposed the Lincoln administration: its direction of the war, perceived abuses of civil liberties, and the influence of Radical Republicans within Lincoln's party. These Democrats, Meagher insisted, had sought to discourage Irish Americans from volunteering, and he was witnessing a Democratic success.[36]

As the North reeled under the horrific losses at the battles at Antietam and Fredericksburg and reacted to the controversial Emancipation Proclamation, opposition to the war escalated. This was especially true in Irish American communities, which would be among the first to increasingly question the war effort and initiate demands for a peaceful resolution.

In September 1862, Confederate and Union armies met again outside Sharpsburg, Maryland, near Antietam Creek. This battle would be remembered as the bloodiest day in American history, with more than 22,000 soldiers killed, wounded, missing, or captured within a twelve-hour period. The fighting in the West Woods devastated the ranks for the Irish 69th Pennsylvania, while Meagher's Irish Brigade suffered from its assault on the Bloody Lane. Both the 63rd and 69th New York, Irish Brigade regiments, lost 60 percent of their numbers, suffering 202 and 196 casualties, respectively, most cut down within the first five minutes of the battle. The 88th New York lost 27 killed and 75 wounded, with the entire brigade suffering 540 casualties.[37] Among these brigade casualties were 75 new recruits who had just joined the brigade the day before the battle.[38]

These losses reflected the valor and skill of Irish American soldiers, but they devastated families and communities at home. Criticisms of Meagher increased, captured in the reflections of one Irish sergeant who described Meagher as "a gentleman and a soldier, but . . . he wanted to gain so much praise he would not spare his men."[39] Further problems arose as rumors spread that Meagher had actually fallen from his horse drunk at Antietam and failed his men. As Union colonel David Hunter Strother of McClellan's headquarters staff noted, "Meagher was not killed as reported, but drunk, and fell from his horse."[40] While largely discounted by Irish Americans, this account circulated through Northern newspapers that fall and contributed to further tensions between nativist and Irish American communities.

The losses from Antietam combined with a series of controversial decisions announced by President Lincoln in the coming months angered the Irish American community. The first event occurred in the aftermath of the battle, when Lincoln announced the Emancipation Proclamation that would free all slaves held in Confederate territory as of January 1, 1863. The new law did not free slaves in slave-owning states loyal to the Union, such as Maryland and Missouri. Nor did it free slaves in formerly Confederate lands now held by Federal forces. Despite this, the proclamation caused the war to evolve from a conflict to preserve the Union to a bloody struggle to abolish slavery and reunite a nation.

Many Northerners had never taken a clear stand on slavery, believing that it had little impact on their lives or the need to save the Union. Some Northerners, including many Irish American Catholics, saw the Emancipation Proclamation as evidence of Lincoln's support for the Irish Americans' sworn enemies, the abolitionists. The Irish linked the abolition of slavery with new labor competition from free blacks in an already difficult market. It meant freedom and a level of respect, though drastically limited, for a group the Irish had prided themselves as being above. Catholic leaders in Irish communities reinforced this racism, and some of the most powerful support came from the influential Archbishop John Hughes of New York. He refused to publicly condemn slavery and rejected any overtures from abolitionist leaders.[41] Within the New York African American Catholic community, there was a powerful sense of rejection from Hughes, who one black leader insisted "hate[s] the black race so much he cannot bear them to come near him." The animosity between Irish and African Americans was powerful, and it was a major factor behind Irish Catholic frustration and disillusionment with the Lincoln administration after the announcement of the Emancipation Proclamation. As Catholic historian Jay Dolan has clarified, the Irish were hardly alone in white America with their prejudice against blacks. He concludes, however, that "the roots of this prejudice in New York and elsewhere can be traced back to the era of John Hughes, when the patterns of discrimination first emerged with a vengeance."[42] Immersed in these racial tensions, and learning of horrifying losses at the Battle of Antietam, the Irish community in America learned that the war was moving in a direction they could not support.

Lincoln's other problem focused on his relief of General George B. McClellan from command of the Army of the Potomac. McClellan had displayed a constant case of what Lincoln called "the slows" throughout the campaign season of 1862, and the president believed he could not win the war with such a conservative commander. His decision, however, was nearly as controversial, for Union volunteers and their families, as the Emancipation Proclamation and added fuel to the fire of complaints across the North.

Much of this unrest was within McClellan's Army of the Potomac, whose soldiers loved the commander who seemed so concerned with sparing their lives, compared with the press and politicians at home who always demanded more battles. As McClellan passed the Irish Brigade during his final farewell, Meagher ordered the Irish men to throw down their green battle flags in an act of devotion. McClellan was honored but insisted that the men retrieve the banners before he passed and obey their orders just as he must accept his. With McClellan's departure, several Irish Brigade officers tendered resignations to protest the president's decision, but Meagher refused to accept them. The Irish men of the Army of the Potomac would obey their orders but not without complaint.[43]

Following McClellan's departure in the fall of 1862, General Ambrose Burnside, who replaced McClellan, marched the Army of the Potomac southward toward Richmond. He lost a dramatic engagement with Confederate general Robert E. Lee's Army of Northern Virginia at the battle at Fredericksburg, Virginia, on December 13. The Union army suffered tremendous casualties, nearly 13,000 men, and the Irish Brigade bore a heavy portion of those losses. As the survivors reflected on their devastating losses, just three months after the bloodletting at Antietam, a dark depression fell over the men.[44]

Father William Corby, the Catholic chaplain in the 88th New York, was horrified by the suffering of the Irish men in his care and declared "the place into which Meagher's brigade was sent was simply a slaughter-pen." Irish Brigade historian and staff member Captain David P. Conyngham went further, challenging the very idea that such fighting deserved the title of a military engagement. "It was not a battle—it was a wholesale slaughter of human beings—sacrificed to the blind ambition and incapacity of some parties," namely, General Ambrose Burnside. Colonel Robert Nugent of the 69th New York agreed with such descriptions of the battle, characterizing that bloody day at Fredericksburg as a "living hell from which escape seemed scarcely possible."[45] Years later he explained to a comrade from the Irish Brigade that his regiment lost two officers killed and fourteen wounded, "so that not a single officer of the sixteen that went into the fight escaped unharmed," including Nugent, who suffered a bullet wound through his right side. "From this you will readily perceive that sad havoc was made in the ranks of the 69th on that day," he argued. As one Irishman from Jersey City, New Jersey, summarized the situation the day after the battle, "The Irish Brigade is completely used up. This morning the whole five regiments together only muster 250 men."[46]

The depleted ranks of the Irish Brigade verified these claims. In days following the battle, the Irish Brigade estimated that it had taken 45 percent losses and recorded fifty-five officers killed or wounded at Fredericksburg, a devastating loss in leadership when added to the twenty-four officers killed and wounded from its New York regiments at Antietam.[47] It would be difficult, if not impossible, for the brigade to recover from this loss and may explain why the remaining men rallied around Meagher, despite rumors questioning his leadership, in their desperate need for guidance amid such turmoil.

These sentiments spread from camp to the Irish American home front within a few weeks. On December 27, 1862, the *New York Irish-American* published a letter Captain William J. Nagle of the 88th New York had sent to his father the day after the battle. In it he spoke well of Meagher but complained of wasted efforts. "Irish blood and Irish bones cover that terrible field to-day," Nagle wrote. "The whole-souled enthusiasm with which General McClellan inspired his army is wanting—his great scientific engineering skill is missing—his humane care for the lives of his men is disregarded. We are slaughtered like sheep, and no result but defeat."[48] John England, an Irish American serving in the 9th New York, described to his family the carnage of Fredericksburg as "one of the most fruitless, destructive, and disastrous battles ever fought on the old or new Continent" and was shocked at the treatment of the wounded, who are "thought no more of than a pack of used up maimed dogs, and treated no better; and hundreds are stiff and cold in death to-day, who would be living and might recover if properly treated and attended."[49] Summarizing the situation, one Irish soldier wrote, "As for the remnant of the Brigade, they were the most dejected set of Irishmen you ever saw or heard of."[50]

The year ended in a dark mood for many Northern Irish Americans. What had begun so gloriously with the formation of the Irish Brigade found many Irish men in December 1862 reexamining the direction of the war and their place in it. With the horrendous losses of Irish men at Antietam and Fredericksburg, combined with Lincoln's controversial Emancipation Proclamation and decision to relieve McClellan, Irish Americans hoping to preserve an American asylum for Irish refugees could no longer believe in these dreams. Those fighting to gain military experience for the future looked about the battlefields and camps, watching their numbers dwindle as they realized that there would be few Irish men left to fight such wars. Those of a similar mind-set at home were shocked to read the casualty reports in the papers that fall, with the lists of killed and wounded filling page after page. For increasing numbers of Irish men, the cost of this war and its goals were creating a nation that could no longer be their home. Men in camp and at home bitterly criticized the Lincoln administration's new abolition policies and expressed equally sharp comments on the inequities of state drafts and the rumors of an upcoming national draft. The cracks within Irish American support for the war burst open during those cold, dark months, foreshadowing an explosion of riots and protests that would characterize Irish frustrations the following year. As 1863 began, an Irish soldier captured the mood that permeated Irish America: "All is dark, and lonesome, and sorrow hangs as a shroud over us all."[51]

Similar sentiments surfaced among Irish soldiers in the Midwest that winter. Peter Casey, of Mulligan's 23rd Illinois (Chicago's Irish Brigade), complained, "Black abolitionism is potent in our times." Expressing his concern over rumors that Colonel Mulligan planned to leave the regiment and would be replaced by a non-Irish Catholic, Casey insisted that the Union high command selected favored, though unqualified, men to lead their units and showed particular prejudice toward Irish Catholics. He feared that the 23rd Illinois, and especially the Irish Catholics in the unit, would suffer from such practices if Mulligan left. "They will not give [Irish Catholics] a chance of that kind," Casey insisted, "[and] others not worthy of confidence will fill the high places which is about all they want or care for. The Negro and not the welfare of the country is what most engrosses their minds and perhaps when all is over they will turn their attention to the burning of convents and churches as they have done before."[52]

Irish sergeant Major M. W. Toale of the 65th Illinois made charges of prejudice as well, claiming that his failure to receive a number of well-earned promotions was due to anti-Irish hostility. He asked Colonel Mulligan to "bring me to a regiment where 'nationality' will [not] debar a 'brave man' from holding the position [he] merits, and where '*35 miles of water*' will no longer separate me from the fellowship of my brother soldiers."[53] Similar reports came from Irish American captain R. T. Farrell fighting near Grand Junction, Tennessee. He had written Mulligan of similar problems two years earlier and now insisted that "an Irishman, particularly a Catholic, has a devilish hard road to tread when not in an Irish regiment."[54]

When Thomas Francis Meagher returned to New York that January for a high mass recognizing the sacrifices of the Irish Brigade, he found evidence of similar disillusionment. Irish newspapers spoke of the community mourning its husbands, fathers, and sons and challenged the idea of sending more Irish men into a cause many had come to question and under the direction of leaders they did not trust. The most popular Irish paper in the city warned Meagher that his visit, which included continued recruiting efforts, would work only "if men can yet be found to volunteer in a war—the conduct of which reflects anything but credit on those who have undertaken its management."[55]

Unknown to many Irish, Meagher faced resistance in several quarters. The Lincoln administration had never liked, and now firmly disapproved of, Meagher's methods in locating and enlisting recruits. The exchange between the president, Secretary of War Edwin M. Stanton, and Meagher indicates that the White House had tired of its political generals. One issue of special concern was leave time for the Irish Brigade. Despite repeated requests, War Department officials did not allow Meagher to lead his brigade home for a well-deserved rest. When Meagher argued that other units were receiving such leaves, the response was silence.[56]

Meagher did manage to secure several brief trips for himself, but then he made the mistake of returning late to camp and having to face trial on charges of being absent without leave before a court-martial. In another order that allowed Meagher a medical leave in Baltimore or Philadelphia, the general traveled instead to New York, where he made several public appearances. Following a brief return to the field in May 1863 to lead his dwindling Irish Brigade, numbering only 520 men, at the Battle of Chancellorsville, Meagher feared the unit would be disbanded, then men shifted to other non-Irish units, and he would lose his command unless he did something dramatic. In a letter indicating his dedicated service and sad frustration with the Lincoln administration, Meagher insisted that it left him no choice but to resign in protest of the administration's unjust behavior. This time the War Department's response was prompt and brief: we accept.[57]

For many Irish Catholic civilian leaders and soldiers, Meagher's resignation was the only honorable response to an ungrateful, prejudiced administration. The general public knew little or nothing of the conversations between Stanton, Lincoln, and Meagher, or of the latter's violations of command. All that Northern Irish Americans knew was that years of Irish sacrifice had not convinced the War Department to even acknowledge Meagher's requests for leave for his men. When individuals argued that the Union was in too precarious a position to allow whole brigades leaves of absence, Irish Americans pointed to units from other states that secured such periods of rest. So while the government responded to the requests of native-born commanders and expressed concern for their Protestant troops, some Irish Americans argued, they failed to grant similar attention to Irish Catholic soldiers. Capturing this mood, the *New York Irish-American* charged, "If the Brigade were not so markedly and distinctively *Irish*, they would not have been treated with the positive injustice and neglect to which they have been exposed."[58]

Irish American community leaders, politicians, officers, and enlisted men resented what they saw as total disrespect from leading Republicans. Editorials in the *Pilot* reflected this: "There is an aching void in our hearts; a sad sense of neglect, if not of wrong done to us and our living comrades; of indifference and coldness toward the memory of our noble immortal dead, whose bones lie on every battle-field from Yorktown to the last and most fatal days at Chancellorsville." The men of the Irish Brigade had fought valiantly and heroically, trusting, as one soldier recalled, that they would be heroes upon their return home. There was, however, little evidence of this. As Captain Nagle of the 88th New York explained, "It was this that made every man determined to excel at Fredericksburg, and prove by our deeds, if any further proof could be necessary, even with our small numbers, how worthy we were of the consideration and kind offices of the government." That May they concluded that their service had achieved none of this.[59] The men of the brigade, Nagle told his father, felt anger, sorrow, and bitterness when they learned of Meagher's resignation. "Am I not right in saying," he asked,

> that in any other country the brigade which had fought and suffered as this has would be gratefully and proudly cherished, its ranks kept full, its deeds of heroism acknowledged and rewarded? We asked neither reward nor favor, only what was right—just to the government, and for the advancement and good of the cause in which we had staked life and reputation. It was denied us, and the Irish Brigade is blotted out of the army of the Union.[60]

Nagle argued that Irish Americans sought only "what was right" in return for their service, and that he viewed this not as a reward or favor but simply as fair treatment that they had earned. The noncommissioned officers of Nagle's regiment went so far as to issue an official statement expressing their regret that Meagher's resignation was the only means possible to maintain the honor and integrity of the brigade. The officers of the 116th Pennsylvania argued that with Meagher's resignation, "we have been deprived of a leader whom we all would have followed to death." Some questioned whether they, too, should resign, and as the general departed from camp, they assured Meagher of their support.[61]

Leading members of Irish American communities at home expressed their anger more boldly. Reflecting the growing disillusionment that spring, the *Pilot* cried, "We are an emigrant race; we did not cause this war; vast numbers of our people have perished in it. . . . [T]he Irish spirit for the war is dead! Absolutely dead!"[62] The editors argued that despite Meagher's countless attempts to strengthen the Irish Brigade, he received no support from the War Department. Secretary Stanton, the editors charged, "has shown his porcine proclivities to their full extent" in this matter, "but not for the first time." Despite the fact that "General Meagher [had] fully informed him of the condition of the gallant brigade . . . Secretary Stanton took no notice of his representations."[63] Such clear disregard for the Irish, the editors warned, would not be forgotten. "The Irish will never forgive this extreme want to decorum. It will remain in their memory with national bitterness, as the deaths of their warriors will with national regret," wrote the *Pilot*. "Such sentiments will have their effect." That effect included diminished Irish support for the war.[64]

While Northern Irish leaders were lamenting, "How bitter to Ireland has been this rebellion! It has exterminated a generation of its warriors," they faced a new challenge: the nation's first federal draft.[65] In March 1863, when Congress passed the Enrollment Act, Irish community leaders in Boston insisted that, unlike the previous state drafts, this law targeted aliens. A close scrutiny of the Enrollment Act revealed that immigrants who had declared their intention to become American citizens had sixty-five days after the passage of the act to leave the country before they became eligible for the draft, and reviews of the law confirmed this. The *Pilot* complained, "Most [aliens] cannot get away in that time. Many of them are here, too, under the advice of Secretary [of State William H.] Seward."[66] This was, declared the editors, "a miserable Yankee trick to entice over here 'food for powder.'"[67]

Irish American volunteer John England agreed, arguing that he was not opposed to the concept of a draft so much as the inequity of this system. The law, he insisted, "was framed for the benefit of the rich and the disadvantage of the poor. For instance—a rich conscript can commute for $300! Now, it is a fact well known to all that there are some rich animals in the northern cities who can afford to lose $300, as much as some poor people can afford to lose one cent." For Irish Americans in the latter category, the Enrollment Act seemed to reveal a war that held nothing for them but further prejudice, sacrifice, and death. England warned that the "conscription law, no matter how constructed, can never become popular, for it is the last alternative of an unpopular cause," and a cause in which many working-class Irish Americans, those most significantly affected by the bill, would refuse to participate.[68]

As Irish Americans increasingly faced perceived injustices from nativists, their opposition to the draft grew. In the Midwest, a Democratic convention pledged, "We will *resist* to the *death* all attempts to draft any of our citizens into the army." New Yorkers were equally determined, with editor James McMaster of the Catholic *Freeman's Journal* proclaiming for himself and the Irish Catholic community, "When the President called upon them to go and carry on a war for the nigger, he would be d—d if he believed they would go." New York's Democratic governor Horatio Seymour supported this as he warned Republicans, "Remember this—that the bloody and treasonable doctrine of public necessity can be proclaimed by a mob as well as by a government."[69]

The New York City draft riots of July 13–17, 1863, unleashed five days of terror as various groups of New Yorkers, including many Irish American Catholic unskilled laborers, voiced their opposition to the draft, emancipation, the Republican administration, and the war in general. When the violence subsided, it was clear that the memory of it, and especially the significant role played by Irish men in those bloody July days, would not be forgotten.

New York diarist George Templeton Strong, representative of prominent New York Republican businessmen, characterized the rioters as "stalwart young vixens and withered old hags . . . swarming everywhere, all cursing the 'bloody draft' and egging on their men to mischief." Strong described the mob as entirely Irish, depicting "thirty-four lousy, blackguardly Irishmen with a tail of small boys . . . [and] a handful of *canaille*." To Strong and many other wealthy native-born New Yorkers, the Irish were "brutal, base, cruel, cowards, and as insolent as [they were] base." Reflecting on the riots, Strong mused, "No wonder St. Patrick drove all the venomous vermin out of Ireland! Its biped mammalia supply that island its full average share of creatures that crawl and eat dirt and poison every community they infest."[70]

In addition to characterizing the rioters as largely Irish savages, Republican papers like the *New York Times* dismissed claims that the participants' main purpose was to protest the draft. By the second day of the riots, the *Times* reported, "'Resistance to the draft' was the flimsiest of veils to cover the wholesale plundering which characterized the operations of the day."[71] Indeed, the *Times* chastised anyone who defended the mob. The *New York*

World, for example, had concluded, "We charge it plainly upon the radical journals of this City" that by supporting the Lincoln administration over the Democratic opposition, papers like the *Times* had only encouraged the draft riots. The *Times* replied in disgust that it was not to blame for simply discussing the political and social aspects of this conflict.[72] When a New York laborer and rioter attempted to explain the mob's perspective, the *Times* was equally impatient. Writing to the paper as "A Poor Man, but a Man for all that," the rioter argued,

> You will no doubt be hard on us rioters tomorrow morning, but that 300-dollar law has made us nobodies, vagabonds, and cast-outs of society, for whom nobody cares when we must go to war and be shot down. We are the poor rabble, and the rich rabble is our enemy by this law. Therefore we will give our enemy battle right here, and ask no quarter. Although we got hard fists, and are dirty without, we have soft hearts, and have clean consciences within, and that's the reason we love our wives and children more than the rich, because we got not much besides them and we will not go and leave them at home for to starve. Until that draft law is repealed I for one am willing to knock down more such rum-hole politicians as [superintendent of police John A.] Kennedy. Why don't they let the nigger kill the slave-driving race and take possession of the South as it belongs to them.[73]

Another letter to the editor, signed "A Poor Man," argued the inequality of the exemption clause, writing, "If this is not releasing the rich and placing the burden of the war exclusively on the poor, I should like to know what would be." Again the *Times* had no sympathy, explaining that substitute fees would be distributed among the poor to induce volunteers, and in the process would increase their pay by hundreds of dollars: "Not a single poor man will be drafted now who would not be if this $300 exemption clause were not in the law. But a great many would miss the $300 which now they can obtain as a bounty for volunteering."[74]

Most Irish Americans defended the motivations behind the Irish rioters, while leading native-born Americans renewed old stereotypes that the Irish were a dangerous, undeserving people who could never be trusted. Nativists ignored the fact that Irish-born Paddy McCafferty helped rescue the young boys and girls from the rioters who destroyed the Colored Orphan Asylum.

Nor did they recognize the service of Irish Catholic officer and Provost Marshal Robert Nugent, who tried to enforce the draft, or Irish American captain Henry O'Brien, who lost his life in an effort to protect New Yorkers' property.[75]

It is significant that not all Irish Catholic volunteers and civilians opposed the draft. Peter Welsh, a member of the 28th Massachusetts and the Irish Brigade, actually supported the draft, even with the exemption clause. "No conscription could be fairer" than that proposed in 1863, Welsh claimed, adding, "It would be impossible to frame it to satisfy every one. And those drafted men may never have to fight a battle." Through conscription, Welsh believed, "the war will either be settled or the skulking blowers at home will have to come out and do their share of the fighting." When those "skulkers" included Irish Americans, Welsh did not change his tone. He commended the use of canister and grapeshot against the draft rioters, and while regretting that many of the rioters were Irish, he regretted more their actions. "God help the Irish," Welsh prayed. "They are too easily led into such snares which give their enemies an opportunity to malign and abuse them."[76] Welsh was more the exception than the rule, but there were Irish American volunteers expressing such thoughts.

Even more, however, spoke out against the draft and the war itself. Boston's *Pilot* had been arguing since 1862 that "aliens are under no obligation to fight our battles; and no one has a right to make the smallest objection to them for refusing to do so. . . . [W]hen a war is raging . . . noncitizens of a country cannot be morally required to expose themselves to mutilation and death for it." The *Pilot* reminded its readers of nativists' abuses, questioning why a recent immigrant would ever wish to offer his service and his life for such a nation. The editors argued:

> It is going too far to *require* an alien—a recent emigrant—to go to battle. We refuse aliens the right of voting, the right of holding office, and if they wanted passports for foreign travel, not one could they get. The aliens who came to vote would be knocked down at the polls, and then imprisoned; the alien who held office, would be hunted from it by every description of violence; and the alien who looked for the protection of our government would not get it. What *right* then have we to be *severe* with aliens for not enlisting?[77]

In response to these developments and culminating with the riots of 1863, native-born Americans stopped celebrating Irish military traditions, fighting abilities, and other examples of ethnic pride, and they returned to the antebellum descriptions of the Irish as "disturbing characters" who upset the "community order."[78] While many Americans equated declining Irish support for the war with betrayal, most Irish Americans considered it an act of loyalty and honor by remaining faithful to their fellow countrymen even if this meant abandoning the Union cause. A sense of responsibility to their heritage and families in Ireland and America had both inspired Irish men to wear Union blue, and these same dual loyalties led to their eventual opposition to that cause.[79]

A combination of all these events contributed to the declining Irish support for the Union war effort and declining Irish enlistments. Those Irish men entering service during the final two years of the war appear to have been much more interested in economic concerns than matters of Irish nationalism or saving America for future generations of Irish refugees. By the summer of 1864, the *New York Irish-American* informed its readers of the despair spreading through the ranks, quoting the sentiments of one soldier that the Irish Brigade "was a Brigade no longer." It appeared that soon the brigade would exist only in the "recollection[s] of its services and sufferings."[80] The brigade did survive, but the veterans noticed that new recruits lacked the determination and discipline of those who had joined two years earlier, and it would be difficult to maintain the unit's superb record.[81]

In October 1864, army officials witnessed similar disinterest in service from large elements of the Irish American community in Schuylkill County, Pennsylvania, where 400 to 500 deserters and drafted men were refusing to report for service. The men systematically attacked cavalry detachments attempting to arrest them, firing upon soldiers and then rushing into the safety of the thickly wooded hills. Officers reported that these were predominantly Irish men who broke into homes and businesses and even attacked wounded soldiers. Many of these men were, indeed, Irish, but the soldiers sent into these hills who made these reports had little understanding of the chaos they entered. While battles raged on distant fields, Irish miners had waged their own war in the anthracite regions of Pennsylvania, with increasing levels of violence, to secure better wages, fewer work hours, and safer working conditions at the collieries that dominated their lives.

Local mine owners, managers, and their supporters saw an opportunity to use the laws that allowed the U.S. Army to arrest draft resisters to crack down on the increasingly organized, determined, and violent Irish miners and their communities. As the Republican editor of the *Miner's Journal*, Benjamin Bannan, explained, "Such poor devils are to be pitied, but it is far better to send them into the army and put them in the front ranks, even if they are killed by the enemy, than that they should live to perpetuate such a cowardly race." He concluded, "Now is the time . . . for the operators . . . to get rid of the ringleaders engaged in threatenings, beatings, and shooting bosses at the collieries, and put better men in their places," and he saw the army as the perfect means to accomplish this. "A good Provost Guard with a battalion," Bannan wrote, "would soon teach the outlaws . . . their duties to the country in which they live." With the army arresting leading Irish workers and unknowingly breaking their labor organization efforts, these soldiers walked into a separate war in the Pennsylvania hills. Reports of the ensuing violence served to further discourage Irish enlistments in an army that seemed to be attacking their communities. Native-born Americans responded to these reports, too, but interpreted them differently, seeing further evidence of Irish disloyalty and violence during desperate times.[82]

Irish Americans continued to voice their discontent with the Union war effort through their support of Democratic presidential candidate George McClellan in 1864. Some hoped his victory would secure an armistice, while others insisted that McClellan would redirect the war away from issues of emancipation and back to the original matter of union. Regardless of his policies, the *Pilot* insisted that he would be an improvement over the Republicans, who saw the Irish as useful for nothing better "than being reduced to dust and being made food for gunpowder."[83] While it is true that Irish Americans were not alone in their exhaustion with the war and concerns over President Lincoln's leadership, they were among the minority who would oppose his reelection bid in 1864. Instead, Irish men turned out in large numbers for McClellan. In some areas of New York, including the heavily Irish Sixth Ward, McClellan received 90 percent of the vote, while the entire city went to him with more than a two-to-one majority.[84] It was not enough, however, to secure his victory. In fact, Irish Americans, at home and at the front, where nearly 80 percent of the soldier vote went for Lincoln, discovered they were in a clear minority of a country that overwhelmingly reelected President Lincoln.

McClellan's defeat was a defeat for the Irish, who would pay the price for their continuing loyalty to the Democratic Party and their criticism of the president and the war in general for years to come. For many Republicans, abolitionists, and African Americans, Lincoln's assassination on April 14, 1865, Good Friday, following Confederate general Robert E. Lee's surrender five days earlier on Palm Sunday, made the president almost Christlike. Anyone who had criticized or challenged the martyred Lincoln was seen as partly responsible for his death and the nation's suffering. For years to come, the Irish would be punished for this and for their loyalty to the Democratic Party, which would be so commonly associated by Republicans with the Confederacy, violence, and treason.[85]

It is essential to understand Irish support for Irish interests when studying their role in the Union war effort, though this should not be overemphasized to the point where readers see every Irish American soldier as a Fenian. Irish Americans acted out of blended familial, cultural, and national influences that defined their identity. That heritage shaped how they viewed the war and how they responded to it. When the cause of union complemented the desires and aspirations of the Irish American community, they supported the Northern war effort. When the interests of Irish America clashed with these goals, however, many Irish men abandoned that cause. The Irish would pay for their perceived disloyalty in the years following the war, despite the challenges they voiced. In the end, though, one could argue that this tenacious, clanlike loyalty of Irish Americans for Irish America paid off. With increasing numbers and unity, they became a powerful force in American politics, economics, and religion. The journey would be long and difficult, but by maintaining their loyalties to Ireland and America, though increasingly in reverse order, they would find success in the United States.

NOTES

1. Christopher Byrne, Vernon Center, Minnesota, to Patrick Byrne, County Monaghan, Ireland, March 31, 1863, Shirley Family Papers, D3531/G/6, Public Record Office of Northern Ireland, Belfast. I wish to thank Dr. Ruth-Ann Harris for making me aware of Christopher Byrne's wonderfully detailed letter and for sharing

her knowledge of his experiences in the Civil War. Byrne is the focus of a forthcoming article by Harris and Sally Sommers-Smith in *Eire-Ireland*.

2. *Chicago Daily Tribune*, April 20, 1861.

3. Harold F. Smith, "Mulligan and the Irish Brigade," *Journal of the Illinois State Historical Society* 56 (1963): 164–66.

4. *Pilot*, January 12, 1861.

5. *Pilot*, February 2, 1861.

6. *New York Irish-American*, February 14, 1861.

7. Michael Cavanagh, *Memoirs of Gen. Thomas Francis Meagher* (Worcester, MA: Messinger Press, 1892), 369.

8. Daniel George MacNamara, *The History of the Ninth Regiment Massachusetts Volunteer Infantry, June, 1861–June, 1864*, ed. Christian G. Samito (New York: Fordham University Press, 2000), 5.

9. Ibid., 16.

10. Ibid., 17.

11. Brian C. Pohanka, *James McKay Rorty: An Appreciation* (New York: Irish Brigade Association, 1993), 20–21.

12. *Souvenir Sketch of St. Patrick's Church Philadelphia, 1842–1892* (Philadelphia: Hardy and Mahony, 1892), 32

13. Monsignor Eugene Murphy, *The First One Hundred Years, 1831–1931: The Parish of St. John the Baptist* (Philadelphia: Church Printing and Envelope Co., 1932), 179–87.

14. John R. G. Hassard, *Life of John Hughes, First Archbishop of New York* (New York: Arno Press, 1969), 439, 487, cited in Jay P. Dolan, *The Immigrant Church: New York's Irish and German Catholics, 1815–1865*, 2nd ed. (Notre Dame, IN: University of Notre Dame Press, 1983), 162. For more on the Romanization of the Catholics of Philadelphia in the mid-nineteenth century, see Dale B. Light's *Rome and the Republic: Conflict and Community in Philadelphia Catholicism between the Revolution and the Civil War* (Notre Dame, IN: University of Notre Dame Press, 1996).

15. General Thomas Francis Meagher to General Edwin V. Sumner, July 2, 1862; *The War of the Rebellion: A Compilation of the Official Records of the Union and Confederate Armies* (Washington, DC: Government Printing Office, 1880–1901), ser. 1, vol. 11, pt. 2, 74–75 (hereafter *OR); see also David Power Conyngham, The Irish Brigade and Its Campaigns, ed. Lawrence Frederick Kohl (New York: Fordham University Press, 1994), 37, 45, 218; Joseph G. Bilby, The Irish Brigade in the Civil War: The 69th New York and Other Irish Regiments of the Army of the Potomac (Conshohocken, PA: Combined Publishing, 1998), 45.*

16. Anon., Ninth Massachusetts Diary, June 27, 1862, *Civil War Times Illustrated*, 29, no. 2 (June 1990): 30; and Stephen W. Sears, *To the Gates of Richmond: The Peninsula Campaign* (Boston: Houghton Mifflin, 1992), 230.

17. *Pilot*, July 19, 1862.

18. Bradley M. Gottfried, *Stopping Pickett: The History of the Philadelphia Brigade* (Shippensburg, PA: White Mane Books, 1999), 93.

19. *Detroit Free Press*, May 31, 1862; quoted in the *Pilot*, July 12, 1862.

20. Smith, "Mulligan and the Irish Brigade," 173.

21. Craig Lee Kautz, "Fodder for Cannon: Immigrant Perceptions of the Civil War—The Old Northwest" (Ph.D. diss., University of Nebraska, Lincoln, 1976), 140–41.

22. *Quincy Herald*, August 4, 1862; quoted in Kautz, "Fodder for Cannon," 141.

23. *Chicago Post*, July 19, 1862; reprinted in the *Pilot*, August 2, 1862.

24. *Pilot*, June 21, 1862; August 9, 1862.

25. *Pilot*, July 19, 1862.

26. *New York Times*, July 26, 1862; also covered in the *Irish-American*, August 2, 1862.

27. *New York Times*, July 26, 1862

28. Frank A. Boyle, *A Party of Mad Fellows: The Story of the Irish Regiments in the Army of the Potomac* (Dayton, OH: Morningside Books, 1996), 167.

29. James B. Turner to the Turner family, July 29, 1862; July 19, 1862, James B. Turner Papers, 1861–1876, New York State Library, Albany, New York.

30. Matilda Sproul, Carn Corn, County Tyrone, Ireland to Andrew J. and Frances Sproul, Fredericksburg, Ohio, July 28, 1862, Sproul Family Papers, Southern Historical Collection, University of North Carolina, Chapel Hill.

31. Hugh Harlin, Laporte, Indiana, to John Harlin, New York, May 28, 1862; August 4, 1862, private collection of Mr. Robert J. and Mrs. Ruth Fitzgerald, Rouses Point, New York.

32. Christopher Byrne, Vernon Center, Minnesota, to Patrick Byrne, County Monaghan, Ireland, March 31, 1863. For details on some of the state drafts and the riots that erupted in the Wisconsin area in response to it, see Lawrence H. Larsen, "Draft Riot in Wisconsin, 1862," *Civil War History* 7 (December 1961): 421–27.

33. *Pilot*, June 14, 1862.

34. *Pilot*, June 14, 1862; July 26, 1862.

35. *Chicago Post*; quoted in the *Pilot*, August 2, 1862.

36. Athearn, *Thomas Francis Meagher*, 115.

37. *OR*, ser. 1, vol. 19, pt. 1, 192; see also Stephen W. Sears, *Landscape Turned Red: The Battle of Antietam* (New York: Houghton Mifflin, 1983; reprint, New York: Book-of-the-Month Club, 1994), 243 (page citations are to the reprint edition).

38. Conyngham, *Irish Brigade and Its Campaigns*, 308; see also Bilby, *Irish Brigade in the Civil War*, 60.

39. Burton, *Melting Pot Soldiers*, 126.

40. Sears, *Landscape Turned Red*, 243–44.

41. Dolan, *Immigrant Church*, 25.

42. Dolan, *Immigrant Church*, 25.

43. *New York World*, November 12, 1862; see also Sears, *Landscape Turned Red*, 342–43.

44. Edward J. Stackpole, *The Fredericksburg Campaign: Drama on the Rappahannock* (Mechanicsburg, PA: Stackpole Books, 1957), 276.

45. Corby, *Memoirs of Chaplain Life*, 132; Conyngham, *Irish Brigade and Its Campaigns*, 343; Bilby, *Irish Brigade in the Civil War*, 67.

46. Robert Nugent, New York City, to St. Clair Mulholland, Philadelphia, Pennsylvania, January 5, 1881, St. Clair A. Mulholland Papers, box 1, Civil War Library and Museum, Philadelphia, Pennsylvania; *New York Irish-American*, December 27, 1862.

47. *OR*, ser. 1, vol. 21, 129; *OR*, ser. 1, vol. 19, pt. 1, 192; Bilby, *Irish Brigade in the Civil War*, 70.

48. *Irish-American*, December 27, 1862.

49. John England to Ellen Hargeddon, December 17, 1862, John England Letters, U.S. Army, 1814–1862, Manuscripts and Archives Division, New York Public Library.

50. Conyngham, *Irish Brigade and Its Campaigns*, 350.

51. *Irish-American*, January 10, 1863.

52. Private Peter Casey, 23rd Illinois, New Creek, Virginia, to Colonel James A. Mulligan, Chicago, Illinois, March 23, 1863, Mulligan Papers, Chicago Historical Society.

53. M. W. Toale, Camp Douglas, Chicago, Illinois, to James A. Mulligan, Chicago, Illinois, 10 February 1863, Mulligan Papers, Chicago Historical Society.

54. Captain R. T. Farrell, Grand Junction, Tennessee, to Colonel James A. Mulligan, February 8, 1863, folder 2, box 2, Mulligan Papers, Chicago Historical Society (emphasis in the original).

55. *New York Irish-American*, December 27, 1862.

56. The entire exchange between Meagher and the Lincoln administration is outlined in my book manuscript, *The Harp and the Eagle: Irish Volunteers in the American Civil War*. See Henry W. Halleck to Edwin M. Stanton, February 18, 1863, Papers of Edwin M. Stanton, Library of Congress, Washington, D.C.; Robert G. Athern, *Thomas Francis Meagher: An Irish Revolutionary in America* (Boulder: University of Colorado Press, 1949; reprint, New York: Arno Press, 1976), 101, 121, 123–25; *OR*, ser. 1, vol. 34, pt. 3, 333; James M. McPherson, *Battle Cry of Freedom: The Civil War Era* (New York: Oxford University Press, 1988), 328; T. Harry Williams, *Lincoln and His Generals* (New York: Knopf, 1952), 217; Assistant Adjutant General S. Williams on behalf of Major General Joseph Hooker to Brigadier General Thomas Francis Meagher, March 3, 1863, Thomas Francis Meagher, M-1064, roll 187, Letters Received by the Commission Branch of the Adjutant General's Office, 1865, National Archives and Records Administration, Washington, D.C. (hereafter NARA); Brigadier General Thomas Francis Meagher to Major John Hancock, Assistant Adjutant-General, May 8, 1863, Thomas Francis Meagher, M-1064, roll 187, Letters Received by the Commission Branch of the Adjutant General's Office,

1865, NARA; Conyngham, *Irish Brigade and Its Campaigns*, 405; *OR*, ser. 3, vol. 3, 372; Brigadier General Thomas Francis Meagher to Edwin M. Stanton, Secretary of War, July 13, 1863, Thomas Francis Meagher, M-1064, roll 187, Letters Received by the Commission Branch of the Adjutant General's Office, 1865, NARA; *Pilot*, May 30, 1863; New York *Irish-American*, March 14, 1863. General Halleck did contact Secretary Stanton on February 18, 1863, expressing his concern over the number of officers and men away from camp, and Halleck said he would approve leaves only for the "very few cases where a refusal would cause great hardship," for "sickness in family," or for "urgent private business." Beyond that, I found no evidence to indicate that Secretary Stanton or anyone within the Lincoln administration announced a general order revising all leave policies. In January 1864, Meagher returned to duty as a major general, assigned to organize a division composed of soldiers recovering from wounds, stragglers, and others. In January 1865 he and his division participated in minor operations in North Carolina until he was relieved of duty for drunkenness in February and returned home to New York. Meagher officially resigned this commission in May 1865.

57. Assistant Adjutant General S. Williams on behalf of Major General Joseph Hooker to Brigadier General Thomas Francis Meagher, March 3, 1863, Thomas Francis Meagher, M-1064, roll 187, Letters Received by the Commission Branch of the Adjutant General's Office, 1865, NARA.

58. *New York Irish-American*, March 14, 1863.

59. *Pilot*, May 30, 1863.

60. Ibid.

61. Cavanagh, *Memoirs of Gen. Thomas Francis Meagher*, 28–32.

62. *Pilot*, May 30, 1863.

63. *Pilot*, May 23, 1863.

64. *Pilot*, May 30, 1863.

65. Ibid.

66. *Pilot*, May 23, 1863.

67. Eugene C. Murdock, *One Million Men: The Civil War Draft in the North* (Madison: State Historical Society of Wisconsin, 1971), 308; *Pilot*, May 30, 1863.

68. John England to Mr. Hargeddon, March 28, 1863, John England Letters, Manuscripts and Archives Division, New York Public Library.

69. McPherson, *Battle Cry of Freedom*, 609.

70. George Templeton Strong, *Diary of the Civil War, 1860–1865* (New York: Macmillan, 1962), 336, 342–43.

71. *New York Times*, July 15, 1863; July 19, 1863.

72. *New York Times*, July 16, 1863.

73. *New York Times*, July 15, 1863.

74. Ibid.

75. Edward K. Spann, "Union Green: The Irish Community and the Civil War," in , eds. *The New York Irish*, ed. Ronald H. Bayor and Timothy J. Meagher (Balti-

more: Johns Hopkins University Press, 1996), 204–5; Iver Bernstein, *The New York City Draft Riots: Their Significance in American Society and Politics in the Age of the Civil War* (New York: Oxford University Press, 1991), 36–37; Barnet Schecter, *The Devil's Own Work: The Civil War Draft Riots and the Fight to Reconstruct America* (New York: Walker and Company, 2005), 189.

76. Lawrence Frederick Kohl and Margaret Cossé Richard, eds. *Irish Green and Union Blue: The Civil War Letters of Peter Welsh* (New York: Fordham University Press, 1986), 110, 113, 115.

77. *Pilot*, 13 September 1862, emphasis in the original.

78. These characterizations are presented in David T. Knobel, *Paddy and the Republic: Ethnicity and Nationality in Antebellum America* (Middletown, CT: Wesleyan University Press, 1986), 76, 78.

79. Lawrence J. McCaffrey, *The Irish Catholic Diaspora in America* (Washington, DC: Catholic University of America Press, 1984), 7–8.

80. *New York Irish-American*, June 2, 1864.

81. Conyngham, *Irish Brigade and Its Campaigns*, 467; *OR*, ser. 1, vol. 36, pt. 1, 72; *OR*, ser. 1, vol. 42, pt. 1, 248. Following the Battle of Spotsylvania in May 1864, for example, Irish-born Colonel Matthew Murphy reported that he could account for 1,600 men of the Irish Brigade, many now draftees rather than volunteers, but "the remainder . . . [were] drunk on the road." After the Battle of Reams' Station in August 1864, Brigadier General Francis C. Barlow, commanding the 1st Division of the Army of the Potomac, complained that when he ordered the Irish Brigade to fill a break in the line during the battle, the Irish men "behaved disgracefully and failed to execute my orders. They crowded off to our right into the shelter of some woods, and there became shattered and broken to pieces."

82. *OR*, ser. 1, vol. 43, pt. 1, 480–82. See also Grace Palladino, *Another Civil War: Labor, Capital, and the State in the Anthracite Regions of Pennsylvania, 1840–1880* (Champaign: University of Illinois Press, 1990), 131–42. Palladino offers detailed analysis of this complex situation throughout chapters 6 and 7.

83. *Pilot*, September 17, 1864.

84. Spann, "Union Green," 208.

85. Several historians have made the argument regarding Lincoln's martyrdom, including James McPherson, *Ordeal by Fire: The Civil War and Reconstruction*, 3rd ed. (Boston: McGraw Hill, 2001), 521.

~ 4 ~

IRISH REBELS,
SOUTHERN REBELS

The Irish Confederates

David T. Gleeson

At Hibernian Hall in Charleston, South Carolina, in late 1877, former congressional candidate Michael Patrick (M. P.) O'Connor was master of ceremonies of an event to raise money for a new monument "to the Irish Volunteers." The Volunteers had served in the Confederate army during the Civil War. O'Connor had been an important member of Wade Hampton's "straight-out" ticket, which had recently "redeemed" the state from Radical Republican rule and ended Reconstruction. The Catholic son of an Irish immigrant had helped certify Irish Charleston's loyalty to the Redeemer cause, and he would win election to Congress in 1878 as a result. The meeting featured speeches from former Irish Volunteer captain Edward McCrady and the Honorable A. G. Magrath, a former federal judge and the last Confederate governor of South Carolina.

The son of an Irish immigrant who had fled political persecution in Ireland, Magrath particularly liked to link the Irish cause with the Southern one. In outlining the history of the unit, he reminded the packed hall that the Volunteers had their roots in the "men of '98" (the United Irish rebellion), "who had been told that their love of country was treason." He listed the litany of Ireland's wrongs at the hands of England and how this had helped Irish immigrants understand the importance of the Southern cause better than many natives. The Irish were also well aware that Carolinians had recognized their oppression and given them refuge. At secession and the outbreak of war, "the day came when the exiles from Ireland testified how well they remembered the justice done to their native land. The Irish immigrant sealed with his life's blood the covenant between his people and the land in which he lived and for which he died."[1] Magrath thus highlighted how the Irish in South Carolina had been rebels in two countries and how the American struggle had actually brought them closer, indeed "sealed," their place in their adopted home.

Therefore, while the Irish experience in the Confederacy was in many ways similar to that of every native-born Confederate, the historical and cultural baggage that they had brought with them from Ireland made theirs somewhat unique as well. First, in terms of motivation, the Irish had different reasons for going into Confederate service. Their experiences of Ireland, leaving it, and settling in the United States marked their opinions of the sectional crisis. Also, as recent arrivals, their roots both social and economic were not very deep in the South. Indeed, before coming to the region, many (especially those in the Atlantic states of the Confederacy) had lived in the North and often retained family and friends there. Second, ardor for the Southern cause among the Irish was often not as strong as that among natives. The Irish realized that in the aftermath of defeat the correct interpretation of their contributions to Confederate experiment was just as important as the actual reality of their participation in it.

On the eve of the 1860 presidential election, Irishman John McFarland of New Orleans, Louisiana, a native of Strabane, County Tyrone, who had come to America in 1839 and settled in Yazoo City, Mississippi, expressed fear about the coming election and its consequences, but he concluded:

> Myself, [and] my destiny were cast in the South 21 years ago. I came to it a stranger and penniless youth. I was taken by the hand by southerners; they have been kind to me. I have prospered beyond my expectations. My affections, my family, my home, are all here and whatever the fortunes of my adopted country mine rises or falls with it, in the South I have made the money that I am ready to offer up as well as my own arms to defend her honor and her rights.[2]

McFarland's rhetoric resonated with many of his fellow immigrants. After the election of Abraham Lincoln and secession, Irish men volunteered in numbers to fight in the Confederate army and often formed their own ethnic companies. They participated in the excitement of what they saw as the birth of a new nation. In New Orleans, the Irish chose the St. Patrick's Day after secession to celebrate both their heritage and their loyalty to the Southern cause. In a city where nativist and immigrant tensions had been very high less than three years earlier, and where Know-Nothings still controlled city hall, Irish men talked of the "fusion of hearts " between themselves and their Crescent City neighbors to defeat the common Yankee threat. Prominent at "Southern rights meetings," the Irish impressed a former journalistic Know-Nothing critic as "true men of the South."[3]

In Charleston the Irish militiamen took part in the "thrilling" activities of forming and defending a new government. In December 1860 some served in nearby Fort Moultrie, preventing Union resupply of the besieged Fort Sumter, while a company led by Edward McCrady had made the first seizure of Federal property when it helped occupy Castle Pinckney in Charleston harbor, a local newspaper noting that the Irish Volunteers were "among the most efficient of our companies" taking part in the "bustle and excitement" that pervaded the city. The use of the term "Irish Volunteers" also had deep meaning for Irish soldiers. The term had first been used by the "Wild Geese," Irish men driven from Ireland by English rule in the seventeenth and eighteenth centuries who fought in the armies of continental Europe. Various Irish Volunteers had achieved glory on the battlefield, and thus, Irish Confederates, embracing their ethnic heritage, aspired to that as well. The other implication was that the Irish of the Confederacy were exiles who like the Wild Geese would return to Ireland one day and free it from British rule.[4]

After the bombardment of Fort Sumter in April 1861, more Southern Irish men prepared to defend the Confederacy. Patrick Ronayne Cleburne, a young Irish lawyer in Helena, Arkansas, joined that state's first volunteer company.[5] Irish migrant levee workers in Washington County, Mississippi, one recruiter reported, "confessed a willingness to fight for the South" and wanted to enlist as soon as possible.[6] Irish in the urban South, believing that Confederate struggles mirrored those of Ireland, created their own ethnic companies. The Mobile Irish formed the Emerald Guards and marched out of the city in their green uniforms holding aloft their banner, which had the official Confederate flag on one side and a harp and wreath of shamrock prominently displayed on the other. The Irish-born bishop of Mobile, John Quinlan, blessed their company flag. Irish Mobilians named another company in honor of Robert Emmet, the failed Irish rebel of 1803.[7] Vicksburg's Irish men set up the Sarsfield Southrons, which they named after the Irish cavalryman Patrick Sarsfield. Like the Emerald Guards, the Southrons, led by Irish farmer Felix

Hughes, used the Confederate Stars and Bars as its company flag. They high-lighted their belief in the similarity between the Irish and Southern causes with a wreath of shamrock and the Gaelic war cry "Faugh a Ballagh" (clear the way) emblazoned on the front of their banner.[8] Individual Irish men often used Ireland's history to inspire their offspring. The Irish-born and reared pas-tor of the Second Presbyterian Church in Charleston, Thomas Smyth, was not very active in Irish affairs in the city. He had quickly considered himself a Carolinian, but when his Charleston-born son decided to enter Confederate service, he reminded the young man to

> remember that your blood is of that richest patriotic character—Scotch Irish—combining the mingled elements of English, Scotch, and North Irish—the Smyths, the chiefs of the first colony under James,—the Mag-ees—and the Stuarts of noble pedigree. Your grandfather Smyth was in early life a soldier; and in middle life a captain of the Irish rebels in the Irish rebellion of 1798, and a prisoner of war who narrowly escaped the same gallows upon which was executed the noble patriot, William Orr, whose execution he witnessed at the hazard of life; and the treason-inspiring card, about whose sacrifice on the altar of tyranny by the hands of perjured wit-nesses and the connivance of partial justice, was in itself a death warrant to its possessor—he cherished as a sacred memento.[9]

The older Smyth, an internationally prominent Presbyterian theologian, believed that his family's and his country's treatment in the aftermath of 1798 rebellion "will account for the genuine hatred of British intolerance and cruel injustice toward Ireland with which every member of our family seemed to be imbued."[10] Smyth's comments highlight that Irish Protestants in the South, like their Catholic countrymen who named their units after Irish national heroes, could remain proud of their Irish heritage and used it to boost their Confederate patriotism.

New Orleans contained the largest Irish population in the South, and it provided the greatest numbers of Irish recruits. Virtually all of the city's volunteer regiments had Irish in their companies, and Irish men dominated some others, such as the 6th Louisiana Infantry.[11] Other Southern cities also had Irish units. The Memphis-based 2nd Tennessee's (5th Confederate) recruits came from the largely Irish Pinch district, while the Irish of Nashville

and Clarksville formed the 10th Tennessee. In Georgia, the Irish in Savan-
nah, Augusta, and Macon formed their own companies. Wilmington, North
Carolina's largest center of Irish immigrants, had an Irish-dominated company, and Irish companies in Virginia came from towns such as Alexandria
and Lynchburg, as well as Allegheny County in the western part of the state.
The Richmond Irish had the Montgomery Guards, who mustered into the 1st
Virginia Infantry Regiment, while others organized the 1st Virginia Infantry
Battalion. An important Irish artillery company formed in East Texas. Apart
from these specific Irish units, individual Irish men who could not get into
an Irish company joined everything from the New Orleans Polish Brigade
to the Jasper Grays of Paulding, Mississippi.[12] Many of the South's numerous Irish boatmen signed up for the Confederate navy. These trained sailors
were invaluable to the nascent Southern navy because most Southerners had
no experience working on the high seas. Seafaring for both merchant and
military ships had always been an important occupation for Irish men who
wanted a better life beyond their homeland. Thus, Southern ports were full of
Irish sailors ready and capable to serve the new Confederate navy.[13]

In general the Irish had a good military reputation when they were "han-
dled" right. For example, General Richard Taylor of Louisiana, who had been
a prominent Know-Nothing, described one Irish regiment (the 6th Louisiana
Infantry) as "stout, hardy fellows, turbulent in camp and requiring a strong
hand." In spite of these control problems, Taylor believed that these "hardy"
Irish men when treated with "kindness and justice [were] ready to follow
their officers to the death."[14] On June 1, 1862, Taylor's Irish soldiers justified
his confidence. Thomas J. "Stonewall" Jackson's troops made an exhausting
march to Strasburg, Virginia, to avoid the entrapment of the Federal forces
in the Shenandoah Valley. Shortly thereafter, harassing Union cavalry attacks
caused them to panic. Taylor and the Irish Louisianians helped restore calm by
providing rearguard action to halt the Union forays.[15] Having restored order,
the Irish men refused relief from post duty for that night. Despite atrocious
weather conditions and continuous skirmishing artillery fire, they cried: "We
are the boys to see it out." This loud assurance "from half a hundred Tipper-
ary throats" made General Taylor, the onetime nativist, in praise of his Irish
troops, remark, "My heart has warmed to an Irishman since that night."[16]

Captain McCrady of Charleston was proud of the discipline his troops
showed and the fact that they were the color company of the 1st South

Carolina (Gregg's) Infantry. Irish native William McBurney, McCrady's business associate, replied to him in one letter: "I was quite pleased to learn that my countrymen under your skillful handling had become a pattern company. I hope they will continue so to the end of the war." When an Irishman of another Irish company from the same city (officially designated as Company C of the Charleston Battalion, later Company H of the Twenty-seventh South Carolina Volunteers), Captain William H. Ryan, died gallantly at the fight at Battery Wagner on Morris Island near Charleston on July 18, 1863, the city mourned him. Before his death Ryan had established himself as a brave and excellent officer in the various fights around Charleston. Thus, the *Charleston Mercury* lamented: "Few men have fallen more universally lamented than Capt. William H. Ryan . . . no nobler soldier fell that bloody day."[17]

There are numerous other examples of Irish gallantry from the war. Captain Felix Hughes of the Sarsfield Southrons died leading a charge at the Battle of Baton Rouge in September 1862; Captain Patrick Loughrey of the Emerald Guards had been killed in similar circumstances at the Battle of Seven Pines in Virginia the previous May. Colonel Henry Strong received a mortal wound rallying his troops of the 6th Louisiana at Antietam, his dead white horse captured eerily on film days later by famed photographer Mathew Brady. Lieutenant Dick Dowling of the Davis Guards (recruited in Galveston and Houston, Texas, and designated as Company F of the 1st Texas Heavy Artillery) lived through the war but received the commendation of both President Jefferson Davis and the Confederate Congress for his own and his Irish unit's action at Fort Griffin on the Sabine Pass on the East Texas Gulf Coast in September 1863 when he and his 40 men halted 5,000 Union troops who attempted to invade Texas through the pass.[18] In his official report, Lieutenant Dowling stated: "All my men behaved like heroes; not a man flinched from his post. Our motto was 'victory or death.'" When news of the Davis Guards' victory reached London, Confederate bond prices jumped three points. Coming just two months after the disastrous defeats at Gettysburg and Vicksburg, Dowling's actions, along with those of his men, were a great boost for the Confederacy.[19]

The most important example of Irish military ability for the Confederacy, however, was Pat Cleburne. Patrick Ronayne Cleburne, the "Stonewall of the West," played a major role in this enhancement of Irish reputations. A native of County Cork who had immigrated to Helena, Arkansas, in 1849, Pat Cleburne had enlisted as a private, but his company soon elected him captain.

By December 1862, he had been promoted to major general and had been given a division in General William J. Hardee's corps in the Army of Tennessee. Among his division were large numbers of Irish soldiers from Arkansas, Mississippi, and Tennessee. He made his division "a model of discipline" while maintaining its loyalty. Cleburne and his division had their finest hour at the Battle of Missionary Ridge on the Tennessee-Georgia border in 1863. While other Confederate forces fell easily to Union attacks, Cleburne's troops held their ground and formed a rear guard to protect the rest of the fleeing Confederate forces. Because these actions were the only bright spot in the disastrous rout near Chattanooga, Tennessee, the Confederate Congress commended Cleburne and his division for saving the remnants of the Army of Tennessee.[20]

Cleburne believed strongly in the Confederate cause. Like the Irish in his division, he was acutely aware of the similarities between Ireland and the Confederacy. A Protestant, he had served in the British army during the Great Famine and spent most of his time defending landlords and their agents from the starving Irish. His career enforcing British imperialism had not been an enjoyable one, and it had only made him aware "how artificial barriers could kill ambition." His youth in Ireland contrasted sharply with the success of his life in the South. Thus, when he believed Northern aggression threatened to turn his future into his past and bring about the "lingering dissolution" he had seen in Ireland, he became an ardent Confederate.[21] He, like many of the Irish Catholics in his division (the 2nd Tennessee, later 5th Confederate, was made up predominantly of Irish Memphians, while Company C of the 3rd Confederate Regiment was the Shamrock Guards from Vicksburg) saw parallels between the South and Ireland. This fear of the South becoming a colony made Cleburne treasure "independence above *every other earthly consideration* [emphasis in original]."

When the Confederacy's prospects looked dire in early 1864, Cleburne even advocated the recruiting of slaves into the Confederate army. He believed that young male slaves should be offered their (somewhat limited) emancipation in return for Confederate military service. Southern nationhood mattered more to him than personal property. The mere broaching of the idea cost Cleburne further promotion, and he remained a division commander until his death at the Battle of Franklin in late 1864.[22] The Irish in the South recognized how important Cleburne had been to their cause, as well as the South's.

His example (he retained a pronounced Cork accent throughout his American life) had increased the stature of all Irish Southerners. Thus, it is not surprising that immediately after the war a Fenian organizer in New Orleans noted that the Cleburne name had "a talismanic effect among the Irish of the South," or that when his body was moved from Tennessee to be reinterred in Helena in 1870, the Irish of Memphis turned out in droves to honor the cortege as it came through their city for transportation down the Mississippi River.[23]

But for every Hughes, Dowling, and Cleburne, there were also poor Irish performances under fire. Most infamously were the actions of the 1st Virginia (Irish) Battalion at the Battle of Cedar Mountain in August 1862. Recruited in Richmond, the battalion fought effectively in the Shenandoah Valley campaign and was part of Colonel T. S. Garnett's brigade. When the battalion came under a strong cavalry attack, almost every man turned and fled.[24] Officers failed to halt this panicked "retreat." The Irish men eventually stopped running far behind the Confederate lines, where their officers managed to rally them to act as a reserve for the remainder of the day. One can sense the anger and frustration of the commanding officers in their official reports. The fact that the unit was constantly referred to as the "Irish Battalion" did nothing to enhance the reputation of Irish Confederates among natives. Nonetheless, while not very effective in combat, the men in the battalion did distinguish themselves as policemen, becoming the provost guard of Jackson's corps. It seems that the stereotype of the Irish policeman in America had some Confederate roots as well. Perhaps this was the only role fit for the battalion rather than an Irish propensity for policing because this seems to be the only example of a dedicated Irish military police unit in the Confederate army. All the other Irish companies, including those in Jackson's corps, remained as frontline units.[25]

Richard Taylor's comment that the Irish soldiers were "turbulent" has a lot of supporting evidence. Even boosters of Irish units such as Edward McCrady's friend William McBurney, a native of Ireland himself, recognized that Irish soldiers and alcohol did not mix well. He warned his friend that "you must confine them to homeopathic doses of the 'creather' John Barleycorn [It] generally [goes?] from their heads to their fists and always spoils their manners." McCrady indeed had some trouble with his popular lieutenant, J. S. Ryan, the nephew of one of Charleston's largest slave traders, for being drunk on duty. Ryan had acted in a "disgraceful" manner in front of the men.

McCrady, with the support of his regimental commander, forced Ryan to resign, a move that was very unpopular with the men and one that nearly got McCrady embroiled in a duel with Ryan's uncle back in Charleston.[26]

A larger problem for Irish units, however, was absence without leave and desertion. Irish units suffered from high desertion rates. Assessing these rates is very difficult because most Confederate muster rolls and duty rosters are incomplete. Nonetheless, the available evidence does point to the Irish deserting in large numbers and, when doing so, expressing allegiance to the United States. For example, of the 103 men of McCrady's Irish Volunteers who signed up "for the War" in June 1861, 33 deserted. Those captured often refused to be exchanged and asked to take the oath of allegiance. A relatively comprehensive study of desertion rates has been done on Louisiana regiments in the Army of Northern Virginia and indicates that Irish soldiers deserted more often than their native-born colleagues. The Irish 6th Louisiana, which General Richard Taylor had admired so much, had a high desertion rate.[27]

Irish soldiers could also on occasion use the "foreign" exemption of the March 1862 Confederate draft law, which allowed foreigners in the South to avoid the draft or leave Confederate service if they could show that they did not or had never intended to take citizenship. For soldiers already in service the new law gave them the right to a discharge. Irish in units such as the Montgomery Guards of the 1st Virginia Infantry took advantage of this loophole. In 1862 many in the company applied for discharges on the basis of not having established "domicile" in the Confederacy. To gain this discharge they had to state that they had never become citizens or had any intention of doing so. They also had to have a witness to support their case. County Limerick native Private William Buckley got one Patrick Moroney of Richmond to swear that he had heard Buckley state that he had only come to America for work and had always intended to return to Ireland. Private Matthew Bresnahan of County Kerry was fortunate enough to get the British consul in Richmond to support his case that he had only come "on a visit," one that had, however, lasted three and a half years. Despite the disingenuousness of the cases—the Irish were the least likely of any nineteenth-century immigrants to return to their homeland—both men were discharged.[28]

This was the ultimate disloyalty and called into question Irish support for the Confederacy. Allied with this reality was the myth of foreigners being the backbone of the Union army. Sergeant W. M. Andrews of the 1st Georgia

Infantry (Regulars), for example, who served with and enjoyed the company of Irish soldiers in his own unit, could state when remembering the Union Irish Brigade at the Battle of Fredericksburg: "The Confederates are now fighting the World, Burnside having German, Irish, and Italian brigades. Every foreigner who puts his foot on American soil joins the Northern Army, for the sake of the bounty paid, if anything."[29] He seemed to have forgotten the Irish men around him in his regiment.

Whether they were brave or cowardly, the fact remains that the Irish did not have a huge military effect on the Confederacy. Somewhere in the region of 20,000 served in the Confederate armed forces, not enough to have a major impact on the war.[30] Undoubtedly, specific Irish units did perform vital tactical tasks at certain times, such as the 6th Louisiana in the Shenandoah Valley, and the Davis Guards at Sabine Pass, and Irish officers such as Patrick Cleburne could be very important commanders. But, apart from halting the Union invasion of East Texas, somewhat of a side theater in the war, Irish Confederates did not have any sizable strategic impact. Their numbers were too small and pale in comparison to the Irish and other ethnic participation in the Union cause.[31] The true importance of the Irish Confederates' story lies in what it tells us about their experience as immigrants trying to adjust to life in a host society. It can also tell us a lot about the host society itself, particularly as white Southerners were creating a new nation and a new nationalism to support it. Irish men and women had to negotiate with that identity in the exciting but also traumatic reality of the Confederacy's birth and the resulting war for its preservation.[32]

Most scholars of Confederate nationalism see the home front as the primary element in the construction of Confederate identity and backing for the war.[33] The support of family, friends, and, importantly, clergy, was very helpful in building a sense of Confederate patriotism among Irish immigrant soldiers, undoubtedly encouraging Irish recruitment into service. Private James McGowan of the Irish Jasper Greens of Savannah (Companies A and B of the 1st Georgia Volunteers), who would lose an arm in battle in 1864, must have been pleased with the support of his younger sister Ellen, who played a key role in the secession pageant at the 1862 graduation ceremony of Savannah's St. Vincent's Academy (operated since 1845 by the predominantly Irish Sisters of Our Lady of Mercy as a school for girls). First performed in 1861, the ceremony in 1862 had a number of the Catholic girls play each Southern state, including the Catholic-influenced Maryland (perhaps reflecting the sisters' wishful thinking), in turn receiving their crown from "South Carolina." Included in the ceremony were "dialogues" entitled "Sewing for the Soldiers" and "Southern Patriotism."[34]

McGowan, along with his fellow Jasper Greens, and his brother who served in another Irish company also had the support of their Irish "betters" in the city. The Savannah Hibernians celebrated St. Patrick's Day 1861 with toasts to Jefferson Davis and the Confederate Constitution as well as Irish patriot and Confederate sympathizer John Mitchel. They also toasted their fellow countrymen, many of whom were at the celebration, preparing to fight for the cause. President D. A. O'Byrne, whose father was from County Mayo, toasted "Irishmen—Ever ready to meet a foreign foe."[35] In Savannah, apparently, it was the Northerners, not the Irish, who were "foreign." Later that year Father Jeremiah O'Neill Sr., the pastor of the Irish in Savannah (a position he had held since the 1830s), collected a sizable $193.45 from his congregation at the Cathedral of St. John the Baptist for the Confederate Treasury. After observing an official "day of humiliation and prayer" and asking God "to bestow his blessing on Southern efforts, now being made to establish those just and constitutional rights, against the infringement and invasion of those rights by Northern ill-advised, and therefore, deluded enemies," O'Neill organized the collection among his predominantly Irish parishioners. Confederate secretary of the Treasury Christopher Memminger, who had once seriously questioned the loyalty of the Irish Catholics to the South, replied that he saw their contribution as further "evidence of the earnest and settled purpose of the community" to help the troops at the front.[36]

The pro-Confederate stance of McGowan's bishop Augustin Verot earned him the title "Rebel Bishop." After Georgia's secession he took it upon himself to "[prove] the legitimacy of slavery." This French bishop would also write a catechism "for the use of Catholics in the Confederate States of America." In the section on the fourth commandment ("Honor thy father and mother"), he added "*Q. Is it forbidden to hold slaves?* A. No, both the Old and New Testaments bear witness to the lawfulness of that institution. Gen. XVI, 9; 1 Tim VI, 1, 2, 8."[37] McGowan and all the Irish men of his unit could have no doubt as to legitimacy of their fight for the Confederacy.

Irish-born bishops such as John Quinlan of Mobile and Patrick Lynch of Charleston echoed the Rebel Bishop's support for the Confederacy. Lynch's

Confederate credentials earned him the Confederate ambassadorship to the Vatican. Confederate recruiters recognized the value of clerical support when they conceded that Irish troops' loyalty could be guaranteed with the aid of a few "good Catholic priests."[38] Irish chaplains were often part of Irish Confederate units, and Confederate officials recognized their great value. Father James McNeilly, chaplain to an Irish unit in the Army of Tennessee, went into battle with his Irish soldiers to perform the sacrament of "extreme unction" for the mortally wounded. Before blessing the deceased, he searched for their crucifixes or rosary beads. During these searches, McNeilly often discovered many Union Catholic soldiers and gave them the last rites as well.[39] Father Abram Ryan gained much of his love for the Southern cause and hatred for the Northern one from his difficult and dangerous service in the Army of Tennessee, while Father John Bannon of St. Louis, Missouri, endured numerous battles, including the siege of Vicksburg, with his Irish Confederate unit. Despite the hardships associated with campaigning, Bannon, as a favor to his soldiers, found the time to take care of their pay. Keeping strict account of their deposits with him on the cover of his diary, Bannon doled out money to the boys when they asked him for it.[40]

Bannon was perhaps the most important nonfighting Irish Confederate in the Civil War. His efforts on behalf of the Confederacy impressed not only the Irish troops he served but also all Irish Southerners. His renown as a Confederate and the "Fighting Chaplain" made him famous throughout the South. Captured after the fall of Vicksburg, Bannon received a pardon from the Union forces and went to Richmond for new duty at the behest of President Davis. With $1,500 in gold in his pocket, he traveled to Europe to attempt to prevent Irish immigrants from signing on with the Union army.[41] Through a vigorous newspaper, poster, and speaking campaign, he achieved some success. With the blessing of Ireland's most important cleric, Archbishop, later Cardinal, Paul Cullen, he posted bills in Dublin churches that outlined the justice of the Southern cause and the dangers of volunteering to "labor" in the North. He also sent letters to every parish in the country outlining how the "dastardly nativist" Republicans had mistreated those of the Catholic faith. In his writings and speeches, he stressed that the Union army used Irish troops as cannon fodder. Although he failed to stop Irish immigration to the Northern states, he did change many Irish residents' opinion of the justice of the Confederate cause and, according to his Confederate superior in London, may have cut the annual Union recruitment in Ireland by two-thirds, thereby keeping thousands of Irish men out of the Union army. In absentia, the Confederate Congress rewarded his efforts with a vote of thanks and a $3,000 bonus.[42]

Irish religious women were also important to the Irish image in the Confederacy. For example, the mostly Irish order of the Sisters of Charity left Natchez to operate a military hospital in Monroe, Louisiana, while the altruistic actions of the Irish Ursulines in Columbia, South Carolina, made them "the mainstay and the comfort of the afflicted people" and the "Church at last popular." In Savannah the Sisters of Our Lady of Mercy established field hospitals in Dalton, Atlanta, and Augusta, where their efforts impressed native-born doctors, nurses, and soldiers. One Bill Fletcher from Texas noted that he lost his anti-Catholic prejudice when these sisters saved his foot from amputation after the Battle of Chickamauga in September 1863. After the war, when he had made a fortune in the lumber business, in gratitude to the sisters he opened a Catholic hospital in Beaumont, Texas.[43] Ultimately, these women's endeavors were often as important as the Irish soldiers' efforts on the battlefield in proving Irish loyalty to the Southern cause.

Again, however, as with the soldiers, Irish civilians also had a mixed record of Confederate patriotism. Among the poorest of the poor, the Irish women and children left behind when their soldiers went to the front often faced destitution. In New Orleans, Mobile, and Richmond, for example, city authorities had to establish "free markets" to feed the starving immigrants and other poor citizens. Initially, these efforts may have eased class and ethnic tensions. Historian of the Confederacy Emory Thomas notes that while these free markets were an added burden to city authorities in the South and achieved only partial success, they were still "indications of heightened social and economic conscience." Indeed, being poor and desperate may have been a sign of Confederate patriotism over those who hoarded and exploited through the black market.[44]

Nonetheless, economic hardship on the home front affected Irish military performance and the Irish image at home. Irish desertion rates often increased when soldiers were moved from around their cities to other theaters. In 1864, for example, the Savannah Jasper Greens saw increased "absents without leave" when the unit was switched from its home city to defend Atlanta against the advance of William T. Sherman's troops.[45] Despite the free markets, poor

Irish women participated in food riots and, as scholar Drew Faust argued, "express[ed] their dissent against the [Confederate] ideology of sacrifice." The most famous disturbance took place in Richmond in 1863. There, some Irish women, or "prostitutes, professional thieves, [and] Irish and Yankee hags, gallows birds from all lands but our own," as one local newspaper unfairly put it, took matters into their own hands with native neighbors and looted local shops. The riot was only quelled by the protests of President Jefferson Davis, who had rushed to the scene from the Confederate White House, and the threat of a volley from Confederate troops mobilized to deal with the disturbance.[46]

Worse than participation in bread riots, which usually featured more native women than immigrants, was the Irish acceptance of Union occupation. For a variety of reasons, many Irish in the South, like numerous other poorer Southerners, accepted the Union victories and resulting occupation with relative ease.[47] They were not particularly upset when Union forces occupied their new homes. Throughout the South, the Irish just seemed to assent to occupation. In New Orleans many Irish welcomed occupation because it meant a revival of the economy. Union commander of the city General Benjamin Butler was seen as the "Beast" by ardent native Confederates, yet many Irish expressed their desire to work with the new man in charge.[48] Reluctant secessionist but ardent Irish Democrat newspaper editor John Maginnis advocated giving a Butler a chance. After all, the "Beast" as a prewar Massachusetts Democrat had stood up for the Irish against the Know-Nothings. John Hughes of Algiers, directly across the Mississippi River from New Orleans, immediately offered his and a number of his staff's shipbuilding services. One Joseph Murphy, "a loyal citizen of Louisiana," desired to "strike a blow for the cause of the Union" by raising a company of soldiers for the United States. Another Irishman, one Jeremiah Hurly, informed Butler that some Union associations had been infiltrated by spies who were encouraging men to leave New Orleans and return to Confederate service. As a result of these Irish and other offers, Butler felt confident that he could raise a number of Union companies in the city.[49]

In Memphis, too, the Irish played the key role in reestablishing city government under Federal control by collaborating with commanding general, William T. Sherman, while in Savannah, which fell to the hated Sherman at Christmas 1864, the Irish were not too upset to hold their first St. Patrick's Day parade since the beginning of the war the following March, even though some of their fellow countrymen from the city were still serving in Virginia and North Carolina.[50]

Along with economic reality, the Irish acceptance of defeat pointed to a rather shallow Confederate nationalism. Inspired by memories of oppression in Ireland of which Irish leaders in the South, religious and secular, constantly reminded them, they had embraced the Confederacy in the excitement of 1861. But when the reality of war hit home, and even though there were exceptions, many found it easy to accept defeat. Hugh Gwynn of Tennessee, who had served honorably, remained proud of his Confederate service at war's end but nevertheless considered himself "a loyal citizen" and boasted that he could "call for Andy Johnson as lustily as any person."[51]

Thus, at war's end, despite the fact that approximately 20,000 Irish men had served in the Confederate cause, and most had done so honorably, the Irish faced the potential of being seen by their neighbors as "scalawags" (white supporters of the Union cause). All the parades, fine speeches, and sacrifices at home and on the battlefield might have been for naught and Irish integration into the white South irretrievably set back. Indeed, the nascent Republican Party in the South saw the Irish as key players in their attempt to reconstruct the South in a Northern image. Some Irish were attracted to these overtures to redefine the region, but ultimately they sided with their "unreconstructed" neighbors in opposing the Radicals. They, for example, played key roles in the infamous Memphis and New Orleans riots, which saw the murder of numbers of innocent African Americans. Race had a large role in this decision. The Irish resented the economic and political competition of the freedmen and thus rallied to their old friends in the party of white supremacy, the Democrats. After 1873, Irish men played key roles in destroying Radical rule in Southern towns and cities.[52]

Crucially, the Irish also used the growing cult of the "Lost Cause" to reestablish their Southern credentials. Former Confederate chaplain Father Abram Ryan was one of the major developers of the Lost Cause, and although he had been born in America of Irish parents, he did it in a very Irish way. The "poet-priest of the Confederacy," as he became known, was the living personification of the dual struggle that Irish Southerners felt during Reconstruction. After the war in which he lost a brother, he pastored for a time in Augusta, Georgia, where he edited the *Banner of the South* in which he extolled the "Confederate Dead" and the "Lost Cause." His poems, such as

"The Conquered Banner" and "The Sword of Robert E. Lee," brought him fame throughout the South and made him the "voice of the Lost Cause."[53] Using religious imagery, he compared Southerners to the persecuted early Christians and eulogized the Confederacy as a legitimate government, which heroes like Jefferson Davis had founded to protect liberty. His "theology" of the Lost Cause profoundly influenced many "unreconstructed" Southerners. Simultaneously, he could extol Irish nationalism against England, thus displaying to all Southerners, native and adopted, how the Irish continued to embrace these parallel struggles.[54]

Thus, it was the Lost Cause as much as actual service in the Confederacy that sealed Irish integration into the post–Civil War South. When the Irish Volunteers prepared to lay the cornerstone of their monument in Charleston on March 18, 1878 (St. Patrick's Day fell on a Sunday that year), they processed through the city to the railroad station. From there they took the short train journey north of the city to the Catholic cemetery, where again A. G. Magrath was the keynote speaker. Father D. J. Quigley of St. Patrick's Church gave the benediction. The event received copious coverage in the local newspaper, the *News and Courier*, one of the more prominent periodicals in the state and region. Its editor, Francis W. Dawson, an English immigrant, Confederate veteran, and leading prophet of the "New South," wrote of the ceremony: "Let the bugle sound . . . but one clear note of Dixie, and the nerves of every man, woman and child within hearing begin to quiver with excitement." This was true because all white Southerners, he believed, were rightly proud of their cause. "Patriotism which is both a sentiment and virtue, shone brightly then," Dawson continued, "and it is a just cause for pride that is still the prominent characteristic of the people of our state." However, "the Irish Volunteers [were] true patriotism personified . . . fighting and dying for the Southern Confederacy with all the ardor and devotion of knights of fair renown, they stand before the people of Carolina the representatives of all that is great and brave and true."[55] The desertions and oaths were forgotten, and this rhetoric suggests that these Irish in the South had become a role model of what was "great and brave and true" and had perhaps established their place as full, if still different, members of the New South. Their new Lost Cause highlighted that they were now as much "Southern rebels" as they had been "Irish rebels." This reality was the most important legacy of the Irish experience in the Confederate States of America and something they would put to good use in the future.[56]

NOTES

1. *The Irish Volunteers Memorial Meeting and Military Hall Festival, October–November, 1877* (Charleston, SC: News and Courier Book and Job Presses, 1878), 11.

2. John McFarland to "Emma," October 9, 1860, Blakemore (Lizzie McFarland) Collection, Mississippi Department of Archives and History, Jackson, Mississippi.

3. Earl F. Niehaus, *The Irish in New Orleans, 1800–1860* (Baton Rouge: Louisiana State University Press, 1956), 158.

4. W. A. Swanberg, *First Blood: The Story of Fort Sumter* (New York: Scribner, 1957), 215–16; W. Chris Phelps, *Charlestonians in War: The Charleston Battalion* (Gretna, LA: Pelican, 2004), 30–31; *Charleston Mercury*, December 29, 1860; Kelly J. O'Grady, *Clear the Confederate Way: The Irish in the Army of Northern Virginia* (Mason City, IA: Savas), 130–36.

5. Charles E. Nash, *Biographical Sketches of General Pat Cleburne and General T. C. Hindeman* (reprint, Dayton, OH: Morningside Books, 1977), 103; Howell Purdue and Elizabeth Purdue, *Pat Cleburne: Confederate General* (Hillsboro, TX: Hill Junior College Press, 1973), 67–69; Craig L. Symonds, *Stonewall of the West: Patrick Cleburne and the Civil War* (Lawrence: University Press of Kansas, 1997), 45–46.

6. William C. Nugent to John J. Pettus, April 18, 1861, quoted in *Mississippi in the Confederacy: As They Saw It*, ed. John K. Bettersworth (Baton Rouge: Louisiana State University Press, 1961), 49.

7. Ella Lonn, *Foreigners in the Confederacy* (Chapel Hill: University of North Carolina Press, 1940), 96; Confederate Muster Rolls Collection, Twenty-fourth Alabama Infantry, Company B, Alabama Department of Archives and History, Montgomery, Alabama.

8. Works Progress Administration (hereafter WPA), Sources on Mississippi History, Warren County, micro. in Mitchell Memorial Library, Mississippi State University, Mississippi State, Mississippi.

9. Thomas Smyth to Augustine Smyth, April 12, 1861, in Thomas Smyth, D.D., *Autobiographical Notes, Letters and Reflections*, ed. Louisa Cheves Stoney (Charleston, SC: Walker, Evans and Cogswell, 1914), 618–19.

10. Smyth, *Autobiographical Notes*, 3–4.

11. Terry L. Jones, *Lee's Tigers: The Louisiana Infantry in the Army of Northern Virginia* (Baton Rouge: Louisiana State University Press, 1987), 238–39; Lonn, *Foreigners in the Confederacy*, 109; James P. Gannon, *Irish Rebels, Confederate Tigers: A History of the 6th Louisiana Volunteers, 1861–1865* (Mason City, IA: Savas, 1998), ix–xiv.

12. Lonn, *Foreigners in the Confederacy*, 496–502; WPA, Source Material on Mississippi History, Jasper County, micro.

13. Lonn, *Foreigners in the Confederacy*, 283–84; Eighth Census, 1860, vols. 5–8 (Orleans Parish, Louisiana), vol. 9 (Mobile County, Alabama); Descriptive List of

Crew on CSS Tennessee (Mobile Squadron), Museum of the Confederacy (hereafter MC), Richmond, Virginia.

14. James I. Robertson Jr., *Stonewall Jackson: The Man, the Soldier, the Legend* (New York: Macmillan, 1997), 323–427; Richard Taylor, *Destruction and Reconstruction* (New York: D. Appleton, 1879), 46.

15. *War of the Rebellion: Official Records of the Union and Confederate Armies* (Washington, DC: Government Printing Office, 1880–1902), ser.1, vol. 12, pt. 1, 649–51 (hereafter *OR*); Robert G. Tanner, *Stonewall in the Valley: Thomas J. "Stonewall" Jackson's Shenandoah Valley Campaign, Spring 1862* (Garden City, NY: Doubleday, 1976), 270–72.

16. *OR*, ser. 1, vol. 12, pt. 1, 650; Taylor, *Destruction and Reconstruction*, 73.

17. William McBurney to Edward McCrady Jr., September 16, 1861, Edward McCrady Jr., to Thomas Ryan, February 13, 1862, both in Edward McCrady Jr. Military Papers, South Carolina Historical Society, Charleston, South Carolina (hereafter SCHS); *Charleston Mercury*, quoted in Phelps, *Charlestonians in War*, 135.

18. Lonn, *Foreigners in the Confederacy*, 655–56; Robert L. Kerby, *Kirby Smith's Confederacy: The Trans-Mississippi South* (Tuscaloosa: University of Alabama Press, 1972), 188–91; Alwyn Barr, "Texas Coastal Defenses, 1861–1865," *Southwestern Historical Quarterly* 65 (July 1961): 24–27.

19. *OR*, ser. 1, vol. 16, pt. 1, 310–12; Kerby, *Kirby Smith's Confederacy*, 190.

20. Thomas L. Connelly, *Autumn of Glory: The Army of Tennessee, 1862–1865* (Baton Rouge: Louisiana State University Press, 1971), 31, 273–76; Symonds, *Stonewall of the West*, 171–76; Peter Cozzens, *The Shipwreck of Their Hopes: The Battles for Chattanooga* (Urbana: University of Illinois Press, 1994), 370–84. See also Mauriel Phillips Joslyn, ed., *A Meteor Shining Brightly: Essays on Maj. Gen. Patrick R. Cleburne* (Milledgeville, GA: Terrell House, 1998).

21. Symonds, *Stonewall of the West*, 22–24.

22. Perdue, *Pat Cleburne*, 289; *OR*, vol. 52, pt. 2, 586–92; Symonds, Stonewall of the West, 32–33, 181–95. Cleburne's plan did not include immediate and full emancipation, but more an interim period of servitude akin to "apprenticeship." Many Northern states had adopted a similar system of gradual emancipation when they had abolished slavery. For more on the "nuanced" nature of Confederate "Emancipation," see Bruce Levine, *Confederate Emancipation: Southern Plans to Arm and Free Slaves during the Civil War* (New York: Oxford University Press, 2007), esp. 90–92, 102–9. See also Leon Litwack, *North of Slavery: The Negro in the Free States, 1790–1860* (Chicago: University of Chicago Press, 1965), 3–29.

23. Patrick Condon to P. J. Downing, February 25, 1866; March 31, 1866, Fenian Brotherhood Records, Archives of the Catholic University of America, Washington, D.C.; Joslyn, *A Meteor Shining Brightly*, 180, 187, 289.

24. Lonn, *Foreigners in the Confederacy*, 117; Robert Krick, *Stonewall Jackson at Cedar Mountain* (Chapel Hill: University of North Carolina Press, 1990), 248, 364.

25. *OR*, ser. 1, vol. 12, pt. 1, 405–7, pt. 2, 205–6; Robert J. Driver Jr. and Kevin C. Ruffner, *1st Battalion Virginia Infantry, 39th Battalion Virginia Cavalry, 24th Battalion Virginia Partisan Rangers* (Lynchburg, VA: H. E. Howard, 1996), 31–37.

26. William McBurney to Edward McCrady Jr., September 16, 1861, Edward McCrady Jr. to Thomas Ryan, February 13, 1862, Edward McCrady Jr., Military Papers, SCHS.

27. Compiled Service Records of Confederate Soldiers Who Served in Organizations from the State of South Carolina, RG 109, First South Carolina Infantry (Gregg's) Regiment, micro., National Archives and Records Administration, Washington, D.C. (hereafter NARA); Jones, *Lee's Tigers*, 233–54; Gannon, *Irish Rebels, Confederate Tigers*, 327–96.

28. Compiled Service Records of Confederate Soldiers Who Served in Organizations from the State of Virginia, RG 109, First Virginia Infantry Regiment, micro., NARA; Kevin Kenny, *The American Irish: A History* (New York: Longman, 2000), 141.

29. Lonn, *Foreigners in the Confederacy*, 390–94, 406–10; W. H. Andrews, *Footprints of a Regiment: A Recollection of the 1st Georgia Regulars, 1861–1865*, ed. Richard M. McMurry (reprint, Atlanta, GA: Longstreet Press, 1992), 99.

30. John Mitchel estimated that 40,000 Irish men served in the Confederate forces. However, the 1860 census lists only 84,000 Irish-born people in the Confederacy. The number of Irish men of fighting age, between fifteen and seventy (initially eighteen to forty five), ranged between 35 and 45 percent of various Southern towns, with the lowest proportions in the entrepôt of New Orleans. Thus, if one goes with an average of 38 percent (New Orleans accounted for nearly a third of the Irish population in the Confederacy), that would leave an eligible population of more than 32,000. Gary Gallagher has estimated a 75 to 80 percent mobilization rate for the entire Confederacy, a remarkable accomplishment by the efficient and often ruthless Confederate recruiters. Taking the lower end of that scale, more than 24,000 Irish would have served. However, many Irish in the region were transient and had connections in the North. Many must have used these connections to get out, although only hundreds, rather than thousands, exploited the foreign exemption clause of the Confederate draft. A still high mobilization of 60 percent would give a total of 19,000. Some Irish in the border states, especially Missouri, also served in the Confederate army, thus bringing the total somewhere above 20,000. Gleeson, *Irish in the South*, 35, 40, 163–65; Miller, *Emigrants and Exiles*, 347; Gary W Gallagher, *The Confederate War* (Cambridge: Harvard University Press, 1977), 28–29.

31. For Irish in the Union army, see Susannah Bruce, *The Harp and the Eagle: Irish American Volunteers and the Union Army, 1861–1865* (New York: NYU Press, 2006). African Americans, in particular, had a huge impact on the war's outcome. See James McPherson, *The Negro's Civil War: How American Blacks Acted and Felt in the Civil War* (New York: Vantage Books, 2003); Dudley Taylor Cornish, *The Sable Arm: Black Troops in the Union Army, 1861–1865* (Lawrence: University Press of Kansas, 1997);

Anne J. Bailey, *Invisible Southerners: Ethnicity in the Civil War* (Athens: University of Georgia Press, 2006), chap. 3.

32. Emory Thomas, in *The Confederate Nation*, first pointed out the importance of studying the Confederacy as a national experience. Other scholars have been skeptical of how successful this creation of a "nation" was. See Richard Berringer et al., *Why the South Lost the Civil War* (Athens: University of Georgia Press, 1991); Drew Gilpin Faust, *The Creation of Confederate Nationalism: Ideology and Identity in the Civil War South* (Baton Rouge: Louisiana State University Press, 1990). Recently there has been a renewal of interest in Confederate nation building, which has reinvigorated the debate. See Ann Sarah Rubin, *A Shattered Nation: The Rise and Fall of the Confederacy, 1861–1868* (Chapel Hill: University of North Carolina Press, 2005); Aaron Sheehan-Dean, *Why Confederates Fought: Family and Nation in Civil War Virginia* (Chapel Hill: University of North Carolina Press, 2007).

33. Gary Gallagher would be the primary skeptic on this point. See Gallagher, *The Confederate War*. Aaron Sheehan-Dean sees a more symbiotic relationship between home and military fronts. Sheehan-Dean, *Why Confederates Fought*.

34. James A. Buttimer, "'By Their Deeds You Shall Know Them': The Sisters of Our Lady of Mercy in Georgia, 1845–1893" (M.A. thesis, Armstrong Atlantic State University, 1999), 64–66.

35. *Savannah Daily Morning News*, March 20, 1861.

36. *Savannah Daily Morning News*, July 9, 1861.

37. Verot also earned the title "rebel" for his vocal opposition to papal infallibility at the First Vatican Council in 1870; see Michael V. Gannon, *Rebel Bishop: The Life and Era of Augustin Verot* (Milwaukee, WI: Bruce, 1964), 31–32, 203–14; Bishop Augustin Verot to [Archbishop Francis Patrick Kenrick], January 18, 1861, copy, Bishop Verot Collection, Monsignor Daniel J. Bourke Memorial Archives, Catholic Diocese of Savannah, Savannah, Georgia; Augustin Verot, *A Tract for the Times* (Baltimore: John Murphy, 1861); *A General Catechism on the Basis Adopted by the Plenary Council of Baltimore for the Use of Catholics in the Confederate States of America* (Augusta, GA: F. M. Singer, 1862), 20.

38. Lonn, *Foreigners in the Confederacy*, 96; Niehaus, *The Irish in New Orleans*, 158–60; David C. R. Heisser, "Bishop Lynch's Civil War Pamphlet on Slavery," *Catholic Historical Review* 84 (October 1998): 681–96; Blair Hoge to Dabney Maury, January 10, 1865, Confederate States of America Archives, War Department, Adjutant and Inspector General's Office, Letters and Papers, Perkins Library, Duke University, Durham, North Carolina.

39. Larry Daniel, *Soldiering in the Army of Tennessee: Portrait of Life in a Confederate Army* (Chapel Hill: University of North Carolina Press, 1991), 121–22.

40. Ed Gleeson, *Rebel Sons of Erin* (Indianapolis: Guild Press, 1993), 276–77; Phillip Thomas Tucker, *The Confederacy's Fighting Chaplain: Father John B. Bannon* (Tuscaloosa: University of Alabama Press, 1992), 61–156; John Bannon Diary, Yates-Snowdon Collection, South Caroliniana Library, University of South Carolina,

Columbia, South Carolina. I am grateful to Dr. Jeremiah Hackett for the reference from Bannon's diary.

41. Tucker, *The Confederacy's Fighting Chaplain*, 133, 157–58, 165, 168; Joseph M. Hernon Jr., *Celts, Catholics and Copperheads: Ireland Views the American Civil War* (Columbus: Ohio State University Press, 1968), 23–25; Kerby Miller, *Emigrants and Exiles: Ireland and the Irish Exodus to North America* (New York: Oxford University Press, 1985), 359–60.

42. Tucker, *The Confederacy's Fighting Chaplain*, 171–77, 181; Hernon, *Celts, Catholics and Copperheads*, 105.

43. Charles E. Nolan, *St. Mary's of Natchez: The History of a Southern Catholic Congregation* (Natchez, MS: St. Mary's Catholic Church, 1992), 139–41; Lonn, *Foreigners in the Confederacy*, 376; Muster Roll, Hospital No. 1, Confederate Army Papers, Georgia Historical Society, Savannah, Georgia; J. J. O'Connell, *Catholicity in the Carolinas and Georgia: Leaves of Its History* (New York: D. and J. Sadlier, 1879; reprint, Spartanburg, SC: Reprint Company, 1972), 268; Buttimer, "'By Their Deeds You Shall Know Them,'" 75–76.

44. Emory M. Thomas, *The Confederate Nation, 1861–1865* (New York: Harper and Row, 1979), 205–6; Sarah Ann Rubin, *A Shattered Nation: The Rise and Fall of the Confederacy, 1861–1868* (Chapel Hill: University of North Carolina Press, 2006), 53–64.

45. Michael Damon Seigle, "Savannah's Own: The Irish Jasper Greens, 1842–1865" (M.A. thesis, Armstrong Atlantic State University, 1994), 45.

46. Lonn, *Foreigners in the Confederacy*, 343–44; Drew Gilpin Faust, *Mothers of Invention: Women of the Slaveholding South in the American Civil War* (Chapel Hill: University of North Carolina Press, 1996), 245, "Altars of Sacrifice: Confederate Women and the Narratives of War," *Journal of American History* 76 (March 1990): 1225; William J. Kimball, "The Bread Riot in Richmond, 1863," *Civil War History* 7 (June 1961): 152–53; Michael B. Chesson, "Harlots or Heroines? A New Look at the Richmond Bread Riot," *Virginia Magazine of History and Biography* 92 (April 1984): 131–75; Thomas, *The Confederate Nation*, 202–4.

47. For native Southern opposition to the Confederacy, see Victoria Bynum, *The Free State of Jones: Mississippi's Longest Civil War* (Chapel Hill: University of North Carolina Press, 2001); and David Williams, Teresa Crisp Williams, and David Carlson, *Plain Folk in a Rich Man's War: Class and Dissent in Confederate Georgia* (Gainesville: University Press of Florida, 2002). For mixed attitudes toward Confederate defeat and Federal occupation, see Laura Edwards, *Scarlett Doesn't Live Here Anymore: Southern Women in the Civil War Era* (Urbana: University of Illinois Press, 2004); Stephen Ash, *When the Yankees Came: Conflict and Chaos in the Occupied South* (Chapel Hill: University of North Carolina Press, 1999), esp. 214–28. The Irish loss of ardor, however, contrasts sharply with the open and violent opposition displayed by the poor whites of piney woods Mississippi and wire grass Georgia even before the "Yankees came."

48. For Butler and New Orleans, see Chester G .Hearn, *When the Devil Came Down to Dixie: Ben Butler in New Orleans* (Baton Rouge: Louisiana State University Press, 1997); Joseph G. Dawson, *Army Generals and Reconstruction, 1862–1877* (Baton Rouge: Louisiana State University Press, 1982), 7–8; Hans L. Trefousse, *Ben Butler: The South Called Him Beast* (New York: Twayne, 1957), 107–34; Howard P. Nash, *Stormy Petrel: The Life and Times of General Benjamin F. Butler, 1818–1893* (Rutherford, NJ: Farleigh Dickinson University Press, 1969), 136–77; Dick Nolan, *Benjamin Franklin Butler: The Damnedest Yankee* (Novato, CA: Presidio Press, 1991), 150–225.

49. *New Orleans Daily True Delta*, September 12, 1862; September 22, 1862; John Hughes to Benjamin Butler, May 13, 1862, Joseph P. Murphy to Benjamin Butler, May 12, 1862, Jeremiah Hurly to Benjamin Butler, August 1, 1862, Benjamin Butler to Henry Halleck, August 27, 1862, all in Benjamin Butler Papers, Library of Congress, Washington, D.C.

50. Gerald M. Capers, *The Biography of a River Town, Memphis: Its Heroic Age* (Chapel Hill: University of North Carolina Press, 1939), 148–49, 157–59; John F. Marszalek, *Sherman: A Soldier's Passion for Order* (New York: Free Press, 1993), 191–93; Joseph H. Parks, "Memphis under Military Rule, 1862–1865," *East Tennessee Historical Society Publications* 14 (1942): 50–58; *Savannah Daily Herald*, March 18, 1865.

51. Hugh S. Gwynn to "Francis," August 7, 1865, Hugh Gwynn Letters, MC.

52. David T. Gleeson, *The Irish in the South, 1815–1877* (Chapel Hill: University of North Carolina Press, 2001), 180–81. Some scholars believe that the Irish were unsure of their "whiteness," and this psychological fear caused them to inflict violence on blacks. On the contrary, the Irish were confident in their "whiteness" and its benefits, and this confidence, along with long-held affection for the Democrats, explains their opposition to black rights. Barrington Walker, "'This Is the White Man's Day': The Irish, White Racial Identity, and the 1866 Memphis Riots," *Left History* 5 (November 1998): 31–55. For more on whiteness theory and its problems, see David R. Roediger, *The Wages of Whiteness: Race and the Making of the American Working Class* (New York: Verso Press, 1991); and Eric Arnesen, "Whiteness and the Historians' Imagination," *International Labor and Working-Class History* 60 (Fall 2001): 3–32.

53. Charles Reagan Wilson, *Baptized in Blood: The Religion of the Lost Cause, 1865–1920* (Athens: University of Georgia Press, 1980), 58–59; Jay B. Hubbell, *The South in American Literature, 1607–1900* (Durham, NC: Duke University Press, 1959), 477–79; Rayburn S. Moore, "Poetry of the Late Nineteenth Century," in *The History of Southern Literature*, ed. Louis D. Rubin (Baton Rouge: Louisiana State University Press, 1988), 189–90. The best biography of Ryan is Donald Robert Beagle and Bryan Albin Giemza, *Poet of the Lost Cause: A Life of Father Ryan* (Knoxville: University of Tennessee Press, 2008).

54. Wilson, *Baptized in Blood*, 23, 59–61, 157.

55. *Charleston News and Courier*, March 18 and 19, 1878. For Dawson's importance, see C. Vann Woodward, *Origins of the New South, 1877–1913* (Baton Rouge: Louisiana State University Press, 1951), 145–47.

56. The Irish in the South retained their ethnicity and indeed heightened it in the years after Reconstruction. They were integrated rather than assimilated into the New South. See David T. Gleeson and Brendan J. Buttimer, "'We Are Irish Everywhere': Irish Immigrant Networks in Charleston and Savannah," in *Irish Migration, Networks and Ethnic Identities since 1750*, ed. Enda Delaney and Donald M. MacRaild (New York: Routledge, 2007), 39–61. For critique of assimilation and its use in American history, see Russell A. Kazal, "Revisiting Assimilation: The Rise, Fall, and Reappraisal of a Concept in American Ethnic History," *American Historical Review* 100 (April 1995): 437–71.

∾ 5 ∾

THE JEWISH CONFEDERATES

Robert N. Rosen, Esq.

In March 1865, Samuel Yates Levy, a captain in the Confederate army and a prisoner of war at Johnson's Island, wrote his father, J. C. Levy of Savannah, "I long to breathe the free air of Dixie." Like the Levy family, Southern Jews were an integral part of the Confederate States of America and had been breathing the free air of Dixie for 200 years.

When the Civil War began, there were sizable Jewish communities in all the major Southern cities. Louisiana boasted more than five congregations. New Orleans had the seventh-largest Jewish population in the United States (Boston was sixth, and Chicago eighth). In Charleston, home to three congregations (one Reform, one traditional, and one composed of Orthodox Polish immigrants), "Israelites occupy the most distinguished places," according to one Jewish traveler. The Jews of Savannah had organized K.K. Mikve Israel in 1735, the third congregation in America following New York and Newport, Rhode Island. There were Jewish communities in Richmond and Petersburg, Virginia; in Atlanta, Macon, and Columbus, Georgia; in Memphis and Nashville, Tennessee; in Galveston and Houston, Texas; and Jews living in dozens of small towns throughout the South.[1]

Louisiana was emblematic of the acculturation and assimilation of Jews in the antebellum South. Judah P. Benjamin served as one of the state's U.S. senators. Lieutenant Governor Henry M. Hyams was Benjamin's cousin, having moved to Louisiana with Benjamin from Charleston in 1828. Edwin Warren Moise, also from South Carolina, served as Speaker of the Louisiana House of Representatives and was about to become a Confederate judge. According to the youthful Salomon de Rothschild, of the great French banking family, "All these men have a Jewish heart and take an interest in me."[2]

Estimates of the Jewish population are wholly unreliable, but in 1860 Louisiana was home to at least 8,000 Jews, and likely many more. The total number of Jews in the eleven states of the Confederacy was in the range of 20,000 to 25,000, which means that Louisiana was home to 25 percent to 40 percent of Southern Jewry. New Orleans in 1860 was the South's largest city by far. Its population of 168,675 dwarfed Charleston's (40,522), Richmond's (37,910), Mobile's (29,258), and Savannah's (22,292). Like the growing cities of the North and West, New Orleans beckoned to immigrants, and they came.[3]

Southern Jews accepted Southern customs and institutions, including slavery and the code of honor. Oscar Straus put it best when he wrote in his memoirs, "As a boy brought up in the South I never questioned the rights or wrongs of slavery. Its existence I regarded as a matter of course, as most other customs or institutions." Mark I. Greenberg points out that Jews adopted the Southern way of life, including the code of honor, dueling, slavery, and Southern notions about race and states' rights. In 1862 Bernhard Felsenthal, a Northern abolitionist rabbi, wrote that "Israelites residing in New Orleans are man by man . . . ardently in favor of secession," and that Jewish German immigrants favored slavery precisely because many non-Jewish German immigrants opposed it. "No Jewish political figure of the Old South ever expressed reservations about the justice of slavery or the rightness of the Southern position," Rabbi Bertram Korn concluded.[4]

Nor is there any evidence that Jews supported slavery as a result of intimidation or fear of reprisals. The Talmud taught the Jews that "the law of the land is the law." According to many rabbis, North and South, the Hebrew Bible allowed for slavery. As we have seen, Rabbi Morris J. Raphall of New York criticized abolitionists and defended slavery as sanctioned by the Bible. Solomon Cohen wrote his aunt, Rebecca Gratz of Philadelphia, that "God gave laws to his chosen people for the government of their slaves, and did not order them to abolish slavery."[5]

Because most Jews in the South in 1861 were struggling or poor immigrants from the Germans states or eastern Europe, few of them owned slaves. Jewish Southerners were peddlers, store clerks, innkeepers, cigar makers, teachers, bartenders, petty merchants, tradesmen, and tailors. A few Jews owned slaves. The Jews of the South lived in a slaveholding society, and they accepted the institution as part of everyday life. Living in cities and towns, those Jews who owned slaves utilized them as domestic servants, as workers in their trades, or they hired them out. "Acceptance of slavery was," Leonard Dinnerstein wrote, "an aspect of southern life common to nearly all its white inhabitants."

Indeed, it was common to its free black inhabitants, who owned more slaves by far than Southern Jews. The free blacks of Charleston, for example, owned three times the number of slaves owned by Charleston Jewry.[6]

In 1840, three-fourths of all heads of families in Charleston owned at least one slave, and the incidence of slaveholding among Jews likely paralleled that of their neighbors. In Richmond, few Jewish auctioneers sold slaves, and there was one Jewish slave dealer, Abraham Smith. Richmond's rabbis supported slavery. George Jacobs of Richmond hired a slave to work in his home, although he owned no slaves. Reverend Max Michelbacher prayed during the Civil War that God would protect his congregation from slave revolt and that the Union's "wicked" efforts to "beguile [the slaves] from the path of duty that they may waylay their masters, to assassinate and slay the men, women, and children . . . be frustrated."[7]

Because Jews accepted Southern customs and mores, Southerners accepted Jews. In general Southerners were tolerant of all religions. The Fundamental Constitution of Carolina written by John Locke in 1699 granted freedom of religion to "Ye Heathens, Jues [*sic*] and other Disenters." Jefferson's celebrated Act of Religious Freedom asserted that "no man shall be compelled to frequent or support any religious worship, place, or ministry whatever." Southern aristocrats, influenced by the Anglican, Episcopalian, Presbyterian, Methodist, and liberal Protestant traditions, had no concern about Jews in their midst. They found their Jewish neighbors to be law-abiding, educated, and cosmopolitan, characteristics they appreciated. Their quality of life was enhanced by Jewish peddlers, teachers, musicians, lawyers, doctors, druggists, merchants, and men of learning. The South attracted few immigrants, and white minorities were therefore readily accepted. Finally, Southerners believed fervently in the God of the Old Testament and respected their Jewish neighbors' knowledge of and historic connection to the Bible. Oscar Straus recalled how his father, who was well versed in biblical literature, translated passages from the Hebrew Bible for the information of local ministers over dinner in their home.[8]

Jews, of course, were white, and Southerners' racist attitudes did not extend to them. In 1859, the traveling journalist I. J. Benjamin explained Jewish acceptance in the South by noting that the white inhabitants "felt themselves united with, and closer to, other whites. . . . Since the Israelite there did not do the humbler kinds of work which the Negro did, he was quickly received among the upper classes and easily rose to high political rank. For this reason, until now, it was only the South which sent Jews to the Senate. Benjamin came from Louisiana; [David Levy] Yulee from Florida." (Yulee was born Jewish, married a Gentile, converted to Christianity, and disassociated himself from his Jewish roots.)[9]

This is not to say that there was no anti-Semitism in the Old South, because there was. Anti-Semitism was a fact of life in the nineteenth century. Emma Holmes of Charleston wrote in her diary that she disliked "Sumter [South Carolina] very much from the prevalence of sand and Jews, my great abhorrences." By 1862, she blamed all of her ills on the Jews. Jews came into conflict with the majority Christian society on issues such as conducting retail business on Sunday. And, of course, Southerners often found Jewish customs strange. Maria Bryan Connell of Hancock County, Georgia, had a Jewish houseguest. "I did not at all comprehend the trouble occasioned by their notions of unclean and forbidden food until I had a daughter of Abraham under the roof. She will not eat one mouthful of the finest fresh pork or the most delicate ham," she wrote. It was not, Maria concluded, "an unimportant consideration with her. Pray let this be entre nous, for I feel as if I am in some respect violating the duties of hospitality in speaking of it."[10]

The Northern states were not as hospitable as the South to Jews prior to the Civil War. The first known Jew in Boston was "warned out" in the 1640s. Unlike colonial Charleston, where Jews flourished, Jews were not allowed to live in early colonial Boston. John Quincy Adams referred to David Yulee as the "squeaking Jew delegate from Florida," and Representative Albert G. Marchand of Pennsylvania as a "squat little Jew-faced rotundity." When the South seceded, the *Boston Evening Transcript*, a Brahmin publication, blamed the decision on Southern Jews. Calling Benjamin "the disunion leader in the U.S. Senate," and Yulee ("whose name has been changed from the more appropriate one of Levy or Levi") an ultra-fire-eater, the newspaper claimed that "this peculiar race, . . . having no country of their own," desired "that other nations shall be in the same unhappy condition." By 1864, the *Times* castigated the Democratic Party because its chairman, August Belmont, was "the agent of foreign jew bankers."[11]

It is difficult to determine the opinion of Jewish Southerners about secession. Whereas Edwin DeLeon was pro-secession, his brother Camden DeLeon, an officer in the army, was clearly uncomfortable with disloyalty to his government. Many were concerned about Lincoln's election and the elevation of an avowed opponent of slavery to the presidency. In a parade to celebrate secession, Simon Baruch, a Prussian immigrant and a medical student, carried a lantern bearing the words, "There is a point beyond which endurance ceases to be a virtue." Solomon Cohen wrote from Savannah that with Lincoln's election, "our enemies have triumphed," and he was worried about control of the federal government by "those who hate us and our institutions."[12]

The irony of Jewish slave owners was not lost on Northern critics of slavery. Benjamin Wade, an antislavery senator from Ohio, called Judah Benjamin, who was a slave owner, an "Israelite with Egyptian principles."[13]

When in April 1861 the *Jewish Messenger* of New York City called upon American Jewry to "rally as one man for the *Union* and the *Constitution*," the Jews of Shreveport responded with a resolution denouncing the newspaper and its editor. "We, the Hebrew congregation of Shreveport," the resolution began, "scorn and repel your advice. . . . We solemnly pledge ourselves to stand by, protect, and honor the flag, with its stars and stripes, the Union and Constitution of the Southern Confederacy, with our lives, liberty, and all that is dear to us." Max Baer, the president of the congregation, asked that newspapers friendly to the Southern cause publish their resolution.[14]

Jewish Southerners perceived New Englanders as abolitionists who were frequently anti-Semitic. Theodore Parker, a leading abolitionist minister, believed Jews' intellects were "sadly pinched in those narrow foreheads," that Jews were "lecherous" and "did sometimes kill a Christian baby at the Passover." William Lloyd Garrison, editor of the *Liberator*, once described Judge Mordecai Manuel Noah of New York as "the miscreant Jew," a "Shylock," "the enemy of Christ and liberty," and a descendant "of the monsters who nailed Jesus to the cross." Similar sentiments came from Edmond Quincy, Lydia Maria Child, William Ellery Channing, and Senator Henry Wilson of Massachusetts, all leading abolitionists. Child thought Judaism rife with superstition, claiming that Jews "have humbugged the world." John Quincy Adams opposed slavery and derided Jews.[15]

It is little wonder, then, that there was no great love lost between Southern Jews, who were accustomed to being treated as equals, and New Englanders. Southern Jews had even more reason to dislike the officious New Englanders than did other Southerners, and this undoubtedly influenced their view of secession. Isaac Harby, the Charleston journalist and pioneer of the Reform movement, was typical in his denunciation of "the abolitionist society and its secret branches." It came as no surprise to South Carolina Jewry to see reprinted in their local newspaper in March 1861 the following from the *Boston Journal*: "The Jew, [Benjamin] Mordecai, at Charleston, who gave ten thousand dollars to the South Carolina Government, had just settled with his Northern creditors by paying fifty cents on the dollar. The ten thousand was thus a Northern donation to secession." The *Charleston Daily Courier* called the story "a willful, unmitigated and deliberate falsehood."[16]

Thus the question of *why* Southern Jews would fight for the Confederacy is no question at all. Why would they *not* fight for their homeland, which had welcomed and accepted them as equals? "We of the South," Solomon Cohen wrote Rebecca Gratz, "feel that prudence and self-defense demand that we should protect ourselves." Jewish Confederates fought for liberty and freedom, including the right to own slaves. They fought to preserve the Southern racial caste system. They fought invaders of their hearth and home. Private Simon Mayer of Natchez wrote his family, "I sympathize with the poor victims of abolition despotism."[17]

Jewish Johnny Rebs were also motivated by a sense of duty and honor, powerful emotions in Victorian America. "Victorians," James McPherson wrote, "understood duty to be a binding moral obligation involving reciprocity: one had a duty to defend the flag under whose protection one had lived." A fallen Jewish Confederate, Corporal Isaac Valentine, mortally wounded in the same battle as his comrade Poznanski, said on his deathbed that he had done his duty and died for his country.[18]

Letters, memoirs, and obituaries all reflect Jewish soldiers' chief reasons for fighting: to do their duty, to protect their homeland, to protect Southern rights and liberty, and, once the war began, to show their loyalty to their comrades in arms. Philip Rosenheim of Richmond had just returned home from marching to the Chickahominy and had "fallen into sweet slumber" when his sister Rebecca awoke him. The bells had tolled, informing his militia company to gather. "I was very weak and had a severe headache," he wrote his family, "but still I dressed myself [and] buckled on my accouterments, thinking I would not shrink from my duty and would follow the company wherever it goes, as our Flag says, when duty calls tis ours to obey." "We were thoroughly imbued with the idea," Moses Ezekiel of Richmond wrote in his memoirs, "that we were not fighting for the perpetuation of slavery, but for the principle of State's rights and free trade, and in the defense of our homes, which were being ruthlessly invaded."[19]

Isaac Hirsch of Fredericksburg, a soldier in the 30th Virginia, visited the battlefield at Second Manassas, where Stonewall Jackson defeated General Pope's army. "It is bad," he wrote in his diary, "that the dead Yankees could not be buried as I don't like to see any human being lay on the top of the earth and rot, but it is a fit emblem for the invader of our soil for his bones to bleach on the soil he invades, especially of a people that wish to be left alone and settle down to their own peaceful pursuits."[20]

It speaks volumes about the South that many a Jewish youth left the German fatherland to avoid military service only to *voluntarily* enlist in the Confederate army soon after arriving in Dixie. Jewish men, like other Southern men, were encouraged to fight by their mothers and sisters. At the start of the war, Catherine Ezekiel, Moses' mother, said "she would not own a son who would not fight for his home and country." Mary Chestnut wrote of her friend "Mem" Cohen's dedication to the cause. "Our soldiers, thank God, are men after our own heart, cries Miriam of the house of Aaron," Mary wrote in her diary in May 1862. Phoebe Pember recalled that the "women of the South had been openly and violently rebellious from the moment they thought their states' rights touched. . . . They were the first to rebel—the last to succumb."[21]

The social pressure to enlist was also a strong factor in many a young Confederate's decision to join the army. According to Gary W. Gallagher, 75 to 85 percent of the Confederacy's available draft-age white population served in the military. And a young Southern male had a difficult time in 1862 and 1863 explaining why he was not in uniform. Simon Baruch, a Prussian from Schwersenz (and Bernard Baruch's father), immigrated to Camden, South Carolina, as did his younger brother Herman. When Simon enlisted, he admonished Herman to stay out of the war. But Herman joined the cavalry because, as he told Simon, "I could no longer stand it. I could no longer look into the faces of the ladies."[22]

There was also the adventure of war and the bounty paid in advance. Young men who worked at jobs they disliked saw a chance to escape. Lewis Leon was such a clerk. An unmarried immigrant who spoke German as well as English, he enlisted for six months at the age of nineteen in the Charlotte

Grays, Company C, 1st North Carolina. (In six months, most Southerners believed, the war would be over.) He was issued a fine uniform. "We were all boys between the ages of eighteen and twenty-one," Leon noted. "Our trip was full of joy and pleasure, for at every station where our train stopped the ladies showered us with flowers and Godspeed."[23]

Jewish Confederates, like other immigrants and African Americans, had a special burden during the war. They had to prove that Jews would fight. One of the staples of nineteenth-century anti-Semitism was that the Jews were disloyal, unpatriotic, and cowardly. The "Wandering Jew" was a staple of anti-Semitism. Jews had lived in ghettos in Europe, had refused to assimilate with their neighbors, and had fled Europe to avoid military service. Many a Southern Jewish boy set out to disprove these calumnies.[24]

Other Jews fought to make a place in Southern society for Jews who would come after them. Philip Whitlock wrote in his memoir that "especially when I was of the Jewish Faith I thought that if I am negligent in my duty as a citizen of this country, it would unfavorably reflect on the whole Jewish race and religion." Charles Wessolowsky said after the war that "sometimes he felt like a Jewish missionary among the Gentiles to show the way for other Jews to follow." Early twentieth-century Jewish historians were anxious to defend the courage and bravery of the generation that preceded them. "There existed no occasion to threaten the young or, for that matter, the middle-aged, with the 'white feather,'" Ezekiel and Lichtenstein wrote. "None held back or hesitated."[25]

Finally, Jewish tradition also played a part. From the book of Esther and from Jeremiah ("Seek the welfare of the city to which I have exiled you" [Jer. 29:7]) to rabbinic law, Judaism taught respect and obedience to the established government. Jews had traditionally aligned themselves with monarchs and conservative regimes for self-protection from the masses. The traditional Jewish prayer for the government, dating to the sixteenth century, called upon God to bless the king, inspire him with benevolence "toward us and all Israel our brethren." In short, because the new Confederacy was now their lawful government, Jewish tradition demanded loyalty to it.[26]

Thus, Jewish Johnny Rebs went off to war for a variety of reasons: patriotism and love of country; to defend their homeland, their yearning for a fatherland they could believe in; Jewish tradition as they understood it; to demonstrate to the North that their rights could not be assailed; hatred for Yankees; social pressure; being caught up in the frenzy of secession and war;

to escape from home and see the world; for adventure and pay; and to prove that Jews would fight. "The Jews of the Confederacy had good reason to be loyal to their section," Rabbi Korn concluded. "Nowhere else in America—certainly not in the ante-bellum North—had Jews been accorded such an opportunity to be complete equals as in the old South."[27]

From the top of the social scale to the bottom, Southern Jews supported the Confederate cause. Former senator Judah P. Benjamin, one of the South's most brilliant lawyers (President Millard Fillmore nominated him to the Supreme Court, but Benjamin declined the honor) became attorney general of the new Confederate States of America. "A Hebrew of Hebrews, for the map of the Holy City was traced all over his small, refined face," Thomas Cooper DeLeon later recalled, "the attorney-general was of the highest type of his race."[28]

There was little legal work for the new attorney general, and Benjamin rapidly became a close confidant of and political adviser to President Jefferson Davis. A wit, a gourmand, and a raconteur, Benjamin became a popular member of Richmond society. When the secretary of war resigned, Davis asked Benjamin to serve as the new secretary.

Unfortunately, Benjamin had no military background. He did bring to the War Department his well-known capacity for hard work and organization, but his tenure was marked by notable failures in the field, for which he received (and accepted) the blame. After the disastrous fall of Roanoke Island, Virginia, in early 1862, Davis promoted Benjamin to secretary of state in "the very teeth of criticism."

Benjamin's Jewish heritage (he did not practice the Jewish religion) was a lightning rod for critics of the Davis administration. One crackpot congressman, Henry S. Foote of Tennessee, a rabid anti-Semite, referred to Benjamin as "Judas Iscariot Benjamin" and the "Jewish puppeteer" behind the "Davis tyranny." John M. Daniel of the *Richmond Examiner* reacted to Benjamin's appointment as secretary of state by remarking that "the representation of the Synagogue is not diminished; it remains full." These, however, were minority opinions.[29]

Benjamin continued to serve Davis as secretary of state. He was to the civilian government what Robert E. Lee was to the military: a loyal, stalwart, indefatigable, and uncomplaining patriot. He was the most well-known Confederate official next to the president and vice president and third in order of succession. Varina Howell Davis called him her husband's "right arm." Historians have called him "the President's most intimate friend and counselor." Eli Evans, his biographer, described Benjamin as Davis's alter ego.[30]

As the war dragged on, the Confederacy's options dwindled. On February 12, 1864, the Confederate Congress voted in secret session to create "bodies for the capture and destruction of the enemies' property." The Bureau of Special and Secret Service came into existence, and funding for these operations went to the State Department. Benjamin, as secretary of state, was the likely head of the bureau and chief of Confederate covert activities. Shortly thereafter, important agents of the Confederacy arrived in Montreal. "A few months later," Roy Z. Chamlee Jr. writes in *Lincoln's Assassins*, "John Wilkes Booth opened a bank account in the same Montreal bank used by the Rebels."[31]

Benjamin had now taken on the most dangerous assignment Davis had given him and his last assignment for the Confederacy—that of spymaster. He established spy rings and sent political propagandists to the North and to Canada. He enlisted the seductive Belle Boyd, the "Cleopatra of Secession," in the cause. He sent agents to Ireland to stem the tide of Irish volunteers entering the Union army. He planned the burning of Federal medical stores in Louisville and the burning of bridges in strategic locations across the occupied South. He also oversaw the suppression of treason against the Confederacy. Special commissioners who investigated and arrested those disloyal to the government reported to Benjamin. For example, Colonel Henry J. Leovy, a close friend of Benjamin's from New Orleans, served as a military commissioner in southwest Virginia. His job was ferreting out traitors.[32]

Benjamin, like many other Confederate leaders, believed the Northern public would not support Lincoln indefinitely. Serious efforts were made to exploit the difference between the eastern and western states, to increase public disaffection in the North for the war, and to raid prisoner of war camps. Provocateurs attempted to capture Federal property in the far north. Confederate agents tried to disrupt the monetary system by urging people to convert paper money to gold. There was even an attempt—probably unknown to Benjamin but involving his agents—to set New York City on fire. Benjamin oversaw the most ambitious mission, a $1 million Canadian covert operation headed by Jacob Thompson. When the war ended, Benjamin fled Richmond with Davis and the Confederate cabinet.[33]

Benjamin's commitment to the Confederate cause was matched by that of the common Jewish soldier in the field. There were about 2,000 Jewish Confederate servicemen. The typical Jewish soldier, like the typical Johnny Reb, served in the infantry. Simon Wolf, a prominent Jewish lawyer, published a book in 1895 containing a list of Jews who had served in the Union and Confederate armies. His list reflects the preponderance of service in the infantry. Of the nearly 1,300 men listed, 967 served in the infantry, 116 in the cavalry, 129 in the artillery, and 11 in the navy or marines. Rabbi Barnett Elzas's more precise list of Jewish South Carolinians shows 117 in the infantry of a total of 167 men. The list in Ezekiel and Lichtenstein's *History of the Jews of Richmond* is consistent, showing approximately 70 of the 100 infantry, as is Eric Brock's Shreveport list.[34]

There were Jewish Johnny Rebs in every aspect of the war. They served as privates in infantry units all over the South and in every major campaign. They were cooks, sharpshooters, orderlies, teamsters, and foragers. They dug trenches, cut trees, guarded prisoners, and served on picket duty. Most of the historical data about Jewish Confederate soldiers is contained in the letters, diaries, reminiscences, and biographies of well-known, powerful, and therefore much older men, such as Judah Benjamin or Raphael Moses, a prominent commissary officer. There is little such documentation for the average soldier.[35]

Yet the average Confederate soldier was in his twenties, and this was undoubtedly true about Jewish Johnny Rebs. We know little about most of these young men except their names and units, but there is information about enough men in the ranks to make some generalizations. The majority enlisted in companies in their hometowns with men whom they knew, often fellow Jews. They preferred serving in units with their friends and relatives. There were seven Rosenbalms in Company H of the 37th Virginia. Philip Rosenheim of the Richmond militia was proud of his service and his friends: "Charley Marx and David Mittledorfer, Julius Straus, Moses Hutzler, Sam and Herman Hirsh, Simon Sycles, Gus Thalheimer, Abr. Goldback, and a good many other Yuhudim all belonged to the same company, which I did."

But unlike Irish and German immigrants, who formed ethnic companies, Jews did not form distinctively Jewish companies because they fervently desired to be seen as citizens of their state and nation, not as a separate nationality. They had no desire to stand out as a group as they had been forced to do in Europe. Unlike for the Irish, who also wanted to be seen as equal citizens, true equality to the Jews meant belonging to the general population. Judaism was a religion, not a nationality, and Jews did not want to seem as a separate nationality. Their mission, therefore, was the exact opposite of other ethnic groups, such as the Irish, who took pride in their ethnic organizations. There were no Catholic or Lutheran units in the Confederate army; therefore, there would be no Jewish units. In addition, as a practical matter, there were few wealthy Jewish men with the military background and political influence needed to organize a company of troops. The majority of Jewish Confederates were recent young immigrants. They were followers, comrades-in-arms, not leaders.[36]

The majority of Jewish Confederates served as privates or corporals in the infantry, but there were Jews in all branches of the service and in all departments. In Wolf's listing for Alabama, for example, 105 served in the infantry and 21 in the cavalry. His Arkansas list shows almost as many cavalry as infantry. Leopold Levy and his brother Sampson served in Company G, 1st Virginia cavalry, commanded by Colonel J. E. B. Stuart. Texas had 73 Jewish infantry men and 21 cavalrymen. As the Jews went west, they rode horseback more often and tended to live in small towns.[37]

Jews also served in artillery units such as the Washington Artillery of New Orleans. Wolf's list for Texas shows five artillerymen; five for Alabama; and eight for Arkansas. Edwin Kursheedt and Eugene Henry Levy served in the artillery. Marx Cohen and Gustavus A. Cohen served in James F. Hart's company (Washington Artillery, South Carolina), initially a part of Hampton's Legion, as did five other South Carolina Cohens. Perry Moses of Sumter served in a number of units, including Culpepper's Battery. In 1863, he was in charge of a twelve-pound Napoleon. "I fought a battery of four guns for over an hour," he wrote his mother, Octavia Harby Moses, in 1863, "giving them gun for gun."[38]

Some Jewish Johnny Rebs served in the local militia or home guards, which were organized for local self-defense. At the beginning of the war, many men who did not want to leave home or serve in the regular army joined the militia. As the war progressed and conscription was instituted, the home guards consisted of those too young, too old, or too infirm to serve, as well as those exempt by virtue of their occupations or political office. Philip Rosenheim of Richmond was a youngster who served in the local militia in the summer or

1863, when Richmond was under attack. Philip and others responded. "I, as well as all the Boys rallied to the call and we stood firmly at our Flag ready to meet the foe," he wrote his sister and brother-in-law, Amelia and Isaac Meinnart.[39]

Jewish soldiers came from varied backgrounds. Some were recent immigrants, and some were from old families. Shreveport, Louisiana, in 1860 is a striking portrait of the Southern Jewish immigrant's contribution to Confederate military service. Eric J. Brock has estimated that 300 Jews lived in Shreveport in 1860 and that 78 served in the Confederate armed forces. Almost all of them were recent immigrants who arrived in Louisiana in the 1850s. Most, like Marx Baer, were born in one of the German states or Alsace-Lorraine. Some were from Poland: Jack Citron, Company I, 3rd Louisiana, from Koval; and Jacob Gall, Company D, 19th Louisiana, from Meschisko. Some were from France: Marx Israel of Company 5, 3rd Regiment, European Brigade, was from Onepie, near Metz.[40]

Leading Jewish Richmonders had been members of the Richmond Light Infantry Blues for generations. The unit participated in quelling the Gabriel slave revolt in 1800 and was called into service in 1807, when the British man-of-war *Leopard* attacked the *Chesapeake* off Norfolk. Thus, when the Richmond Blues left the city for the war on April 24, 1861, fifteen of its ninety-nine members were Jewish, including Ezekiel J. ("Zeke") Levy, its fourth sergeant.

The Blues served as Company A, 46th Virginia, in West Virginia and saw combat at Roanoke Island in February 1862. "Soon a ball [bullet] came from the Yankees," the company's record states, and "one of our boys, Mr. L. Wasserman, replied." Henry Adler was mortally wounded. Isaacs, Lyon, Levi Wasserman, and Joseph Levy were captured. They were exchanged in August. Adler, after suffering a great deal from his wounds, died at the naval hospital in Portsmouth and was buried by the Blues, who turned out en masse to honor their first private killed in the war. The Blues served throughout the war in Virginia and North Carolina, in the defense of Charleston, and later in the defense of Richmond and Petersburg. They fought to the end at Appomattox. In June 1864, the Blue's captain killed and first lieutenant wounded, Lieutenant Ezekiel J. Levy became commanding officer.[41]

There were dozens of Jewish officers in the Confederate service, including the quartermaster general of the Confederate army, Colonel Abraham Charles Myers, the great-grandson of the first rabbi of K.K. Beth Elohim in

Charleston. After graduating from West Point, Myers became a career army officer and served in the Mexican War. Fort Myers, Florida, then literally a fort, was named in his honor by his father-in-law, General David Emanuel Twiggs.

In 1861 Myers set up his offices on the southwest corner of Ninth and Main streets, near Capitol Square in Richmond. The Quarter-Master Department included quartermasters in each state, paymasters and quartermasters in the field, manufacturing plants, special units such as the Tax-in-Kind Office, purchasing agents abroad, and depot and post quartermasters. Colonel Myers reported to the secretary of war.[42]

Public concern, then anger, then outrage at the Commissary Department and Quartermaster Department would be a constant theme in the Confederacy as the war went on. It was understandable, if unjustified, that the officers in charge of food, clothing, and supplies would be blamed for the ills of the army. The head commissary was the Confederate Congress's main scapegoat. His nomination to full colonel and confirmation as commissary general provoked heated debate. Myers's nomination to full colonel and confirmation as quartermaster general was immediately approved. T. C. DeLeon believed that Myers's "bureau was managed with an efficiency and vigor that could scarcely have been looked for in so new an organization." Early in the war, Myers enjoyed a good reputation as a competent and honest department head.

But it soon became clear that the war would not be short, and even clearer that supplying an army of up to 400,000 men would prove to be a formidable task. Prices rose as the blockade tightened and Northern sources of supply dwindled. States' rights played a part in the Confederacy's problems. North Carolina, for example, supplied its own troops in return for an agreement that the quartermaster would not purchase clothing from its factories. The Southern economy could not keep pace with the army's huge appetite for supplies.

The Union victories of 1862 were a disaster for the Confederacy and especially for the quartermaster general. The loss of key border states, New Orleans and other coastal areas, and the Mississippi Valley constricted the area from which supplies, manufactured goods, and raw materials could be obtained. Blockade-running was severely curtailed, interfering with the importation of European goods. By August 1862, Lee complained that his army lacked "much of the materials of war, . . . [was] feeble in transportation, the animals being much reduced, and the men . . . poorly provided with clothes, and in thousands of instances . . . destitute of shoes."

As the war dragged on, the Quartermaster Department came in for severe criticism. The *Savannah Daily News* noted the suspicion in the public mind "that peculation and plunder, and misuse of authority for private purpose, have often been put before public duty and public service." The *Richmond Enquirer* complained that "quartermasters sometimes get rich. . . . Unfaithful, incompetent, or dishonest quartermasters or commissaries could plunge the country into ruin." Despite the criticism, the leading historian of Confederate supply, Richard Goff, concluded that the Quartermaster Department under Myers "appears to have been as well organized and as efficient as circumstances would allow."[43]

Myers's friends in Congress sought to promote him to brigadier general, and in March 1863 the Congress passed a law providing that the rank and pay of the quartermaster general "shall be those of Brigadier General in the provisional army." Seventy-six members of Congress sent the president a letter recommending that Colonel Myers be promoted to general. Ironically, the law was used by Jefferson Davis to dismiss Myers from office altogether. On August 7, 1863, Jefferson Davis replaced Abraham Myers with his old friend Alexander R. Lawton.

The only reason Davis gave was that it was in the interest of efficiency. There does seem to be some basis for the charge. Some said that Myers and Davis had feuded in the old army years earlier. But the true reason, according to Richmond gossip, was that Marian Myers, who considered herself the social superior of Mrs. Davis, had called the president's wife "an old squaw," Mrs. Davis being of a somewhat dark complexion. Assistant Secretary of War A. T. Bledsoe passed along the insult in early 1862. The remark was repeated and became well known. "The Congress of 1863," Mary Chestnut wrote, "gave up its time to fighting the battle of Colonel Myers–Mrs. Myers."[44]

There is no evidence that anti-Semitism played any role in Myers's firing, despite the glee expressed by John Beauchamp Jones, a clerk in the War Department whose memoir, *A Rebel War Clerk's Diary*, was published in 1866. Jones called Myers the "Jew Quarter-Master General" and claimed he replied "let them suffer" when told of soldiers' pleas for blankets. But Sallie Putman, who had no love for the Jews, thought Myers was mistreated; most important, Jefferson Davis not only had no prejudice against Jews but, to the contrary, maintained warm relationships with many Southern Jews.[45]

Adolph Proskauer of Mobile was among the few Jewish immigrants who became a high-ranked Confederate officer. Proskauer had been educated at the gymnasium in Breslau until he came to America. In May 1861, he enlisted in Captain Augustus Stikes's company, the Independent Rifles, for twelve months. He was appointed first corporal. The company went to Richmond and became Company C, 12th Alabama Infantry. The 12th Alabama was a cosmopolitan regiment that included a large portion of Germans, French, Irish, and Spanish sailors and dockworkers from Mobile, and mountain boys from north Alabama. They were noted as foragers, recalled one of its officers, Captain Robert Emory Park, "and the vast majority of them suffered very little from hunger" despite limited rations.[46]

By December, Proskauer had been promoted to sergeant. In April 1862 he was commissioned as a first lieutenant. He served in that rank for only twenty-six days before being promoted to captain in May, replacing Stikes, who became a major of the regiment. As captain, Proskauer was remembered as handsome and the "best dressed man in the regiment."

Proskauer participated in many of the fiercest battles of the war. As lieutenant of Company C, he fought in the siege of Yorktown (April–May 1862). He helped lead the 12th Alabama at the Battle of Seven Pines, where the regiment made a "gallant charge . . . into the very jaws of death."

Proskauer and his regiment marched north in Lee's Maryland campaign as part of Rodes's brigade. Proskauer was in combat at the Battle of South Mountain and Sharpsburg (Antietam), where he was wounded. On September 17, 1862, the single bloodiest day in the Civil War, Lee's Army of Northern Virginia faced George B. McClellan's Army of the Potomac. There were 4,710 men killed and 18,440 wounded. Proskauer was among the wounded, having been shot in the abdomen during intense fighting along the Sunken Road, later called the "Bloody Lane." He recuperated from September until January 1863 and returned to his company at Orange Court House, Virginia.

While the 12th was encamped near Fredericksburg in 1863, Proskauer, now the senior captain in the regiment, formally applied to become major. Proskauer was a popular officer with his men. He was at the Battle of Chancellorsville in May 1863 when the 12th fought as a part of Stonewall Jackson's famous flanking attack on Major General Hooker's Union army. On the morning of May 3, Proskauer led the regiment as Colonel Pickens assumed command of a portion of the brigade after the commander was wounded.

Proskauer was wounded in the battle. He was promoted to major by Colonel Pickens while he was in the hospital, with the promotion confirmed by the Confederate Congress in early 1864.

Major Proskauer caught up with his command on the road and was fit for duty at the Battle of Gettysburg on July 1, 1863. A part of Rodes's division, the 12th suffered heavy casualties at Oak Ridge, northeast of Gettysburg. Years later, Captain Park wrote Mrs. Proskauer: "I can see him now, in mental view, as he nobly carried himself at Gettysburg, standing coolly and calmly, with cigar in his mouth, at the head of the Twelfth Alabama, amid a perfect rain of bullets, shot and shell. He was the personification of intrepid gallantry, of imperturbable courage."

On July 4, 1863, Lee retreated from Pennsylvania. Major Proskauer and the 12th Alabama, "suffering, wet and anxious," on a dark, dreary, rainy night retreated south. They camped near Orange Courthouse during the remainder of the summer of 1863. Fighting continued in Virginia, and in October Major Proskauer led a force of half the regiment on a mission to destroy railroad tracks near Warrenton Junction. In late December, Proskauer led the regiment to Paine's Mill to help saw planks for the Orange Road. The regiment saw action again on May 8 at Spotsylvania Court House, where Major Proskauer received his third wound of the war. The war was over for Adolph Proskauer.

Jewish Confederates were able to turn to their faith to sustain them during the war. Southern rabbis supported the Confederate war effort. Rabbi Max Michelbacher of Richmond's Beth Ahabah Synagogue led the Confederate capital's Jewish community in assisting Jewish boys in the army. He ministered to their needs, requested furloughs on their behalf for Jewish holidays, and even published a "prayer of the C[onfederate] S[tates] Soldiers." Beginning with the Shema, it called upon the God of Israel to "be with me in the hot season of the contending strife; protect and bless me with health and courage to bear cheerfully the hardships of war. . . . Be unto the Army of this Confederacy, as thou wert of old, unto us, thy chosen people!"[47]

Rabbi James K. Gutheim of New Orleans also supported the Confederacy. The spiritual leader of Dispersed of Judah congregation, home to the more assimilated Jews of New Orleans, Gutheim refused to swear allegiance to the Union when the Crescent City was occupied by the Federal army. He left the city, with many of his congregation, for Montgomery, where he prayed from the pulpit, "Regard, O Father, in Thine abundant favor and benevolence, our beloved country, the Confederate States of America. May our young Republic increase in strength. . . . Behold, O God, and judge between us and our enemies, who have forced upon us this unholy and unnatural war."[48]

The revolution wrought by the Civil War—the freeing of the slaves, the collapse of the ancient regime, the death, destruction, and impoverishment of Southern cities—was devastating to Southern Jewry. Those most committed to the cause lost the most. Judah P. Benjamin left the country for Europe. Union officials tried to implicate him in Lincoln's assassination. Abraham C. Myers lost his career. Many families lost fathers, brothers, and sons. Businesses suffered. Many were destroyed. Those few Jews who had owned slaves lost them. Reconstruction was as bitter for the Jewish community as it was for the rest of the white South. "As Israelites," Henry Hyams, the former lieutenant governor of Louisiana, wrote a family member in April 1868, "we are passing through another captivity which relives and reenacts all the troubles so pathetically poured forth by the inspired Jeremiah." Emma Mordecai of Richmond could not abide the occupying army. "Richmond is a strange place," she confided to her diary. "Everything looks unnatural and desecrated."[49]

Like other Southerners, Jewish Southerners licked their wounds, rebuilt their lives, and memorialized their honored dead. The Jewish women of Richmond, for example, formed the Hebrew Ladies Memorial Association for the Confederate Dead. A circular was sent out "To the Israelites of the South" seeking funds to create a cemetery and to erect a monument to the Jewish Confederate dead. Time was of the essence, the circular said. "While the world yet rings with the narrative of a brave people's struggle for independence," it began, and while the story of their noble sacrifices for liberty was fresh, the graves themselves were neglected. This was not a situation that Southern Jewry should allow. Southern Jews should remember "the myriads of heroes who spilled their noble blood" in defense of the "glorious cause." The circular was also designed to appeal to Southern Jewish readers' fear of anti-Semitism. "In time to come," it concluded, "when the malicious tongue of slander, ever so ready to assail Israel, shall be raised against us, then, with a feeling of mournful pride, will we point to this monument and say: 'There is our reply.'"[50]

While the focus of this chapter is the understudied experience of Southern Jews in the Civil War era, it is important to note that during the war the majority of Jewish Americans lived in states in the North, the Midwest, and the West loyal to the Union. In 1860, there were approximately 150,000 Jews in the United States, all but 25,000 of them living in states that remained in the Union. The centers of Jewish life were in the large Northern cities—New York, Philadelphia, Cincinnati, Chicago, and Boston. These Jewish Americans, like their Southern coreligionists, supported their section. Thus, 6,000 to 7,000 Jewish men served in the Union army, some rising to the rank of general. Several enlisted men received the Medal of Honor. Because little has been written specifically about the Northern or Union Jewish experience during the Civil War, it is important to provide for the reader a brief overview of that experience as well as the Confederate experience.[51]

Jews in the North could be found on both sides of the political divide, some Democrats, some Republicans. Prominent Jewish leaders supported President Lincoln and the Republican Party. According to Howard M. Sachar, Jews, "like their middle-class neighbors, and their fellow German immigrants...welcomed the new Republican party, the party of free men and free soil, of vigorous business enterprises." Many German-language Republican clubs were founded by Jewish immigrants. Moses Dropsie helped found the Republican Party in Philadelphia, and Abram J. Dittenhöffer was a presidential elector from New York in 1860. When war came, Jews in the North, the Midwest, and the West rallied to the cause of the Union.

Northern Jews could be found at all points along the spectrum in the debate over slavery. Some, like Michael J. Heilprin, a Polish Jewish intellectual, Rabbi David Einhorn of Baltimore, Rabbi Bernhard Felsenthal of Chicago, and Isidor Busch of St. Louis (a member of the Missouri legislature), were fervent abolitionists. Einhorn believed it was blasphemy for proponents of slavery to identify God and the Bible with slavery. August Bondi fought with John Brown in Bloody Kansas in 1855 and 1856 and later served in the Union army.[52]

Others, like Rabbi Isaac Mayer Wise of Cincinnati and Rabbi Morris J. Raphall of New York City, were vigorous opponents of the abolitionists. Indeed, Rabbi Raphall delivered a controversial sermon entitled "The Bible View of Slavery" in which he said: "How dare you . . . denounce slave holding as a sin? When you remember that Abraham, Isaac, Jacob, Job—the men with whom the Almighty conversed . . . all these men were slaveholders." It is worth noting, however, that when war broke out, the rabbi's son became an officer in the Union army and lost an arm at Gettysburg. Michael Heilprin replied to Raphall in the *New York Daily Tribune* in 1861, disagreeing with his views and also citing biblical verses. "Must the stigma of Egyptian principles be fastened on the people of Israel," he wrote, "by Israelitish lips themselves." Jewish Americans in the North, the Midwest, and the West, like Southern Jewry, reflected the views of the society in which they lived.[53]

Northern, midwestern, and western Jews, like most Civil War soldiers, joined companies and regiments with their friends, relatives, and neighbors. In New York, many young Jewish men joined the New York 68th Volunteer Infantry, which had three Jewish sergeants, three Jewish lieutenants (Adolph Birnbaum, Adolph J. Joseph, and Louis Spitzer), and two Jewish captains (Abram Cohen and Louis Simon). Half of the men of the 11th New York were Jews. There were Jewish soldiers in the infantry, cavalry, and artillery.[54]

Many Jews served in the Ohio 37th under Captain Herman Rosenbaum and Lieutenant Moritz Fleischman. Jewish officers served in the Ohio 35th, 88th, 108th, and many other units. Marcus Spiegel of Akron served as colonel of the 120th Ohio Infantry. Spiegel immigrated to the United States from Abenheim near Worms in the spring of 1849. He moved to Chicago in 1850 and took up peddling. He met and married a young Quaker girl from Ohio who converted to Judaism. Soon he moved to Ohio, where he was active in the Democratic Party and a supporter of Stephen A. Douglas. When war came, he enlisted, and by December 1861 he was the captain of Company C of the 67th Ohio Volunteer Infantry. He was killed in action on May 4, 1864, in a surprise attack on his regiment near Alexandria, Louisiana.[55]

The story of Louis A. Gratz, while hardly typical, illustrates the opportunities for young Jewish immigrants to serve in the Union army. Gratz arrived in New York from Posen in the German states in 1861 speaking no English and began his new life as a peddler. He enlisted in the army shortly thereafter. He wrote his uncle that when the war began, "all the young folks flocked to the colors," and carried away "by the general enthusiasm, I became a soldier. I studied English with great zeal until I could talk fairly fluently." In less than two years, Gratz had become a major, the commanding officer of the 6th Kentucky Cavalry. His heroism at Chickamauga in September 1863 brought him further promotion.[56]

Numerous Jewish officers served in the Union army, including Brigadier General Edward S. Salomon, who enlisted as a lieutenant in the 24th Illinois and rose to the rank of colonel of the 82nd Illinois, which had more than a hundred Jewish soldiers. Company C of the 82nd was officially known as the "Israelite Company" and consisted of German Jewish immigrants living in Chicago. It was a part of the 82nd Illinois Infantry, a regiment made up chiefly of German Americans. Colonel Salomon, who saw action at Chancellorsville and Gettysburg, successfully commanded the regiment in the thick of the fight at Cemetery Ridge and in the Atlanta Campaign.[57] Frederick Kneffler of Indianapolis rose to the rank of major general and commanded the 79th Indiana. He was the highest-ranking Jewish officer in the Union army. There were seven other Jewish generals. Leopold Karpeles was awarded the Medal of Honor for his conspicuous bravery as color sergeant of the 57th Massachusetts during the Battle of the Wilderness, where he saved part of the army by rallying troops around his colors.[58]

When Congress enacted the Volunteer Bill to raise an army in July 1861, the law required chaplains to be ordained ministers of "some Christian denomination." Many Pennsylvania Jews had enlisted in Cameron's Dragoons, the 65th Regiment of the 5th Pennsylvania Cavalry. Its commanding officer was Max Friedman, a German Jew. When the men of the regiment elected a rabbi as chaplain, his commission was refused. Jewish organizations protested, and Congress amended the law in September 1862 to allow chaplains to adhere to some "religious denomination," thereby allowing Jews to serve.[59]

The most anti-Semitic incident of the Civil War occurred not in the South but in the army of General Ulysses S. Grant. In December 1862, Memphis, Tennessee, became a flash point of controversy because, while it was occupied by the Union army, the city became a notorious center of illegal trading, especially in cotton. On December 11, 1862, Grant issued his infamous Order Number 11 expelling all Jews from the military district because "the Jews, as a class," were "violating every regulation of the trade established by the Treasury Department." Jewish families were forced out of some towns. Grant's superiors backed his order, but Jewish leaders protested directly to President Lincoln, who immediately countermanded the order and denounced discrimination against Jews as a class.[60] The incident, while unfortunate, was not typical of either the Lincoln administration or Grant's command.

NOTES

1. "Kahal Kadosh" (Holy Congregation), traditionally the first two words of all early Sephardic congregations, is usually abbreviated "K.K.," as in the previous sentence with K.K. Mikve Israel. Yates Levy to J. C. Levy, March 16, 1865, Phillips-Myers Papers no. 596, Southern Historical Collection, University of North Carolina,

Chapel Hill; Robert N. Rosen, *The Jewish Confederates* (Columbia: University of South Carolina Press, 2000), 9–31; Eli Faber, *A Time for Planting: The First Migration, 1654–1820* (Baltimore: Johns Hopkins University Press, 1992). Some of the better works on local Jewish history are as follows: Mark I. Greenberg, "Becoming Southern: The Jews of Savannah, Georgia, 1830–1870," *American Jewish History* 86, no. 1 (March 1998): 1997; Myron Berman, *Richmond's Jewry, 1769–1976: Shabbat in Shockoe* (Charlottesville: University Press of Virginia, 1979); Steven Hertzberg, *Strangers within the Gate City: The Jews of Atlanta, 1845–1915* (Philadelphia: Jewish Publication Society of America, 1978); Ruthe Winegarten and Cathy Schechter, *Deep in the Heart: The Lives and Legends of Texas Jews* (Austin: Eakin Press and Texas Jewish Historical Society, 1990); James W. Hagy, *This Happy Land: The Jews of Colonial and Antebellum Charleston* (Tuscaloosa: University of Alabama Press, 1993); Belinda Gergel and Richard Gergel, *In Pursuit of the Tree of Life: A History of the Early Jews of Columbia, South Carolina, and the Tree of Life Congregation* (Columbia, SC: Tree of Life Congregation, 1996); Bertram Wallace Korn, *The Jews of Mobile, Alabama, 1763–1841* (Cincinnati, OH: Hebrew Union College Press, 1970); Bertram Wallace Korn, *The Early Jews of New Orleans* (Waltham, MA: American Jewish Historical Society, 1969); Selma S. Lewis, *A Biblical People in the Bible Belt: The Jewish Community of Memphis, Tennessee, 1840s–1960s* (Macon, GA: Mercer University Press, 1998); Janice O. Rothschild, *As but a Day: The First Hundred Years, 1867–1967* (Atlanta, GA: Hebrew Benevolent Congregation, The Temple, 1967); Melvin I. Urofsky, *Commonwealth and Community: The Jewish Experience in Virginia* (Richmond: Virginia Historical Society and Jewish Community Federation of Richmond, 1997); Rabbi Newton J. Friedman, "A History of Temple Beth Israel of Macon, Georgia" (Ph.D. diss., Burton College and Seminary, 1955).

2. Rosen, *Jewish Confederates*, 23–25; Jacob Rader Marcus, ed., *Memoirs of American Jews*, vol. 3 (New York: Ktav, 1974), 104.

3. Rosen, *Jewish Confederates*, 25; Richard C. Wade, *Slavery in the Cities: The South, 1820–1860* (Oxford: Oxford University Press, 1964), appendix; Elliott Ashkenazi, *The Business of Jews in Louisiana 1840–1875* (Tuscaloosa: University of Alabama Press, 1988), 9–11.

4. Greenberg, "Becoming Southern," 57–58; Rosen, *Jewish Confederates*, 37; Bertram W. Korn, *Jews and Negro Slavery in the Old South, 1789–1865* (Elkins Park, PA: Reform Congregation Kenesseth Israel, 1961), 123.

5. Rosen, *Jewish Confederates*, 37. Numerous rabbis and Jewish leaders in the North answered Rabbi Raphall's defense of slavery. The majority of Jews in the North opposed slavery, and there were a number of Northern Jewish abolitionists.

6. Ibid., 382–83; Bertram Korn, *American Jewry and the Civil War* (Philadelphia: Jewish Publication Society of America, 1951), 15–31, and Korn, *Jews and Negro Slavery in the Old South*, published also as a chapter entitled "Jews and Negro Slavery in the Old South, 1789–1865," in *Jews in the South*, ed. Leonard Dinnerstein and Mary Dale Palsson (Baton Rouge: Louisiana State University Press, 1973), 89–134; Hagy,

This Happy Land, 93; Avraham Barkai, *Branching Out: German-Jewish Immigration to the United States, 1820–1914* (New York: Holmes and Meier, 1994), 109–11.

7. Rosen, *Jewish Confederates*, 16; Wade, *Slavery in the Cities*, 20; Korn, *Jews and Negro Slavery in the Old South*, 111–13; Korn, *American Jewry*, 29.

8. Rosen, *Jewish Confederates*, 15, 31–33; Howard M. Sachar, *A History of the Jews in America* (New York: Knopf, 1992), 26–27; Oscar S. Straus, *Under Four Administrations* (Boston: Houghton Mifflin, 1922), 10.

9. Rosen, *Jewish Confederates*, 31; I. J. Benjamin, *Three Years in America, 1859–1862*, vol. 1, ed. Oscar Handlin, translation from German by Charles Reznikoff (Philadelphia: Jewish Publication Society of America, 1956), 76.

10. Rosen, *Jewish Confederates*, 34; John F. Marszalek, ed., *The Diary of Miss Emma Holmes, 1861–1866* (Baton Rouge: Louisiana State University Press, 1979), 162, 209, 306; Carol Bleser, ed., *Tokens of Affection: The Letters of a Planter's Daughter in the Old South* (Athens: University of Georgia Press, 1996), 343.

11. Rosen, *Jewish Confederates*, 35. See, generally, Jacob Rader Marcus, *Early American Jewry*, vol. 1 (Philadelphia: Jewish Publication Society of America, 1951), chap. 5 ("it is . . . a matter of record that the New Englanders, with rare exception, had no use for Jews. The original Puritans were interested in Hebrew and in ancient Hebrews . . . but not in their descendants as long as they remained Jews").

12. Rosen, *Jewish Confederates*, 35; Gergel and Gergel, *Tree of Life*, 33–35; *Confederate Veteran*, 23 (August 1915): 343. This is in a letter from Simon Baruch to the *Confederate Veteran*. Samuel Proctor and Louis Schmier, eds., with Malcolm Stern, *Jews of the South: Selected Essays from the Southern Jewish Historical Society* (Macon, GA: Mercer University Press, 1984), 37; Louis Schmier, "Georgia History in Pictures. This 'New Canaan': The Jewish Experience in Georgia," *Georgia Historical Quarterly* 73, no. 4, pt. 2 (Winter 1989), 820; Greenberg, "Becoming Southern"; Lewis, *A Biblical People*, 34.

13. Eli N. Evans, *Judah P. Benjamin: The Jewish Confederate* (New York: Free Press, 1988), 96–97.

14. Rosen, *Jewish Confederates*, 38; Morris U. Schappes, ed., *Documentary History of the Jews in the United States, 1654–1875*, rev. ed. (New York: Citadel Press, 1952), 436–41.

15. Rosen, *Jewish Confederates*, 38. Korn, *American Jewry*, 250n, 48; Frederic Jaher, *A Scapegoat in the Wilderness: The Origins and Rise of Anti-Semitism in America* (Cambridge, MA: Harvard University Press, 1996), 138, 200–3, 215; John Weiss, *Life and Correspondence of Theodore Parker* (New York: D. Appleton, 1964): Theodore Parker, "Journal," March 1843, 1:214, and Parker to Dr. Francis, May 26, 1844, 1:236, "Letter to the Members of the 28th Congregational Society of Boston" (1859), 2:497, and "Some Thoughts on the Charities of Boston" (1858), 1:397, and to Rev. David Wasson, December 12, 1857, 1:395–96. See also Egal Feldman, *Dual Destinies: The Jewish Encounter with Protestant America* (Urbana: University of Illinois Press, 1990), 56–59; *Liberator* 15 (May 20, 1842): 1, 19; (May 18, 1849): 77; (September 21, 1849): 751.

Edmond Quincy, "A Jew and a Christian," *Liberator* 18 (August 11, 1848): 126. Quincy, a Boston Brahmin and a cousin of John Quincy Adams, wrote a novel, *Wensley: A Story without a Moral*, published in 1854, in which the villain is a forger and cheat named Aaron Abrahams. The book is laced with every cliché of old-fashioned Boston anti-Semitism: the Jew as a liar, cheat, and coward (see pp. 275–91). See also Jonathon D. Sarna, "The 'Mythical Jew' and the 'Jew Next Door' in Nineteenth-Century America," in *Anti-Semitism in American History*, ed. David A. Gerber (Urbana: University of Illinois Press, 1986), 57–78; David A. Gerber, "Cutting Out Shylock: Elite Anti-Semitism and the Quest for Moral Order in the Mid-Nineteenth-Century American Market Place," *Journal of American History* 69 (December 1982): 615–37.

Lydia Maria Child, *Letters from New-York* (New York: Charles Francis; Boston: James Munroe, 1843), 12–13, 26–29, 31, 33–34, 217–18, 225 (Judaism was rife with superstition, vengeance, blindness; its ceremonies "strange . . . spectral and flitting"). See also Patricia G. Holland and Milton Meltzer, eds., *Guide to the Collected Correspondence of Lydia Maria Child, 1817–1880* (New York: Kraus Microform, 1980), s.v. "Jews," especially letters to Louisa Gilman Loring (September 4, 1846) and Ellis Gray Loring (March 5, 1854).

As to Henry Wilson's views, see *Congressional Globe*, 36th Cong., 2nd sess., February 21, 1861, 1091; and 37th Cong., 2nd sess., February 13, 1862, 789; Korn, *American Jewry*, 168; Robert Douthat Meade, *Judah P. Benjamin: Confederate Statesman* (London: Oxford University Press, 1943), 139; Jacob Rader Marcus, *United States Jewry, 1776–1985*, 4 vols. (Detroit, MI: Wayne State University Press, 1985–93), 3:36.

16. Rosen, *Jewish Confederates*, 121; Sachar, *History*, 73; *History of the Jews of Louisiana, Their Religious, Civic, Charitable and Patriotic Life* (New Orleans: Jewish Historical Publishing Company of Louisiana, 1903), 33; Scherck to J. L. Meyer, Columbus, Georgia, September 9, 1864, American Jewish Archives, Cincinnati (hereafter AJA); *Charleston Daily Courier*, March 11, 1861.

17. Rosen, *Jewish Confederates*, 13–14, 49–54; Schmier, "Georgia History in Pictures," 820; Isaac Hermann, *Memoirs of a Veteran Who Served as a Private in the 60s in the War between the States, Personal Incidents, Experiences, and Observations* (Atlanta, GA: Byrd Printing Co., 1911), 192–93; letter, April 17, 1864, Simon Mayer Papers, box 1, Tulane University.

18. James M. McPherson, *For Cause and Comrades: Why Men Fought in the Civil War* (New York: Oxford University Press, 1988); Young, *Where They Lie*, 39.

19. Rosen, *Jewish Confederates*, 49. Letter dated July 8, 1863, addressed to "Dear Brother Isaac and Sister Amelia" (Mr. and Mrs. Isaac Meinnart) in Richmond from Philip Rosenheim, AJA; Leo E. Turitz and Evelyn Turitz, *Jews in Early Mississippi*, 2nd ed. (Jackson: University Press of Mississippi, 1995), xvii; typewritten autobiography of Sir Moses Ezekiel, 75–76, Beth Ahaba Archive (Richmond, Virginia). See also Joseph Gutman and Stanley F. Chyet, eds., *Moses Jacob Ezekiel: Memoirs from the Baths*

of Diocletian (Detroit, MI: Wayne State University Press, 1975); *VMI Alumni Review* 49, no. 3 (Spring 1973): 1; Stanley F. Chyet, "Moses Jacob Ezekiel: A Childhood in Richmond," *Publications of the American Jewish Historical Society* 62 (1973): 286–94.

20. Berman, *Richmond's Jewry*, 194–95.

21. Rosen, *Jewish Confederates*, 50; autobiography of Moses Ezekiel; Vann C. Woodward and Elisabeth Muhlenfeld, eds., *The Private Mary Chestnut: The Unpublished Civil War Diaries* (New York: Oxford University Press, 1984), 350; Phoebe Yates Pember, *A Southern Woman's Story: Life in Confederate Richmond*, ed. Bell Irvin Wiley (Jackson, TN: McCowat-Mercer Press, 1959; reprint, Wilmington, NC: Broadfoot, 1991), 24.

22. Rosen, *Jewish Confederates*, 52; Gary W. Gallagher, *The Confederate War* (Cambridge: Harvard University Press, 1997), 28; Bernard M. Baruch, *My Own Story* (New York: Henry Holt, 1957), 5.

23. Lewis Leon, *The Diary of a Tar Heel Confederate Soldier* (Charlotte, NC: Stone Publishing Co., 1913), 1; Marcus, *Memoirs of American Jews*, 3:197; Schappes, *Documentary History*, 481, 707–8.

24. Jaher, *Scapegoat*, 3–4, 117–18, 135–36.

25. Philip Whitlock Recollections, 1843–1913, p. 92, Virginia Historical Society, Richmond; Herbert Ezekiel and Gaston Lichtenstein, *The History of the Jews of Richmond from 1769 to 1917* (Richmond, VA: Herbert Ezekiel, 1917), 183, 16, 175.

26. Jonathan D. Sarna, "American Jewish Political Conservatism in Historical Perspective," *American Jewish History* 87 (June/September 1999): 113–22.

27. Bertram W. Korn, introduction to "The Jews of the Confederacy," *American Jewish Archives* 13, no. 1, "Civil War Centennial Southern Issue" (April 1961): 4.

28. Rosen, *Jewish Confederates*, chap. 2; Thomas Cooper DeLeon, *Belles, Beaux, and Brains of the '60's* (New York, 1909), 91–93.

29. Richard S. Tedlow, "Judah Benjamin," in *"Turn to the South": Essays on Southern Jewry*, ed. Nathan M. Kaganoff and Melvin I. Urofsky (Charlottesville: University Press of Virginia, 1979), 46; Evans, *Judah P. Benjamin*, 147–49; S. I. Neiman, *Judah Benjamin: Mystery Man of the Confederacy* (Indianapolis: Bobbs-Merrill, 1963), 145–46; Meade, *Judah P. Benjamin*, 235; George C. Rable, *The Confederate Republic* (Chapel Hill: University of North Carolina Press, 1994), 130.

30. A. J. Hanna, *Flight into Oblivion* (Richmond, VA: Johnson, 1938), 194; Louis Gruss, "Judah Philip Benjamin," *Louisiana Historical Quarterly* 19 (October 1936): 1046; Pierce Butler, *Judah P. Benjamin* (Philadelphia: W. G. Jacobs, 1907), 332; Robert Selph Henry, *The Story of the Confederacy* (Indianapolis, IN: Bobbs-Merrill, 1931), 85, 87; Charles P. Roland, *The Confederacy* (Chicago: University of Chicago Press, 1960), 83, 111; Evans, *Judah P. Benjamin*, xi–xxi.

31. Roy Z. Chamlee Jr., *Lincoln's Assassins: A Complete Account of Their Capture, Trial, and Punishment* (Jefferson, NC: McFarland, 1990), 401.

32. Meade, *Judah P. Benjamin*, 297–305; Evans, *Judah P. Benjamin*, 193; Rosen, *Jewish Confederates*, 137. Colonel Henry J. Leovy's activities are briefly described in

William M. Robinson Jr., *Justice in Grey: A History of the Judicial System of the Confederate States of America* (Cambridge: Harvard University Press, 1941), 409–11. His activities as a special commissioner are described in the *Official Records* IV, 4:802–15; and Kenneth W. Noe, "Red String Scare: Civil War Southwest Virginia and the Heroes of America," *North Carolina Historical Review* 69 (July 1992): 301–22. Noe has Leovy's name as "Leory" because the *Official Records* made the same mistake. On the flight of the cabinet, see Hanna, *Flight into Oblivion*. See Leovy's obituary, *Daily Picayune*, October 4, 1902, 10, col. 2; letters from Jefferson Davis to Leovy dated May 26, 1877, and November 10, 1883, Historic New Orleans Collection (Henry J. Leovy Papers, 1859–1900).

33. Meade, *Judah P. Benjamin*, 301–4; William A. Tidwell, *Come Retribution: The Confederate Secret Service and the Assassination of Lincoln* (Jackson: University Press of Mississippi, 1998), chap. 8; William A. Tidwell, *April '65: Confederate Covert Action in the American Civil War* (Kent, OH: Kent State University Press, 1995), 127–29.

34. Simon Wolf, *The American Jew as Patriot, Soldier, and Citizen* (Philadelphia: Levytype, 1895); Barnett A. Elzas, *The Jews of South Carolina from the Earliest Times to the Present Day* (Philadelphia: Lippincott, 1905); list of Shreveport Jewish Confederate soldiers compiled by Eric Brock, Rosen Papers, Jewish Heritage Collection, College of Charleston Library; Ezekiel and Lichtenstein, *History of the Jews of Richmond*, 176–88. The authors, writing in 1916, believed their list of Jewish Confederate soldiers to be "the best that has ever been printed, and it is safe to assume that no more complete or accurate one will ever be published" (176); Bell I. Wiley, *The Life of Johnny Reb: The Common Soldier of the Confederacy* (Garden City, NY: Doubleday, 1971), 331.

35. Rosen, *Jewish Confederates*, 162–63.

36. Ibid., 163–65. Another reason there were no Jewish units is that many Jews were afraid to admit they were Jews. As Korn points out, "Hundreds and hundreds of Jewish men and officers in the Union and Confederate armies . . . thought they would avoid trouble by attempting to hide their background." Rabbi Isaac Leeser observed that some (Union) soldiers "would scarcely confess their Jewish origin . . . there was, on the whole, a hesitancy to confess our religion" (Korn, *American Jewry*, 96–97). Korn contends that Jews of this generation were mostly immigrants who had experienced serious prejudice and discrimination in Europe and "were afraid to call attention to themselves" even by creating a national Jewish organization (Korn, *American Jewry*, 13). An anonymous letter from a Jewish soldier dated February 1862 pointed out, "As a general rule, the Jews do not care to make their religion a matter of notoriety . . . some of our brethren fear that, were they known as Hebrews, it would expose them to the taunts and sneers of . . . their comrades" (Schappes, *Documentary History*, 465–66). "The fact that so few Jewish companies were organized," Korn observed, did not stem from any lack of patriotism among Jews, but from a reluctance to form Jewish enclaves in the army (121). An exception to this rule appears to be Company C ("The Israelite Company") of the 82nd Illinois, which

consisted primarily of Jewish men from Chicago (Schappes, *Documentary History*, 469–72).

37. Wolf, *American Jew*, passim; *Encyclopedia of the Confederacy*, 266–67; Rosen, *Jewish Confederates*, 166.

38. Wolf, *American Jew*, passim; as to the Cohens, see 374; Ashley Halsey Jr., "The Last Duel in the Confederacy," *Civil War Times Illustrated* 1, no. 7 (November 1962): 7; Elzas, *Jews of South Carolina*, 226; Joseph H. Crute, Sr., *Units of the Confederate Army* (Gaithersburg, MD: Olde Soldier Books, 1987), 271–72; Dorothy Phelps Bultman, "The Story of a Good Life" (November 1963, Sumter, South Carolina), 1, Jewish Heritage Collection, College of Charleston.

39. Ernest B. Furguson, *Ashes of Glory: Richmond at War* (New York: Knopf, 1996), 212. Letter dated July 8, 1863, from Philip Rosenheim to the Meinnarts, Korn file, AJA.

40. Rosen, *Jewish Confederates*, 174–75; Eric Brock, "The Jewish Cemeteries of Shreveport, Louisiana" (Shreveport, LA: privately printed, 1995), Jewish Heritage Collection.

41. John A. Cutchins, *A Famous Command: The Richmond Light Infantry Blues* (Richmond: Garrett and Massies, 1934), passim; Berman, *Richmond's Jewry*, 93–97; Ezekiel and Lichtenstein, *History of the Jews of Richmond*, 129, 149–152; Darrell L. Collins, *46th Virginia Infantry* (Lynchburg, VA: H. E. Howard, 1992), 151.

42. Rosen, *Jewish Confederates*, 118–125. The best source on Abraham C. Myers is Richard D. Goff, *Confederate Supply* (Durham, NC: Duke University Press, 1969). Walter Burke Jr. has written a useful pamphlet entitled "Quartermaster: A Brief Account of the Life of Colonel Abraham Charles Myers, Quartermaster General C.S.A.," published in 1976. William C. Davis, *Breckinridge: Statesman, Soldier, Symbol* (Baton Rouge: Louisiana State University Press, 1974); Davis, *Jefferson Davis: The Man and His Hour* (New York: Harper Collins, 1991); and Davis, *A Government of Our Own: The Making of the Confederacy* (New York: Free Press, 1994). Thomas Cooper DeLeon, the irrepressible author of *Belles, Beaux, and Brains of the '60s* and *Four Years in Rebel Capitals: An Inside View of Life in the Southern Confederacy, from Birth to Death* (Mobile: Gossip Printing Co., 1890), knew Myers personally and was well acquainted with his family, as was true of Mary Chestnut, who was also from South Carolina and knew the Jewish community through her close friendship with Miriam DeLeon Cohen. Thus, her diary, *Mary Chestnut's Civil War*, is a good source on Myers.

See also Karl H. Grismer, *The Story of Fort Myers: The History of the Land of the Caloosahatchee and Southwest Florida* (Fort Myers, FL: Southwest Florida Historical Society, 1949); Samuel Bernard Thompson, *Confederate Purchasing Operations Abroad* (Chapel Hill: University of North Carolina Press, 1935); Clement Eaton, *A History of the Southern Confederacy* (New York: Macmillan, 1954); Ellsworth Eliot Jr., *West Point in the Confederacy* (New York: G. A. Baker, 1941); Robert C. Black III, *The Railroads of the Confederacy* (Chapel Hill: University of North Carolina Press,

1952); John Beauchamp Jones, *A Rebel War Clerk's Diary at the Confederate States Capital*, 2 vols., ed. Howard Swiggett (New York: Old Hickory Bookshop, 1935).

43. Rosen, *Jewish Confederates*, 132, 142.

44. Eaton, *History of the Southern Confederacy*, 138; Davis, *Jefferson Davis*, 537–38; Goff, *Confederate Supply*, 142; Woodward, *Mary Chestnut*, 437n5.

45. Woodward, *Mary Chestnut*, 532; Sallie B. Putnam [A Richmond Lady], *Richmond during the War: Four Years of Personal Observation* (New York, 1867; reprint, Alexandria, VA: Time-Life Books, 1983), 275. Jones was a native of Baltimore. *A Rebel War Clerk's Diary*, condensed edition, edited by Earl Schenck Miers (New York: Sagamore Press, 1958), see 1:186; 2:8; Berman, *Richmond's Jewry*, 187.

46. Rosen, *Jewish Confederates*, 107–10; Joseph Proskauer, *A Segment of My Times* (New York: Farrar, Straus, 1950). Adolph Proskauer's daughter Jenny Proskauer wrote an unreliable recollection in 1948, which is at the AJA. The chief source of this material is Robert Emory Park, *Sketch of the Twelfth Alabama Infantry of Battle's Brigade, Rodes Division, Early's Corps, of the Army of Northern Virginia* (Richmond, VA: W. E. Jones, 1906), originally printed in *Southern Historical Society Papers* 33 (1905): 193–296. The details of Proskauer's military career are derived from his compiled service record at the National Archives, as well as the *Official Record*, where his name is misspelled "Proskaner." See ser. 1, vol. 25, pt. 1, 960 (Reports of Col. Samuel B. Pickens, 12th Alabama, May 5, 1863); ser. 1, vol. 36, pt. 1, 1083 (May 9, 1864); 1:27, 563; 1:25, 950–53 (Reports of Col. Edward A. O'Neal, May 12, 1863); 1:29, 891–92 (Reports of Maj. A. Proskaner, January 22, 1864). Also see Young, *Where They Lie*, 76, 78–79; Robert K. Krick, *Lee's Colonels: A Biographical Register of the Field Officers of the Army of Northern Virginia* (Dayton, OH: Morningside House, 1992), 266; Korn, *American Jewry*, 176; obituary of Adolph Proskauer, AJA (the AJA has an extensive file on Proskauer); Park, *Sketch*, 5.

47. Rosen, *Jewish Confederates*, 209–13.

48. Ibid., 249, 256–57.

49. Ibid., 333–37. Letter from Hyams dated April 19, 1868 to "My Dear Caroline," AJA; Marcus, *Memoirs of American Jews*, 3:341.

50. Undated clipping, George Jacobs scrapbook, AJA; Rosen, *Jewish Confederates*, 338–40 (the circular is reproduced on p. 339). See also Korn, *American Jewry*, 110–12.

51. The best history of the Jews in the Civil War remains Bertram Wallace Korn's classic work, *American Jewry and the Civil War* (Philadelphia: Jewish Publication Society of America, 1951). A paperback edition was published in 1961 that contained a new preface with much new material. The paperback edition was reissued in 2001. It addresses the experience of the Jewish community on the home front, North and South. Like much Jewish history, it focuses on religious and organizational issues (the chaplaincy controversy, for example) and anti-Semitism and, unfortunately, does not address or even discuss the Jewish military experience. There are, as Korn acknowledges, "severe limitations . . . inherent in this approach" (xi). Korn described

in detail the slavery question, how the Jewish leadership, North and South, came to take sides, and the home front. A third of the book is devoted to anti-Semitic incidents and the response to them. There is a chapter on Lincoln and the Jews.

Aside from biographies of leading personalities (such as Stephen Birmingham's *Our Crowd: The Great Jewish Families of New York* [Syracuse, NY: Syracuse University Press, 1967]; James G. Heller's *Isaac M. Wise: His Life and Work* [New York: Union of American Hebrew Congregations, 1965]; Irving Katz's *August Belmont: A Political Biography* [New York: Columbia University Press, 1968]) and local Jewish histories, few books have been published that discuss Jews of the North during the Civil War. Simon Wolf detailed the contribution of Jews to both the Northern and the Southern cause in *The American Jew as Patriot, Soldier, and Citizen* (New York: Levy Type Co., 1895). This book is flawed in many ways, but it does contain a great deal of useful information and attempts to list each Jewish soldier in the Civil War. (For a discussion of Wolf's work, see Rosen, *Jewish Confederates*, 459–60. Given the popularity of Civil War history, this is rather bizarre. It seems that academic historians of the American Jewish experience, clustered in the Northeast and overwhelmed by notions of political correctness, shy away from the history of the Civil War, and indeed the nineteenth century, in favor of more "liberal" and "Jewish" topics, such as immigration; anti-Semitism; the labor movement; left-wing, radical, and socialist causes; feminism; and the Holocaust. But see the relevant chapters in Marcus, *United States Jewry*, vol. 2; Jonathan D. Sarna, *American Judaism: A History* (New Haven: Yale University Press, 2004); Sachar, *History*, chap. 3; Barkai, *Branching Out*; Naomi W. Cohen, *Encounter with Emancipation: The German Jews in the United States, 1830–1914* (Philadelphia: Jewish Publication Society of America, 1984); Leonard Dinnerstein, *Anti-Semitism in America* (New York: Oxford University Press, 1994); Hasia Diner, *A Time for Gathering* (Baltimore: Johns Hopkins University Press, 1992); Diner, *The Jews of the United States, 1654 to 2000* (Berkeley: University of California Press, 2004); and Martin Litvin, *The Journey: A Biography of August M. Bondi* (Galesburg, IL: Galesburg Historical Society, 1981). For the diary of one Jewish Union officer, see Marcus M. Spiegel, *A Jewish Colonel in the Civil War: Marcus M. Spiegel of Ohio* (Lincoln: University of Nebraska Press, 1995).

Rabbi Korn's mentor, Jacob Rader Marcus, published, and helped others publish, letters, diaries, and memoirs about the Northern experience. See Marcus, *Memoirs of American Jews*, which contains much primary source material on this period. For a pioneering work that discusses all the Jewish men killed in the Civil War, see Mel Young, *Where They Lie, Someone Should Say Kaddish* (Lanham, MD: University Press of American, 1991). The opportunities for further research and writing are manifold and exciting. How did the large Jewish communities of New York City, Chicago, Cincinnati, and Philadelphia react to the war? Who served in the Union armed forces and why? Who were officers, and how did they fare? Especially intriguing are the untold stories of New York and Chicago, where large numbers of Jews enlisted, sometimes making up a majority of companies. See, for example, Schappes, *Docu-*

mentary History, 469–70 (Company C, "The Israelite Company"). The stories of the careers of notable Jewish Union soldiers, both officers and enlisted men, are yet to be told.

52. Sachar, *History*, 73; Rosen, *Jewish Confederates*, 35–37; Korn, *American Jewry*, 17–23; Jayne A. Sokolow, "Revolution and Reform: The Antebellum Jewish Abolitionist," *Journal of Ethnic Studies*, no. 1 (1981): 26–41; Barkai, *Branching Out*, chap. 5.

53. Korn, *American Jewry and the Civil War*, 2nd ed. (Philadelphia: Jewish Publication Society, 1957), 18–23; Sachar, *History*, 72–74; Schappes, *Documentary History*, 405–28. For a recent, brilliant study of the biblical foundations of the pro-slavery argument, see Stephen R. Haynes, *Noah's Curse: The Biblical Justification of American Slavery* (Oxford: Oxford University Press, 2002); Rosen, *Jewish Confederates*, 37.

54. Wolf, *American Jew*, 3, 237–41, 263, 294–95.

55. Jean Powers Soman and Frank L. Byrne, *A Jewish Colonel in the Civil War* (Lincoln: University of Nebraska Press, 1985), 1–19, 335–37; Wolf, *American Jew*, 237–41, 305–44. Spiegel's brother, Joseph, who also served in the Union army, survived the war and founded the well-known Spiegel Catalogue Company.

56. Marcus, *Memoirs of American Jews*, 3:226–35.

57. Schappes, *Documentary History*, 469–71; Sachar, *History*, 74; Wolf, *American Jew*, 2–3, 184–85. See also www.illinoiscivilwar.org (82nd Illinois) and www.geocities.com (82nd and Salomon).

58. Wolf, *American Jew*, 5, 106, 178, 204; Sachar, *History*, 74.

59. Barkai, *Branching Out*, 118–19; Korn, *American Jewry*, 56–97.

60. Sachar, *History*, 78–80; Korn, *American Jewry*, chap. 6; Schappes, *Documentary History*, 472–75; Rosen, *Jewish Confederates*, 265, 431.

❦ 6 ❦

NATIVE AMERICANS IN
THE CIVIL WAR

Three Experiences

William McKee Evans

In 1861, when news of the Confederate attack on Fort Sumter swept the country, Native Americans could have had few illusions about being on the winning side. They had been on the losing side in all the white men's wars. In the Seven Years' (or French and Indian) War, the Indians had sided with the French, whom they experienced not as land-grabbing settlers but as merchants who bought their furs and sold them European goods. The French and Indians lost. Then, in the American War for Independence, the Indians sided with the British, who had taken over the French fur trade and behaved toward Indians much like the French had, buying their furs and selling them European goods instead of settling on their land.[1] The British armed the Indians against the rebellious settlers. Again, Native Americans found themselves on the losing side.

In the War of 1812, although the Catawbas, the Cherokees, and some of the Creeks sided with the Americans, Indian nations again sided overwhelmingly with the British. The charismatic Shawnee chief Tecumseh, whom the British had made a general, was having some success organizing an Indian confederation that would stretch from the Great Lakes to the Gulf. British arms poured in. At first the war went well for them. The war had divided white Americans into pro-war and antiwar factions, and this split had deepened when an army of Indians and Canadians turned back an American invasion of Canada and captured Detroit. The Americans sued for peace. British terms were harsh. Concerning Indians, they demanded the division of the Mississippi Valley into two Indian confederations under British protection. They also demanded the "internationalization" of the Mississippi River, in practice putting it under control of the British navy. Underscoring their demands, they captured and burned Washington.

Fortunately for the Americans, the British people were weary from twenty years of war in Europe. The government, burdened by a towering war debt and now having troubles with its European allies, softened its terms, offering the Americans the status quo ante bellum, terms eagerly accepted. The two sides signed the Treaty of Ghent. But unknown to the negotiators at Ghent, the war in America had taken a sharp turn. General Andrew Jackson, heading an army of frontiersmen and Indians, had defeated the pro-British Indians on the Gulf Coast and the British at the Battle of New Orleans.[2] So despite the Treaty of Ghent, the situation on the ground had decisively changed in favor of the Americans. There would be no more British arms to Indians, no Indian confederations under British protection. Now Native Americans stood alone against the land-hungry whites.

After the American victories, General Jackson, a rich land speculator, large planter, and slaveholder, gave the Indians a foretaste of things to come. He punished the pro-British Creeks by confiscating half of their lands. He also confiscated half of the lands of the pro-American Creeks. For the next generation, American Indian policy most often consisted in ignoring existing treaties but offering Indians new treaties in which they gave up their ancestral lands in exchange for land grants beyond the frontier of white settlement, grants that would be valid "forever" in the ancestral territory of other Indians.

In 1848, with American victory in the Mexican War, in which Indians hardly participated, this policy ended. The United States conquered the northern half of Mexico, advancing the American frontier to the Pacific. With this final frontier, there was no more land beyond white settlement where Indians could be exiled. They had to be subdued and confined to "reservations" or exterminated as American pioneers settled the western territories. Indians resisted. But the "Indian wars" in the West reported in the press were often the indiscriminate slaughter of entire Indian communities. From 1850 to 1860, the gold rush of fortune seekers to California, scrambling for mining claims and livestock range on Indian lands, reduced California's Indian population from 100,000 to 35,000.[3]

Yet, despite their experience with white men's wars, some 20,000 Native Americans served in the Civil War on one side or the other. Some went to war as individuals for the same reasons as some common white folk, enticed by recruitment bounties or hired as a substitute by some wealthy person, or pressured by loyalty to some powerful protector or patron. But many Indians acted collectively, and their loyalty was more to their own nations rather than to either the Union or the Confederacy. The Ottawa, and some of their neighbors, for example, hoped that their formation of a company of the 1st Michigan Sharpshooters would help them in their struggle against removal.

For Indians, due to the overwhelming power of the whites, there was no winning strategy, only strategies to reduce or postpone their losses. As in earlier white men's wars, Indian groups everywhere sought to survive by one or the other of two conflicting strategies: either by accommodating white power or by resisting it. In the wartime histories of the Cherokees, both the Western Band and the Eastern Band, as well as that of the Lumbees, one can see how Indians came to adopt these strategies and how their choices affected their lives and their future.

The Western Cherokees: Indians Fight Indians

Of all Native American peoples, the Cherokee Nation contributed the largest number of fighters. As with other Indian groups, their involvement followed from conflicting strategies for survival: accommodation or resistance. They were one of the Five Civilized Nations of the Southeast, "civilized" because their lifestyle resembled that of their white neighbors.[4] Especially "civilized" were the slaveholding Cherokee planters. These were the "mixed-bloods," the people who had most fully assimilated white customs.[5] Far more numerous were the "full-bloods," who cultivated small farms and raised livestock. By the 1820s, the lands that the Cherokees held by treaty had been reduced to the southern Appalachians and neighboring parts of Georgia and Alabama.

In the 1830s, a crisis erupted for the Cherokees with the discovery of gold in their territory, bringing in a flood of white squatters. The Cherokee Nation's leaders took legal action in the federal courts to uphold their treaty rights against the invaders. But Congress and the administration of President Andrew Jackson, instead of enforcing the existing treaty, proposed a new one: the surrender of Cherokee land in the Southeast in exchange for "grants" of land already occupied by other Indians beyond the Mississippi. Overwhelmingly, the Cherokees opposed such a treaty. With some support from white missionaries, the National Council continued legal resistance in the courts.

But federal representatives, bypassing the Cherokee National Council, negotiated with the accommodating "mixed-blood" Ridge Party. Under an 1807 Cherokee law, it was a capital crime to surrender tribal land without the authorization of the National Council, a law that, ironically, John Ridge had helped write. Yet in 1835, leaders of the Ridge Party signed the Treaty of New Echota.[6] Then, with their black slaves, they migrated west to establish cotton plantations on virgin land in Indian Territory, present-day Oklahoma.

In 1838, the new president, Jackson's protégé, Martin Van Buren, took the same hard line as Jackson. He ordered General Winfield Scott to remove the antitreaty Cherokees. Except for one small band living on the less valuable land near the Great Smoky Mountains of North Carolina, Scott, with a force of 7,000, rounded up those who refused to recognize the legality of the Treaty of Echota and forced them to take the "trail of tears." Almost one-quarter died in this forced migration.[7]

Upon the arrival of the survivors in Indian Territory, a bloody feud erupted between the antitreaty Cherokees and the Ridge Party. The two sides signed a peace treaty in 1846, but underlying tensions continued. Indeed, tensions increased as North-South issues sharpened. The Nationalist Party of Principal Chief Ross consisted mostly of antiremoval "full-bloods" who owned few or no slaves. In 1859, led by an abolitionist preacher, they founded the secret Keetowah Society to promote nationalist feelings among the "full-bloods" and to oppose the assimilationist tendencies of the "mixed-bloods." Despite their nominally Christian orientation, they retained ancient Cherokee religious rites.

In 1860, with the secession of the Deep South, the Nationalists formed a secret Loyal League to promote Cherokee treaty rights, friendly relations with the United States, and the abolition of slavery. They opposed the election to public office of anyone suspected of treason to the Cherokee Nation or to the United States.[8]

The pro-slavery Ridge Party was also organizing, founding the Blue Lodge and a chapter of the nationwide Knights of the Golden Circle. During the 1850s, the Knights had sponsored "filibusters": paramilitary bands that made raids into neighboring countries of Latin America, where they attempted to extend the South's slaveholding pattern of society.[9]

With the outbreak of war, the Confederate government moved more quickly than the Union to secure its position in Indian Territory. Confederate president Jefferson Davis, former U.S. secretary of war, was experienced in the politics of Indian diplomacy. To Indian Territory, he dispatched a Confederate general, the learned New England–born Albert Pike, who spoke several Indian languages. Pike persuaded a number of the smaller Indian nations to sign treaties that included their creation of Confederate military units. These, reinforced by the white North Texas Cavalry, gave him the military muscle to persuade such larger nations as the Cherokees.

Before the Confederates approached the Cherokee National Council, however, they reached an understanding with the pro-slavery Ridge Party. They authorized the talented Stand Watie to raise a Confederate regiment, commissioning him first colonel, later general. Ross and his supporters also formed a regiment, the 2nd Indian Mounted Rifles, which recruited from the secret societies, the Nationalist Keetowah, and the Loyal League. But faced with armed Confederates both within and around the Cherokee Nation, they were in a corner. The Confederates were now in a position to replace Ross as principal chief with Stand Watie.

The treaty they offered the Cherokees had attractive features. The federal government had defaulted on the annuity payments it had agreed to pay for lands the Cherokees had surrendered. The Confederates promised to honor these payments. Also, the treaty stipulated that Cherokee troops would be used only in defense of the Indian Territory and would not be subject to duty elsewhere.[10] The Nationalists, however, wanted no treaty with the Confederates. It had been Southerners, not Northerners, who had carried out massive expulsions of Indians from the East, and they had done so with the help of "mixed-blood" Cherokee slaveholders.

Ross was in a difficult position. Like many leaders of the Ridge Party, Ross himself was a "mixed-blood" who owned a hundred slaves. His office as principal chief was at stake. Caught between the military threat of the Confederates and the stiff nationalism of his "full-blood" supporters, he wavered and proposed that the Cherokee Nation should remain neutral in the Civil War. Yet his position grew weaker as his supporters fled northward to join Union forces that were mobilizing in Kansas. Then came news of Union defeats at Bull Run and at nearby Wilson's Creek, Missouri. Ross capitulated and signed the treaty.[11]

The Confederate treaty proved to be like other treaties that the Cherokees had signed. The promised annuity payments were scant and infrequent. Despite the provision that Cherokees were not to serve outside of Indian Territory, scarcely eight months later the Confederate high command ordered the Cherokee forces to Arkansas to take part in a Confederate offensive aimed at capturing the state of Missouri. The Union forces turned back the offensive, defeating the Confederates at Pea Ridge. In the wake of this defeat, the 2nd Indian Mounted Rifles defected to the Union, and the Union forces captured Principal Chief Ross.[12]

The Union paroled Ross, but General Watie, claiming that Ross had abdicated his office of principal chief, declared himself head of the Cherokee Nation. Ross protested that he was still the legitimate chief, but he was now in his seventies and compromised among his supporters by his signing the Confederate treaty. Increasingly, younger leaders took charge, repudiating the treaty and declaring the abolition of slavery.

Now Cherokee fought Cherokee, and the victims on both sides were mostly small farmers and ranchers. The war reduced their numbers from 22,000 to 15,000. One-third of the married women were now widows, and one-quarter of the children orphans. Their farms and ranches were devastated, and they had lost 300,000 head of cattle.[13] The Cherokees had lost more than a quarter of their people in the conflict. No other ethnic group in America suffered such losses.

The Eastern Cherokees: Indians Fight the Unionists

For the small Eastern Band of Cherokees the war was less divisive. They supported the Confederacy. This is surprising because in the southern Appalachians, plantations were rare, and even the whites held few slaves. According to a federal census taken in 1835, Cherokee masters, mostly "mixed-bloods," held 1,592 slaves. But only 37 of these slaves were in North Carolina, where the "full-blood" future Eastern Band lived.[14] Indeed, the Union recruited many soldiers from among the whites of the southern Appalachians. The support that the Confederacy enjoyed from the Eastern Cherokees appeared to have resulted from the influence of a single, remarkable individual, William Holland Thomas. The Eastern Band was more pro-Thomas than pro-Confederate.

Thomas was born to white parents in the tiny mountain community of Waynesville, North Carolina. His father died before he was born. When he was twelve, Cherokee neighbors, the family of the influential chief Yonaguska adopted him, although he continued living most of the time with his mother, who taught him to read, write, and do arithmetic. The Cherokees gave him the name Wil-Usdi, "Little Will." He grew up fully bilingual and appeared equally comfortable with customs of the whites or of the Cherokees.[15] At twelve, he was working at a trading post. Five years later his mother sold some land and set him up in his own trading post and general store. Perhaps as the result of the influence of his adoptive family, the business prospered, and within a few years he owned a half dozen such establishments.

Wil-Usdi/Thomas presents a paradox: he grew rich in a land where most people, white and Indian, were poor, and he did so while continuing to enjoy the respect of most of his neighbors. The natural beauty of the Appalachians masked much of the ugly poverty of its people. Farms were small, often little more than gardens. Even livestock herds were small, as winter forage was not as abundant as in the warmer lowlands. People lived near the edge: sometimes crops failed and winter storms killed animals. To survive one needed credit at some store.

Wil-Usdi/Thomas offered credit to both races. Sometimes he waited months or years for repayment. But his customers repaid with 10 percent interest. They repaid with deerskins, with medicinal herbs, with gold flakes representing countless hours in the lean mines of the region, or with livestock. Some repaid with their own labor in his growing empire of stores, sawmills, gristmills, and tanneries or by tending his farms and herds.[16] The needy survived, and Wil-Usdi/Thomas grew rich.

While still in his twenties, he began an activity that would serve him well in his later military career. He led bands of mounted men on "long drives" of cattle from western North Carolina to markets in the port cities of Charleston and Savannah. Some cattle were from his own herds, others he sold on commission. Along with the "long drives" went wagon trains carrying mountain commodities to market.[17]

During these years, he also began to practice law. When he was only fifteen, the trading post where he worked suffered bankruptcy. The owner, in place of salary, paid him with a set of law books. He began "reading law." In time, he became one of the many self-taught lawyers who practiced in North Carolina courts. Highlanders, Cherokees especially, suffered a hefty share of legal injuries. The North Carolina Constitution of 1835 stripped "people of color" of their civil rights.[18] Past federal treaties, however, guaranteed certain rights to Indians. But whites often brushed aside like cobwebs Indian treaties and the rights they granted. Wil-Usdi/Thomas listened to grievances in Cherokee and pled causes in English.

He followed the accommodationist survival strategy of his foster father, Chief Yonaguska, who struggled to convince whites that Cherokees were "civilized." While the chief was devoted to the Cherokee myths, which interpreted the natural features and wildlife of the Cherokee homeland, at the same time he regarded the Christian missionaries as friends and allies.[19] They wanted to distribute Cherokee-language Bibles and hymnbooks among his people.

Before giving his permission, the chief insisted on acquainting himself with this material. He had his black servant, Cudjo, whom he called "his brother," read to him in Cherokee the Gospel of St. Mathew. After listening carefully to several chapters, he commented, "Well it seems to be a good book—strange that the white people are not better, after having it so long." Also, he and his white son promoted a temperance society that reduced liquor sales at Wil-Usdi's stores. Wil-Usdi collected testimonials from whites that Cherokees were sober Christian citizens.[20]

But nothing protected the Eastern Band more than the scant resources of their mountainous home. There was no flood of whites eager to share in the poverty of the highlanders. The Cherokees in Georgia were more "civilized" but also more vulnerable. They occupied valuable gold fields and plantation lands and were facing removal. In 1835, Wil-Usdi/Thomas hurried to the Cherokee capital, New Echota, for discussions with the accommodationist Ridge leaders. By bargaining away tribal land behind the back of the National Council, they were committing a capital crime. They needed all the Cherokee support they could get. As the agent of Chief Yonaguska's people, Thomas persuaded them to include in their New Echota Treaty Article XII, stipulating that Indians who "qualified" for state citizenship not only would be exempted from expulsion but also would be entitled to the same federal compensation as those actually removed. The Indians who became the Eastern Band claimed to be North Carolina citizens. Now, under a federal treaty, they could each claim $53.33 in federal compensation, as if they had actually moved to Indian Territory.[21] With such claims, Wil-Usdi/Thomas the lawyer would have much work to do.

He had become a large land speculator by the time the army removed the main body of the Cherokees. The expulsion of Indians created a feast for speculators. He bought up thousands of acres for himself, but unlike other speculators, he also bought thousands of acres that he held in trust for the Indians he represented, whose legal rights to land or virtually anything were at best uncertain. Some Cherokees paid all or in part for farms; others hoped to pay for farms he held in trust for them. Yonaguska died in 1839, willing the chieftaincy to his white son, who appointed the new subchiefs of the various towns. In 1848, he was elected to the North Carolina senate, where he blocked efforts to remove the Eastern Band. His marriage to Sarah Love increased still further his influence. She was the daughter of a longtime white friend and business associate, one of the wealthiest men in western North Carolina.[22]

His extensive mountain real estate was becoming more valuable because of the growing North-South tensions. Wealthy southern planters did not spend their summers in the unhealthy environment of the coastal low country. During the hot "sickly season," many vacationed in Saratoga Springs, New York or Newport, Rhode Island, or other cool and pleasant resorts in the North. But as the "irrepressible conflict" between the North and the South sharpened, many planters found northern vacations less agreeable and turned to the cool and healthy climate of the southern Appalachians, the "American Switzerland," where Thomas owned much land. When planters built summer homes and hunting lodges in the highlands, they increased his wealth and widened his connections among the Old South elite. They also brought money and jobs into an area where both were scarce.

Wil-Usdi/Thomas's business activities may help explain his growing commitment to "southern rights" politics. His friendship with John C. Calhoun appears to date from 1826, when he accompanied Calhoun and other South Carolina leaders on an unsuccessful expedition to locate a railroad route through the Great Blue Ridge that would connect South Carolina with the Tennessee River Valley.[23] Also, in the Democratic Party Calhoun was the principal rival of Andrew Jackson, the most uncompromising enemy of Indians. By the time of the Civil War, Wil-Usdi/Thomas was fully committed to the cause of the planter South.

With the outbreak of war, the now Colonel Thomas began recruiting what came to be called "Thomas's Legion of Indians and Highlanders," which, at its height, consisted of 2,800 men. While many Cherokee Confederates in Indian Territory, especially full-bloods, deserted to the Union, Cherokees in the Thomas Legion, although thoroughly full-blood, had a substantially lower desertion rate than the Confederate army at large.[24] Undoubtedly, the colonel's Indian and white followers appreciated his services to their community, but there were other ties that bound them to their leader. Many looked to his empire of business enterprises, and those of his wealthy father-in-law, for jobs and credit. Also, at the outbreak of war he was holding in trust thousands of acres of Indian land and $21,334.20 in federal money not yet distributed to Indians.[25] The election of 1861 on the issue of secession suggests that Thomas's economic power and that of his wife's family may have been more important than pro-Confederate sentiment in rallying recruits to his legion, for the Union vote was large in western North Carolina: 60 percent or more in eight counties.[26]

In East Tennessee, especially, the Thomas Legion performed invaluable services for the Confederacy. The area between the Cumberland Mountains and the Great Smokies was of unusual strategic importance. Through this valley passed the Richmond-Chattanooga railroad, a "lifeline" of the Confederacy, the only direct rail connection between the Confederate East and the Confederate West. The line passed through a land where plantations were rare and friends of the Confederacy few. While in the Tennessee elections of June 1861, the state voted for secession, in East Tennessee the Unionists trounced the secessionists two to one. The Confederate minority in this region, nevertheless, was in control, if only barely, because of better arms and more experienced military leaders.

In April 1862, the Thomas Legion crossed over the Great Smokies to reinforce the fragile Confederate power in East Tennessee. The Confederate general there, Felix K. Zollicoff, did not trust some of his own troops. These were local recruits, who had enlisted out of fear, and he suspected they were cooperating with the Unionists. Unionists at Strawberry Plains had stoned a troop train carrying Mississippi soldiers to Virginia, and the soldiers had fired on the crowd. A rumor circulated that Lincoln had shipped 10,000 muskets to Cincinnati, and these were being smuggled into East Tennessee. Union guerrillas had burned five railroad bridges and had attacked three others.[27]

East Tennesseans looked on Thomas's Indian units with curiosity or anxiety. They were reassured on a Sunday when soldiers crowded into a Knoxville church for services conducted in the Cherokee language. Less reassuring were the frightening war whoops of a traditional Cherokee ballgame, much like lacrosse.[28] The Legion camped at Strawberry Plains, a center of Union guerrilla activity near Knoxville, with the responsibility of protecting the railroad. When a regular federal force attempted to break into the Tennessee Valley, the Legion turned them back at Baptist Gap.

The Thomas Legion angered Unionists by enforcing the Confederate conscription acts, which the poor hated because they exempted large slaveholders and men of wealth.[29] Furthermore, they seized provisions and hunted down Unionists. Throughout the Appalachians the inequities of the conscription acts and the heavyhanded tactics of the military eroded support for the Confederacy. Union guerrillas appeared even in Wil-Usdi/Thomas's home territory in North Carolina.[30]

Both sides organized guerrilla bands, sometimes calling themselves "home guards." The Confederate and the Union guerrilla bands had different social compositions. Confederate bands were mostly town-based, composed of substantial property owners or professional men who were approaching middle age, and often led by a slaveholder. Union bands were more rural-based, younger men who held little or no property.[31] In September 1863, Union forces under General Ambrose Burnside drove into the valley from Chattanooga, forcing the Thomas Legion back into the Great Smokies, where from these heights they continued to harass Unionists.

The Thomas Legion held out until after Lee's surrender at Appomattox. When Union officers came to the Battle House, a resort hotel in Waynesville, to receive its capitulation, Wil-Usdi/Thomas, for the moment, had superior forces around the town. So he gave the negotiators one last display of defiance. He and twenty Cherokees, all stripped to the waist and feathered in full battle dress, appeared at the hotel. After two days of such posturing, however, he surrendered. The Union officers allowed him and his followers to return home with their weapons.[32]

For generations the people of the highlands had lived near the brink of calamity, but war brought famine. The Confederates had seized livestock under their tax-in-kind law. Marauding guerrilla bands, ostensibly fighting for the Union or for the Confederacy, had seized even more. Conventional troops in the highlands, where roads and supply lines were often nonexistent, "lived off the country" like guerrillas. Hungry soldiers ate the food of suspected enemies and suspected friends. To save the Union or save the Confederacy or simply to survive, neighbor had injured neighbor, injuries not healed by the Confederate surrender. The legendary feud between the "Hatfields and the McCoys" was just one example of the shattered unity of the highlands. Returning veterans ignited a smallpox epidemic.

Wil-Usdi/Thomas tried unsuccessfully to obtain state aid for the destitute; he brought in a doctor for the smallpox victims, but he was now bankrupt and was having doubts about having led his people into a disastrous war. At times, he lapsed into insanity. In 1869, he resigned the chieftaincy and spent his last years in a mental hospital. For all the service that the Cherokees rendered to Confederate North Carolina, state authorities were little impressed. In 1866, the legislature conceded their right to remain in the state but stopped short of granting them citizenship.[33] The Fourteenth Amendment to the U.S. Constitution made blacks citizens, but excepted "Indians not taxed," presumably those with tribal governments. Under the 1868 Radical Constitution of North Carolina, however, the Eastern Band did indeed pay taxes and vote, and continued to vote until 1900, when the state amended its Constitution to disfranchise both them and the blacks.[34]

The Lumbees: Indians Fight the Confederacy

The orientation of the Lumbees of southeastern North Carolina toward the Civil War, like that of other Native American peoples, was an outgrowth of their history. The origin of the Lumbees is wrapped in legend. The name "Lumbee," which did not come into general use until the twentieth century, derives from the Lumbee (sometimes "Lumber") River, which when it crosses into South Carolina becomes the Little Peedee. Historically they were concentrated in the swampy and relatively inaccessible area between the Cape Fear and the Great Peedee rivers. At first, European immigrants bypassed this region to settle more accessible land in the Piedmont. It was not until the 1760s that Highland Scots began to move into the area, where the small plots of productive land were fragmented by intervening swamps.[35] The inhabitants they found were "mixed-bloods" who spoke a distinctive type of English, were Christians, and generally had English family names.

Some have theorized that these might be, in part, the descendants of "John White's lost colony," an English settlement on Roanoke Island that disappeared mysteriously in the 1580s. Others have suggested that they were survivors of a series of smallpox epidemics that annihilated many Native American peoples in the seventeenth and eighteenth centuries.[36] As elsewhere, "mixed-bloods" more often survived these genocidal European diseases than "full-bloods." When entire tribes were all but annihilated, the remnants of different tribes sometimes consolidated. And since survivors spoke different languages but had long used English as a language of trade, it is plausible that a consolidated group would adopt English as their spoken language.[37] Gerald M. Sider has observed how, beginning in the seventeenth century,

> [n]ative peoples were moving into relatively isolated regions, especially swamps in the borderlands between different colonies, and taking up, at least superficially, Euro-American characteristics: European names; usually the English language; cabins of Euro-American design with horizontal rather than vertical logs; and some components of European agriculture, at first orchards and hog raising. This Europeanization of native peoples was not simply acculturation but the framework for social isolation—for being left alone, for being seen as neither Black nor Indian nor, in some profoundly ambiguous ways, White—an isolation revealed by the long-lasting separateness of many of these peoples who have endured as distinct groups until the present.
>
> It was a relatively successful strategy. The whole coastal plain from New Jersey southward to northern Florida and westward around the southern end of the Appalachians is dotted with these semi-separate groups, semi-hidden by their social and cultural quietness to all but local eyes. The Lumbee, in the most favorable location for this adaptation, are the most populous representatives of this general social form.[38]

A curious feature of the region was that for almost half of the nineteenth century, most whites spoke Gaelic whereas the natives spoke English. Since whites adopted English later, and a later form of English, a difference in speech continued to distinguish the two populations. More than a century later, speech is often a more reliable indication of one's "race" than is one's appearance.

The War for Independence, as in much of the backwoods South, exacerbated conflicts between ethnic groups. The Scottish Highlanders produced naval stores, and the British Crown subsidized their tar, pitch, and turpentine. In addition, their English-speaking gentry and clan leaders were often commissioned British officers receiving half pay. Overwhelmingly, Highlanders were Tories, while most of the natives sided with the Patriots. The result was eight years of bloodletting that was less about loyalty and liberty than about livestock herds and land. If the Treaty of Paris of 1783 settled differences between America and Great Britain, in the low country along the Lumbee, the blood feuds set in motion by the War for Independence continued for another half century.

In the nineteenth century, the level of violence remained high, but much of the conflict was now settled by the courts. Here, the Lumbees fared badly.[39] The county courts governed as well as settled important judicial disputes. They consisted of the justices of the peace, or the "squires," of the county. The governor appointed them for life, and they were always white. In property disputes with whites, Lumbees lost. Their fields grew smaller, their livestock herds shrank.[40] Lumbee families have traditions of whites planting stolen property on their land, then suing and taking their possessions in legal settlements.[41] For the Lumbees as for the Eastern Band of Cherokees, life became worse still with the adoption of the North Carolina Constitution of 1835, which stripped "people of color" of civil rights. It deprived nonwhites of the right to vote, and their testimony against a white person was not admissible in court.

With the coming of secession and war, Wilmington, a port eighty miles to the east of the Lumbees, near the mouth of the Cape Fear River, was of even greater strategic importance to the Confederacy than their "lifeline" railroad in eastern Tennessee defended by the Thomas Legion. Wilmington was the only port in the South that the Union blockade was unable to close. Cape Fear, at the mouth of the river, was well named. The constantly shifting shoal waters were treacherous for ships. But local Cape Fear pilots could guide blockade-runners through the shoals and elude the Union warships.[42] Not only did Wilmington receive the bulk of the Confederate war materials arriving from Europe, but it also had direct rail a connection with northern Virginia. Unlike any other port in the South, Wilmington could make these materials quickly available to Lee's forces. It was the headquarters of the Confederate navy and the home port of the state-of-the-art, British-built warships that attacked Union commerce.[43]

Confederate leaders recognized the strategic importance of Wilmington from the outset. During the Crimean War, their military engineers had gone to Russia to study new advances in fort construction. At the mouth of the Cape Fear, they began the most extensive engineering project that the

Confederacy ever carried out, a system of seven forts, the centerpiece of which was the mile-long Fort Fisher, with its electrically controlled minefields.[44]

The big problem was labor. At first, soldiers did much of the work. But soldiers were increasingly needed elsewhere. Also, the Confederacy hired free workers, paying them with Confederate money. As its value declined, however, wage labor became harder to find. Even worse, a yellow fever struck in 1862, killing some 10 percent of the people in the Wilmington area and precipitating the flight of countless others for higher and healthier ground.[45] Confederate leaders, thinking that the Union would strike the moment the epidemic lifted, pressed grimly forward with the project. They conscripted slaves and Lumbees.[46] When slaves died, their owners complained to the legislature. But there were no complaints when Lumbees died.

After 1863, the yellow fever epidemic subsided, but around the forts, misery continued. In reply to a resolution of the legislature about the harsh conditions in the labor camps, General Braxton Bragg made no effort to minimize the problem. He pointed out, however, that these conditions were not confined to slaves, but "to a great extent had been shared" by Confederate soldiers. Rations were too light for men engaged in heavy work; they were inadequately clad for winter, and they had to work in water when gathering sod and rafting timber.[47]

All suffered hardships, but the experience of conscripted Lumbees converted hardships into rage. To them, it must have appeared that they had at last reached the degradation toward which their people had been pressed for a century. Once independent farmers and herdsmen, they were now doing the work of slaves, yet their miseries were causing the authorities fewer concerns. Some fled the labor camps and returned home.

To avoid capture by the Confederate Home Guard, they began "lying out," living in secret camps where relatives brought them food. In the region along the Lumbee River, plantations were few, and the poor many. Others were also "lying out." There were the pro-Union Heroes of America, in North Carolina called the "red strings" because of a system of signals they used.[48] There were also Union soldiers who had escaped from a Confederate prison camp. Others "lying out" were escaped slaves and Confederate deserters. Local civilians brought them food and kept an eye out for the Home Guard.

For most of the war the swamp refugees were less resisting than hiding from the Confederates. But by 1864 such a survival strategy was becoming more and more difficult. There were too many men "lying out" and too few women growing corn. To make matters worse, Confederate currency was nearly worthless, and the government imposed the "tax in kind." The Home Guard now collected taxes in corn, rice, potatoes, smoked pork, and the like.[49] By the winter of 1864–65, the poor faced a famine.

Out of this crisis the Lowry Band emerged. The core of the group appears to have been four of the ten sons of Allen and Mary Cumbo Lowry, and others who were kinsmen or connected to the Lowrys by marriage. Had this Scottish-Tuscarora family been treated as "white," they might well have served the Confederacy, as did some Lumbees in South Carolina. But the abuse of workers at the forts, the conscription acts that exempted large slaveholders and men of wealth, the "tax in kind," and, finally, the heavyhanded searches by the Home Guard had turned many in the Lumbee River region against the Confederacy.

A contemporary white writer describes how the Lowrys and their supporters changed their survival tactics from subsisting on food provided by their desperately impoverished kin to subsisting on that exacted from prosperous neighbors:

> It is a notorious fact that the inhabitants of Scuffletown [which Indians called "the Settlement"] live for days with nothing to eat except Huckle Berry's [*sic*]; and in the winter season they have been known to live for days without anything whatsoever to eat. These Scuffletonians . . . regarded the [federal government] and its soldiers as their best friends, consequently they were more than proud when these escaped prisoners came amongst them to show them every attention they could and to entertain them as highly as possible. . . . The refusal of our state and Genl Govt [the Confederacy] . . . to accept them as soldiers produced feelings of bitterness . . . and aroused their feelings of enmity against their white neighbors who were their best friends.[50]

Also the escaped prisoners, "by reading and talking to" these Scuffletonians, "presented such pictures to their minds . . . to strengthen their feeling of friendship" toward the Lincoln government. The big problem was food. The Lumbees wishing

> to entertain them a little better than they were themselves accustomed to live . . . [they] determined to have meat to eat. Old Allen Lowry whose

guests these escaped prisoners were . . . sent his sons Henry Berry, Steve, & Bill to Mr. Barns' fields where his fattening hogs were . . . they killed two of the finest and carried them home.[51]

By the winter of 1864–65, the Lowry conflict was under way. The written accounts of this violence bristle with the hostility of state and local authorities. But this record also reveals that the poor of the region faced near starvation and that the Robin Hood tactics of the Lowry Band won them broad popular support among all three races. The Lowry movement became a unifying tradition and a focus of identity for the Lumbee people, who formed its core. Yet others were always involved. Besides the escaped Union prisoners, names that often appeared were those of the teenage Scot Zachariah McLaughlin; the black bricklayer George Applewhite; and the white schoolteacher, Amanda Nash, who cared for their wounded.

The newspapers reported the activities of the Lowery Band as if they were ordinary robbers. Yet details appear that do not fit that mold. When they raided the plantation of the rich widow Elizabeth Ann McNair, for example, they confiscated her wagons and horses to carry away provisions and to move a Union soldier, wounded in the raid. But the next morning they returned the wagons and horses to her.[52] When they robbed a planter, they sometimes left him with a receipt that exempted him from further seizures for a time. Their robberies had a class bias. A prospective victim could sometimes convince them that he could not afford to be robbed. They shared their booty with the poor of all three races.

Early in 1865, the Home Guard raided the homestead of Allen and Mary Cumbo Lowry. Among those they seized were William Lowry, presumed leader of the Lowry Band, and his parents. They convened a hurried "court-martial" and condemned to death William and his father, the elderly and widely respected patriarch, Allen. They formed a firing squad and executed the two men. After the execution, Mary took refuge in the home of her son Sinclair, a carpenter whom the authorities did not connect with the guerrillas. But three weeks latter, the Home Guard again found her. When she failed to give information about her other sons and their weapons caches, they bound her to a stake and blindfolded her, and the commander gave the command to fire. The fire was misdirected and intended to make her more cooperative. When the smoke cleared, she had fainted. They cut her bonds and revived her, but they still failed to exact any information about her sons or their weapons.[53]

After the capture and execution of William, the leadership of the band passed to the youngest of the ten Lowry brothers, the enigmatic and legendary Henry Berry. It is difficult to see why in a society where people normally deferred to age, the Lowry family and others accepted the leadership of a youth who was only about seventeen. It could have been his famous marksmanship and boldness. Another problem is his silence. Although years later, admirers would ascribe to him heroic speeches, written sources show that he rarely spoke. Yet he appears to have had an unusual charisma. A Presbyterian minister, held captive for a time by the band, described him as

> one of those remarkable executive spirits that arise now and again in a raw community, without advantages other [than those] nature gave him. He has passions, but no weaknesses and his eyes are on every point at once. . . . No man who stands face to face with him can resist his quiet will and assurance and his searching eye. Without fear, without hope, defying society, he is the only man we have knowledge of down here who can play his part.[54]

In March 1865, the forces of General William Tecumseh Sherman passed through Robeson County. This was no blessing for the Lowrys and other local Unionists. Their friends, the federal prisoners, departed with the Northern army. Sherman's forces "lived off the country" in a region already stressed to the point of famine. And knowing nothing of local politics, they had seized provisions and draft animals from Unionists and Confederates alike. Their depredations energized a fearful backlash against Unionists.

Even worse, the Reconstruction government set up by President Andrew Johnson restored at the local level virtually the same people who had held power under the Confederates. In Robeson County, the Home Guard became the County Militia and pursued the anti-Lowery war with renewed energy, attempting to convict them in court for hostile actions against the defeated Confederacy. Along the Lumbee River, the Civil War thus continued. When the Republicans came to power in 1868, they inherited a guerrilla war in Robeson County, which technically was no longer against the Confederates but against post–war civil authorities. Many, perhaps most, Republicans in the state accepted news accounts that depicted the Lowry Band as common criminals.

In Robeson County, where nonwhites and the white poor were numerous, the Republican Party won large majorities, but the party enjoyed more support than actual power. For one thing, the Reconstruction Constitution, to prevent local officeholders from absconding with public funds, required a substantial bond. But Republicans were poor and sometime could not provide the bond for officials they elected. They elected a sheriff, for example, but could not secure his bond, and the courts awarded the office to a member of the Conservative (later Democratic) Party.[55]

Even more, the local Republicans were divided over the Lowry Band. Most wanted to see a rule of law that would replace the violent seizures of property and summary executions that had prevailed. Other Republicans perceived that the legal system worked in favor of those who could afford lawyers and could negotiate out-of-court cash settlements. Thus Henderson Oxendine was captured, convicted, and hanged for Lowry Band crimes, but the men who had ridden first with the Home Guard, later with the County Militia, and now with the Ku Klux Klan were untouched by the law. For some, the best prospects for justice lay not in the courts but in the avenging weapons of the Lowrys. A black woman showed a Northern reporter that she had only two teeth left. When she was a slave, her master had knocked out the others "with an oak stick," and she added, "Oh dis was a hard country, and Henry Berry Lowry's jess a paying 'em back. He's only payin' 'em bac! It's better days for the black people now."[56]

Supporters of Henry Berry Lowry were also supporters of the Republican Party. But the band was an embarrassment to Republican leaders, who represented themselves as the defenders of law and order and pointed out the ties that their rivals, the Conservatives, had to the Ku Klux Klan. In 1870, when the Conservatives gained control of the legislature, they regarded the Lowry Band as the Republican equivalent to the Klan. Republican governor W.W. Holden, faced with impeachment, succumbed to Conservative pressure and called upon President U. S. Grant for Federal troops not to suppress the Klan, which was terrorizing a dozen Piedmont counties, but to suppress the Lowrys in Robeson County. On October 12, 1870, an artillery battery arrived in Lumberton to "aid the civil authority."[57] But the Conservatives expected more from the Federal troops. The editor of the *Wilmington Journal*, whose predecessor had headed the state Ku Klux Klan, wrote:

> We know the officer in command of the United States troops in Lumberton will do all he can, but he is powerless in a strange country without guides and without the sympathy and aid of every citizen. . . . If one company is insufficient, let a regiment be sent. If a regiment cannot do the work, let us have a brigade, and let the Scuffletown district be burned and devastated until not even a dry twig remains rather than the entire country suffer as it has done.[58]

But the Federal forces were under orders to prevent such an assault on the community.[59]

The Lowry Band benefited from a one-way flow of information. Sympathizers, including some conscripted into the militias that hunted them, kept them informed. Children sometimes served as Lowry scouts, keeping an eye on troop movements and getting word to the leaders by what was called the "grapevine telegraph." The one-way flow of information enabled them to carry out spectacular feats of defiance, appearing publicly at one place when the military was searching for them at another. If Henry Berry was a man of few words, he was a master of dramatic deeds that thrilled his supporters. When reports of guerrilla activity drew troops away from Lumberton to some distant point, the leaders of the band appeared at the county court and sat through the trials that were taking place. When the soldiers returned, they had vanished. The Lowry leaders often attended church. They once treated a congregation to the spectacle of seeing the state's most wanted men standing singing hymns side by side with one of the men who most wanted them. On another occasion they invited themselves to a family breakfast with a prominent planter who had been trying to capture them "dead or alive," causing him to violate Southern custom by sharing his table with guests of all three races.[60] They organized the escape of prisoners from the jail in Lumberton, and also in Wilmington, which was considered the most secure jail in the state.

Finally, the North Carolina legislature placed large bounties on the heads of Henry Berry and his principal lieutenants. Yet even though the Lumbee River region was desperately poor, these offers did not produce results for a considerable time. When the legislature raised its offer for Henry Berry from $10,000 to $12,000, the highest bounty that the state had ever offered, he responded characteristically not with words but with a deed. Within the week, when the Wilmington, Charlotte and Rutherford train stopped at the Moss Neck station, the passengers were astounded to see the famous outlaw standing on the platform surrounded by a crowd of friends. But they had not come to rob the train. They had brought a barrel of cider and treated the passengers to drinks.[61]

In the end the princely rewards worked. By 1874, all the outlaws either had been assassinated or had disappeared. The bounty on the head of the black leader, George Applewhite, went uncollected. There is evidence that he escaped and returned to his trade as a bricklayer. Nor did anyone ever collect the even larger reward for Henry Berry. The man who appeared and disappeared many times never reappeared in public after February 1872. Despite an abundance of stories giving vivid details about how he was killed or how he survived, he seems to have vanished into hearsay. Out of a Civil War struggle against forced labor and famine, the Lowry Band forged a heroic legend, a wealth of lore that has inspired history and fiction.[62]

In the eighteenth century, the remnants of the native peoples decimated by European diseases and weapons had been forced to consolidate, some by joining what was left of a surviving tribe, such as the Catawbas. Others consolidated by forming a new group, the Lumbees. Like the tradition of "White's lost colony," the folk memory of the Lowry Band has contributed to this unifying process. Today more than 50,000 people identify themselves as Lumbees, and near the heart of that identity is the towering image of Henry Berry Lowry.

The Lowry Band disappeared, but they left behind an empowering legacy. In 1900, the white supremacist tide that had swept the South, indeed the nation, disfranchised both the blacks and the Eastern Band of Cherokees. But the Lumbees continued to vote. And they remembered the deeds of their ancestors. In 1870, Henry Berry had assassinated the local leader of the Ku Klux Klan. In 1957, when the reconstituted Klan attempted to reorganize in Robeson County, the Lumbees armed. The showdown came in the "battle of Maxton field," a near-bloodless shootout that once again drove the Klan from the county.[63] These are traditions that give Lumbees the sense of being a distinct people.

Accommodation or Resistance?

Native Americans were besieged by overwhelming forces; thus, neither accommodation nor resistance could in the end win. The experience of the Cherokees and the Lumbees suggests, however, that resistance offered better prospects than accommodation for cutting one's losses. In 1835, had the Cherokees closed ranks behind the large Nationalist Party, they certainly would have lost their valuable plantation lands and gold fields, but they might have consolidated most of their nation in their ancestral highlands.[64] Instead, in 1835 and again in 1860, the smaller pro-slavery Ridge Party tried to accommodate white planters. As a result, Cherokee killed Cherokee first in a blood feud and later in the Civil War. Still later, when the government opened the Cherokee treaty lands in the West to white settlers, Cherokees were in no position to resist.

The government granted the Eastern Band of Cherokees a small reservation in the Great Smokies, a grant that may owe more to the scant resources of those highlands than to the accommodation efforts of Chief Yonaguska and Usdi-Wil/Thomas. Their support for the planter cause in a land where planters were few shattered the unity of the highlands. A savage war set neighbor against neighbor, devastated the land, and left the Cherokee leadership torn by faction. The case of the Lumbees, on the other hand, is different. Like many Native Americans, they are disproportionately poor. But their resistance and tradition of resistance has enabled them to better overcome much of the degradation that they suffered at the time of the Civil War.

NOTES

1. In the Royal Proclamation of 1763, the British drew a line, roughly following the Appalachian Mountains, which established the western limits of white settlement.

2. Arsène Carrière Latour, *Historical Memoir of the War in West Florida and Louisiana, 1814–1815*, trans. H. P. Nugent (Philadelphia: John Conrad, 1816).

3. The holocaust of the Indians is often explained as an accidental result of their contact with settlers carrying Old World diseases to which Indians had little resistance. But there had been some white settlers in California for decades. Certain Indian deaths indeed may have come from Old World diseases, as there are reports of deliberate sales to Indians of smallpox-infested blankets.

4. Grant Foreman, *The Five Civilized Tribes* (Norman: University of Oklahoma Press, 1934).

5. Annie Heloise Abel, *The Slaveholding Indians*, 3 vols. (Cleveland: Arthur H. Clark, 1915–1925), 1:158–80; Theda Perdue, *Slavery and the Evolution of Cherokee Society* (Knoxville: University of Tennessee Press, 1979).

6. W. Craig Gaines, *The Confederate Cherokees: John Drew's Regiment of Mounted Rifles* (Baton Rouge: Louisiana State University Press, 1989), 3–4. It is "unfounded to suppose that Major Ridge & and others associated with him in their doing at New Echota, have been appointed by the General Council of the Cherokee Nation." Delegation of the General Council to Lewis Cass, U.S. Secretary of War, February 29, 1836, in *The Papers of Chief John Ross*, vol. 1, *1807–1839*; vol. 2, *1840–1866*, ed. Gary E. Moulton (Norman: University of Oklahoma Press, 1984), 1:389.

7. Stanley W. Hoig, *The Cherokees and Their Chiefs: In Wake of Empire* (Fayetteville: University of Arkansas Press, 1998), 171–72.

8. Ross to his nephew, William P. Ross, undated, c. June 1860, in *Papers of Chief John Ross*, 2:449; Laurence Hauptman, *Between Two Fires: American Indians in the Civil War* (New York: Free Press, 1995), 45–46; Gaines, *Cherokee Chiefs*, 21–22.

9. Virtually every year for a decade before the Civil War, "American adventurers would formulate schemes to invade, or actually invade some part of the Caribbean region." See Robert E. May, *Southern Dreams of a Caribbean Empire, 1854–1861* (Baton Rouge: Louisiana State University Press, 1973), 29.

10. Hauptman, *Between Two Fires*, 48; Brad R. Clampitt, "'An Indian Shall Not Spill an Indian's Blood': The Confederate Indian Conference at Camp Nelson," *Chronicles of Oklahoma* 83, no. 1 (2005): 36.

11. Hauptman, *Between Two Fires*, 48; Wilfred Knight, *Red Fox: Stand Watie and the Confederate Indian Nations during the Civil War Years in Indian Territory* (Glendale, CA: Arthur H. Clark, 1988), 65–66; Gary E. Moulton, *John Ross, Cherokee Chief* (Athens: University of Georgia Press, 1978), 172. See also Ross's "Annual Message," October 9, 1861, *Papers of Chief John Ross*, 2:492–95.

12. Hoig, *Cherokees and Their Chiefs*, 227; Moulton, *John Ross, Cherokee Chief*, 175.

13. Hauptman, *Between Two Fires*, 42.

14. John R. Finger, *The Eastern Band of Cherokees, 1819–1900* (Knoxville: University of Tennessee Press, 1984), 16.

15. Wil-Usdi may have influenced the creation of the fictional character "Wil," who from his youth interacted with the Cherokee people. See Charles Frazier, *Thirteen Moons: A Novel* (New York: Random House, 2006).

16. E. Stanley Godbold Jr. and Mattie U. Russell, *Confederate Colonel and Cherokee Chief: The Life of William Holland Thomas* (Knoxville: University of Tennessee Press, 1990), 35.

17. Ibid., 29.

18. North Carolina Constitution (1835), art. I, sec. 3, col. 3.

19. James Mooney, "Myths of the Cherokee," in *U.S. Nineteenth Annual Report of the Bureau of American Ethnology, 1897–98, Part 1* (Washington, DC: Government Printing Office, 1900), 11–578.

20. Godbold and Russell, *Confederate Colonel and Cherokee Chief,* 11, 20.

21. Ibid., 57, 59.

22. Ibid., 40, 78.

23. Ibid., 32.

24. Hauptman, *Between Two Fires,* 108–9.

25. Godbold and Russell, *Confederate Colonel and Cherokee Chief,* 97.

26. Sean Michael O'Brien, *Mountain Partisans: Guerrilla Warfare in the Southern Appalachians, 1861–1865* (Westport, CT: Praeger, 1999), xiv.

27. Noel C. Fisher, *War at Every Door: Partisan Politics and Guerrilla Violence in East Tennessee, 1860–1869* (Chapel Hill: University of North Carolina Press, 1997), 4, 42, 47, 55–56.

28. Finger, *Eastern Band of Cherokees,* 74, 85–86, 94.

29. Confederate States of America, *Statutes at Large,* 1862, chap. 45.

30. Finger, *Eastern Band of Cherokees,* 87–88. Confederate general Robert Tooms warned that the impressing agents have, "in many cases, robbed the families of their meager support . . . the soldiers . . . have become discontented and desertions have taken place." O'Brien, *Mountain Partisans,* xvi.

31. O'Brien, *Mountain Partisans,* xx.

32. Hauptman, *Between Two Fires,* 119; O'Brien, *Mountain Partisans,* 35. This episode appears out of character with Thomas's earlier life. At the end of the war, he was already suffering lapses of rationality, signs of his later mental illness.

33. Finger, *Eastern Band of Cherokees,* 98, 100–103.

34. Ibid., 174–75.

35. Duane Gilbert Meyer, *The Highland Scots of North Carolina, 1732–1776* (Chapel Hill: University of North Carolina Press, 1961); William McKee Evans, *To Die Game: The Story of the Lowry Band, Indian Guerrillas of Reconstruction* (Baton Rouge: Louisiana State University Press, 1971), 25–30.

36. The Catawba tribe, living just west of the "mixed-bloods" who became the Lumbees, survived as a tribe. But whereas in 1700, they had been able to count 1,500 fighting men, their leader, "King Haglar," reported that by about 1750 their number had been reduced to just 60. Alexander Gregg, *The History of the Old Cheraws . . .* (New York: Richardson and Co., 1867), 18–17. See also William L. Sauders, ed., *The Colonial Records of North Carolina* (Raleigh: State of North Carolina, 1886–90), 5:143, 581; 6:616. Perhaps because of their reduced numbers, the Catawba took in fragments of a number of Native American groups. See Douglas Summers Brown, *The Catawba Indians: The People of the River* (Columbia: University of South Carolina Press, 1966), 3–5; Charles M. Hudson, *The Catawba Nation* (Athens: University of Georgia Press, 1970), 46 and passim.

37. Karen I. Blu, *The Lumbee Problem: The Making of an American Indian People* (Lincoln: University of Nebraska Press, 1980), 44.

38. Gerald M. Sider, *Lumbee Indian Histories: Race, Ethnicity, and Indian Identity in the Southern United States* (Cambridge: Cambridge University Press, 1993), 243.

39. During the Revolution, many of the ancestors of the Lumbees fought on the winning side. Testifying before the Joint Congressional Committee Investigating Conditions in the Insurrectionary States, a Robeson County lawyer stated that some of them emerged from the conflict with substantial property, including slaves. But "they were indicted for violations of the law and were known as lawless men. . . . I think the last of their slaves were sold from them; I do not think they have owned any slaves within about thirty years." Quoted in Blu, *Lumbee Problem*, 50–51.

40. U.S. Bureau of Census, *Eighth Census of the United States* (1860), Free Population, North Carolina, XIII, Robeson County (unpublished reports in National Archives).

41. Gerald Marc Sider, "The Political History of the Lumbee Indians of Robeson County, North Carolina: A Case Study of Political Affiliations" (Ph.D. diss., New School for Social Research, 1970), 36.

42. Rod Gragg, *Confederate Goliath: The Battle of Fort Fisher* (New York: Harper-Collins, 1991), 4–12; William Mckee Evans, *Ballots and Fence Rails: Reconstruction on the Lower Cape Fear* (Chapel Hill: University of North Carolina Press, 1966), 3–5.

43. Evans, *Ballots and Fence Rails*, 3–4.

44. Gragg, *Confederate Goliath*, 21; John G. Barrett, *The Civil War in North Carolina* (Chapel Hill: University of North Carolina Press, 1963), 259.

45. Evans, *Ballots and Fence Rails*, 7; Barrett, *Civil War in North Carolina*, 259. A Wilmington resident remembered that on October 18, 1862, "there had been five hundred new cases in the past week and 150 interments. . . . The streets were entirely empty, nothing broke the sickly silence save the rolling sound of a hearse or the physicians' vehicles or, here and there, a solitary footfall." *Wilmington Review*, February 15, 1889.

46. Officially, conscripted "free people of color" worked for wages paid in Confederate money. Although by 1863 their "pay" had fallen to five cents a day hard money, army clerks continued to record "wages" paid to workers. These records include the family names of the large Lumbee clans. See U.S. War Department, Captured Confederate Records, Payrolls (RG 109, National Archives). See also anonymous manuscript on the origins of the Lowry Band among the papers of Colonel Francis Marion Wishart and in possession of his grandson Clifton Wishart, White Plains, New York, p. 6, hereafter Anonymous, "Origins of the Lowry Band." (This manuscript was treated as authoritative by Colonel Wishart, the best informed of the authorities attempting to hunt down the Lowry Band.)

47. Don Carlos Seitz, *Braxton Bragg: General of the Confederacy* (Columbia: SC State Co., 1924), 506–7.

48. O'Brien, *Mountain Partisans*, 23; Joseph Gregoire de Roulhac Hamilton, "The Heroes of America," *Publications of the Southern Historical Association* 11 (1907): 10–11 and passim.

49. Maud Thomas, *Away Down Home: A History of Robeson County, North Carolina* (Lumberton, NC: Historic Robeson, 1982), 116–17.

50. Anonymous, "Origins of the Lowry Band," 2–3.

51. Ibid., 3.

52. Evans, *To Die Game*, 44.

53. Ibid., 14–15, 50–51.

54. Quoted in George Alfred Townsend, comp., *The Swamp Outlaws* (New York: Robert M. De Witt, 1872), 14.

55. Evans, *To Die Game*, 136.

56. Townsend, *Swamp Outlaws*, 27.

57. Special Order 228, in U.S. War Department, Headquarters of Department of the East (RG 94, National Archives).

58. *Wilmington Journal,* January 15, 1871.

59. General Charles Hale Morgan to Captain Evan Thomas, February 17, 1871, in U.S. War Department, Records of the Army Command, Post of Lumberton (RG 393, National Archives).

60. Evans, *To Die Game*, 198.

61. Ibid., 207.

62. The outlaw chief was so elusive and left such a scant paper trail that he is a daunting subject for biography or even convincing fictional biography. In a task almost as difficult, a novelist has written a fictional biography of his wife, Rhoda Strong Lowry. See Josephine Humphreys, *Nowhere Else on Earth* (New York: Penguin, 2000).

63. *Lumberton Robesonian*, January 16, 1958; January 20, 1958; January 23, 1958; January 30, 1958; *Newsweek,* January 27, 1958, 27.

64. This is suggested by the contemporary Second Seminole War in the Florida Everglades. Political support in Washington was declining for a costly war to win land of little value.

THE AFRICAN AMERICAN STRUGGLE
FOR CITIZENSHIP RIGHTS IN
THE NORTHERN UNITED STATES
DURING THE CIVIL WAR

Joseph P. Reidy

B etween the Revolution and the Civil War, successive generations of Americans debated the meaning of citizenship. The vocabulary drew upon the legacy of the Revolution and similar struggles for national independence and republican government in the Atlantic world during the late eighteenth century and early nineteenth century. The language addressed both the broad relationship between citizens and governmental institutions and the specific rights and responsibilities of citizens, particularly the most cherished prize of republican citizenship, the elective franchise. Yet, given the strong association of the vote with property-owning white, male household heads, citizenship rights necessarily affected domestic as well as public institutions. Specifically, the concept that patriarchs virtually represented their dependents in public affairs both reflected and reinforced long-standing cultural prescriptions—including biblical ones—about proper household relationships. Although voting citizens decisively shaped the outcome of these discussions in the Revolutionary era, propertyless men, women, enslaved African Americans, Indians, and immigrants began to voice their aspirations in similar terms even before the founding of the Republic. By the dawn of the nineteenth century, citizens and noncitizens were well versed in the language of citizenship, even if not all could speak it fluently.[1]

Following Abraham Lincoln's election to the presidency in November 1860, the slaveholding states in the Deep South cast the accepted notions of citizenship into disarray by leaving the Union. Secession unilaterally annulled the existing relationship between the inhabitants of the seceded states and the national government in Washington. From its birth in February 1861, the Confederate States of America claimed their allegiance and expected the loyalty of citizens and noncitizens, voters and nonvoters alike. In the mobilizations that followed the outbreak of war between the United States and the Confederate States, the two national governments made unprecedented demands on their populations. In turn, citizens and noncitizens alike made claims on government institutions and public officials that quickly outgrew the antebellum concept of citizenship and its assorted manifestations. Persons of African ancestry especially desired to take advantage of the opportunities presented by the war.[2]

On the Northern side of the contest, President Lincoln's unprecedented call for 75,000 volunteers to suppress the rebellion—the pretext for the secession of the Upper South—and the subsequent suspension of habeas corpus and imposition of a military draft illustrate the ways in which the national government's relationship with its citizens changed. But even more significantly, the mere hint of slave emancipation threatened to undermine private property, a fundamental right of citizens under modern governments. Far more than a concept with implications for the Confederacy, emancipation would have direct implications for the United States, given that more than 425,000 slaves resided in the states that remained within the Union.[3] If slave property could be confiscated, what would prevent the government from confiscating any form of private property? Even more troubling, emancipation would destroy the domestic authority of the slaveholder-citizen over his dependent family members. If slaves could be freed from their masters, would wives and children be freed from their husbands and fathers?

Finally, if persons of African ancestry, whether free or enslaved, enfranchised or not, were mobilized in the fight to defeat the rebellion, what rights might those who served expect in return? The prior service of African American soldiers in the Revolutionary War and the War of 1812 served as vague precedents (and ones with little practical significance outside of New England), largely due to the vastly grander scale of the Civil War mobilization. By war's end, approximately 200,000 persons of African ancestry fought to save the Union and destroy slavery. They expected—indeed, demanded—the government to reward this loyalty by granting full and unqualified citizenship to black men and appropriate rights, privileges, and protections to all African Americans. Over the course of the war, government officials at both state and national levels contended with this demand, at times recognizing its legitimacy and at other times resisting it. Out of these interactions emerged a new understanding of citizenship that departed radically from everything that came before, despite the familiar rhetoric of freedom, democracy, and equality.[4]

On the eve of the Civil War, free African Americans in the Northern United States took neither freedom nor civic rights for granted. In addition to family ties that many shared with enslaved loved ones, they faced daily reminders of the Peculiar Institution's national reach and its lingering influence in the North. New York and New Jersey did not take steps to abolish slavery until the nineteenth century and even then enacted gradual emancipation, such that as late as 1850 more than 200 persons were held as slaves in New Jersey, and in 1860, 18 of that number remained "Colored apprentices for life by the act to abolish slavery passed April 18, 1846," according to the official census report.[5] Laws in the various Northern states restricted access to the suffrage, to the courts, and to the publicly funded schools. Several states also required payment of security bonds or special taxes. The exceptions to this rule, such as black manhood suffrage in several New England states, grew out of historical circumstances not present in other regions, particularly the old Northwest Territory.[6]

Private individuals and businesses reinforced the pattern of second-class treatment that state and local governments prescribed. "We are oppressed everywhere in this slavery-cursed land," observed John S. Rock, an abolitionist attorney in Massachusetts; "while colored men have many rights, they have few privileges here." Reflecting on the deplorable state of available housing in Boston, Rock noted "We are colonized," an image fraught with irony in the cradle of liberty.[7] During the 1850s, federal legislation added new weight to the burden of inequality. The Fugitive Slave Act of 1850 threatened the liberty of all African Americans, and the infamous Dred Scott decision of 1857 declared that they had no rights that a white man was bound to respect.[8]

Besides these legal and customary restrictions, black Northerners were also enmeshed in networks of relationships based on kinship, geography, and voluntary association that bound individuals with families and families with communities. The resulting social and psychological ties could be both liberating and restricting. In many areas, white patronage figured prominently in these relationships. The families of former slaves often remained linked with those of their former masters for years, if not generations. One African

American frankly acknowledged "a strong attachment to the whites with whom our blood has been commingling from the earliest days of this country." [9] Despite these potentially restrictive aspects, attachments to family and community provided a buffer against the notion of atomized individualism that was gaining popularity in nineteenth-century America.

Within African American communities, personal relationships and community organizations provided both needed social services and a structure for the development of skills and tactics in the cause of equal rights. These organizations constituted the backbone of the state and regional networks that joined the national debates over slavery and citizenship initiated by the abolitionist movement and the state convention movement of black men. African Americans throughout the North took a spirited interest in the political issues of the day. They subscribed to William Lloyd Garrison's *Liberator*, Frederick Douglass's *North Star*, the African Methodist Episcopal Church's *Christian Recorder*, and other antislavery publications. They attended abolitionist lectures and sheltered fugitives from bondage. They retained an intense interest in the individual and collective rights of African-descended people and in the future of the American republic.

Despite the local emphasis of these issues, the abolitionist and state convention movements provided the seedbed for an increasingly sophisticated national campaign for manhood suffrage as the embodiment of civic equality. Men from all backgrounds and states desired the suffrage as a means of establishing an equal footing with all other men in controlling the machinery of self-government and safeguarding their dependent wives and children. Indeed, the rhetoric African American men employed to achieve equal citizenship drew upon patriarchal imagery to suggest that they could not properly support and protect their domestic charges without political equality. If anything, men of humbler circumstances felt even more strongly about their patriarchal rights and responsibilities than did their counterparts from the middle class.[10] The Civil War provided an opportunity to advance these objectives. Several months after Fort Sumter, the editor of the *Weekly Anglo-African* reflected on "What We Are Fighting For"; besides life, liberty, and the pursuit of happiness, he specified the right "to our wives and little ones."[11]

As scholars of the civil rights movement of the twentieth century have discovered, both the objectives of the struggle and its ultimate success depended on leaders and actors with firm roots in specific communities.[12] The struggle for citizenship rights in the Civil War era followed a similar pattern, in large part because the essence of nineteenth-century citizenship had local implications that were at least as significant as the national ones. Until the landmark federal legislation of the post–Civil War era—particularly the Civil Rights Act (1866) and the Fourteenth Amendment (1868) and Fifteenth Amendment (1870)—state legislatures controlled those aspects of citizenship most meaningful in the lives of their inhabitants, not least of which were the criteria for voting.[13] While not obviating the need for a national agenda and leaders to advance it, this reality required locally grounded leaders with a keen awareness of opportunities and obstacles at the state and local levels.

For all their powers of insight, the chief contemporary spokesmen of African American Northerners did not always acknowledge this complex reality. Indeed, many enjoyed considerable personal freedom and, by virtue of their mobility, attenuated ties to specific local communities. Furthermore, their adherence to Protestant Christianity's emphasis on individual rights and responsibilities and their involvement in the antislavery movement (and the related social movements influenced by the Second Great Awakening) reinforced those tendencies. Secular manifestations of this cultural influence— the popular image of the "self-made man," for instance—celebrated making a mark on the world through business or the professions, and numerous African American men did so during the antebellum era despite the obstacles and the odds. The most prominent African American personality of the time, Frederick Douglass, referred to himself as "in some sense a 'self-made man.'"[14] African American leaders traveled in circles of self-made men who were their friends and role models, even if at times also their rivals.

Applauding human ambition did not necessarily deny the abiding hand of God in human affairs. As the clouds of war gathered, African American Northerners viewed unfolding events as a providential intervention against slavery and racial discrimination. The apocalyptic nature of the war and the similarities between the African American predicament and that of the children of Israel provided strong religious moorings for the cause of emancipation and equal rights. For example, resolutions from a meeting of the Genesee Conference of the African Methodist Episcopal Zion Church, held in Binghamton, New York, in September 1863, characterized the military contest as "a holy war, because it is God's war; for it is really a righteous visitation of the provoked wrath of Him who has said, 'I will remember their iniquities against them,' and who has promised that Ethiopia should stretch forth her hands . . . without the galling yoke of slavery, but free to act and worship God according to the dictates of an enlightened conscience."[15]

Besides this religious sentiment, commentators also reflected the secular spirit of the nineteenth century. Like their white counterparts, many black observers likened the Civil War to a revolution, frequently coupling that analogy with the axiom that "revolutions never go backward," as Frederick Douglass did in May 1861.[16] Two years later, Sattira A. Douglas, a Chicago abolitionist, observed, "This revolution, like all others is to act as a national purifier. We are now undergoing a process of fermentation, and all those false and unwholesome theories which have and do possess the American mind in regard to the relation which the colored race is to sustain towards the other nations of the world, are to work to the surface and pass off." [17] Others noted the apparent compression of time during the war. "Every day," observed John S. Rock in October 1864, "seems almost to be an era in the history of our country."[18] Buoyed by the progressive spirit of the age, these leaders also strove to advance it. "The world must know we are here, and that we have aims, objects and interests in the present great struggle," argued Alfred M. Green, an antislavery activist from Philadelphia. "Without this we will be left a hundred years behind this gigantic age of human progress and development."[19] The war uncoupled the struggle for emancipation and civic equality from conventional time and presented a chance to overcome centuries of past wrongs in the blink of an eye.

Whether of biblical or secular bent or some combination of the two, progressives implicitly believed that freedom and equality would thoroughly vanquish slavery and discrimination. Others hedged their bets, fearful that the United States would never live up to its egalitarian rhetoric. This skepticism took several forms, but perhaps none as significant as the recurring interest in emigration. For all its unattractive connections to pro-slavery politics, emigrationism had strong roots. The notion of repatriation to the distant homeland, however realistic or fanciful, engaged African Americans no less than other diasporic communities. Yet from early in the nineteenth century, and particularly from the founding of the American Colonization Society in 1816, most black leaders condemned African emigration as at best a foolish scheme designed to distract attention from the quest for equality in the United States and at worst a racist plot. Although these leaders sometimes endorsed migration to Canada as an antidote to the imperfect freedom of the Northern states, they staunchly opposed settlement to distant lands, whether across the Atlantic Ocean or the Gulf of Mexico. This opposition eased somewhat during the 1850s with the rise of prominent advocates of Africa such as H. Ford Douglas and Martin R. Delany.[20] Over the course of the nineteenth century, African emigrationist sentiment ebbed and flowed as the prospects of realizing life, liberty, and the pursuit of happiness in the United States alternately waxed and waned.

President Lincoln's reluctance to declare war on slavery from the start of hostilities prompted renewed interest in emigration. In September 1861, for instance, the editors of the New York *Weekly Anglo-African* noted that "many of our readers would like to be well informed in regard to the actual condition of Hayti," and pledged to provide information.[21] The president's own support for removing liberated slaves from the United States, best exemplified in his plans for a settlement in Chiriqui, Central America, in the summer of 1862, first fanned this interest but ultimately stifled it. The prominent black abolitionist George B. Vashon, who had lived for a time in Haiti, acknowledged that

Liberia, with the bright and continually growing promise for the regeneration of Africa, will allure many a colored man to the shores of the motherland. Haiti, with her proud boast, that, she alone, can present an instance in the history of the world, of a horde of despised bondmen becoming a nation of triumphant freemen, will by her gracious invitation, induce many a dark hued native in the United States to go and aid in developing the treasures stored away in her sun-crested hills and smiling savannahs. And, Central America, lying in that belt of empire, which Destiny seems to promise to the blended races of the earth, will, no doubt, either with or without federal patronage, become the abiding place of a population made up, in great measure, of persons who will have taken refuge there from the oppression which they had been called upon to undergo in this country.[22]

Vashon's ultimate goal, however, was to challenge Lincoln's plan: victory depended on mobilizing black soldiers to reinforce "our heart-stricken armies" and emancipating the slaves, not on exiling the sons and daughters of Africa.[23] Pressing Vashon's suggestion one step further, black Philadelphians advocated "giving the four millions of slaves their freedom, and the land now possessed by their masters."[24] After Lincoln issued the Emancipation Proclamation, colonization and emigration sentiment went dormant, not to awake again until after the war when the prospects for meaningful social change grew dim under Andrew Johnson's presidency.

Although impatient with President Lincoln's refusal to declare slavery the root cause of the nation's woes, many African American Northerners also trusted that a strong display of patriotism would help to change his mind. Even before the first shots, black men from various Northern states began making the case for African American participation in the impending conflict. Following the president's call for troops to suppress the rebellion, small numbers managed to enlist in the volunteer regiments organized in the various Northern states; although some faced opposition, others served with the tacit consent of their officers and comrades.[25] In small towns and large cities across the North, black men formed militia units and began training for war. They wrote to officials in Washington and the various state capitals offering their services in suppressing the rebellion. The letters stressed the significance of the struggle to African Americans, their historic loyalty to the United States, and their willingness to make every sacrifice for the Union. At a time when national leaders saw at best only an indirect connection between slavery and the war, African American Northerners believed that a Confederate victory would nationalize slavery. Meunomennie L. Miami, a man of mixed ancestry who had enlisted in a white volunteer regiment from Connecticut, cautioned his wife that if the Confederacy prevailed, "then you may bid farewell to all liberty thereafter and either be driven to a foreign land or held in slavery here."[26] Preventing such an outcome required the full participation of black men in the armed forces of the United States.

In May 1861, an anonymous writer in Boston reported that "as in revolutionary times—in the times of old Sam Adams, and of Crispus Attucks the black," the blood of the black man "boils, ready to flow" in defense of the country, asking "only for his rights as an equal fellow-countryman."[27] W. T. Boyd and J. T. Alston of Cleveland, Ohio, wrote in November 1861 on behalf of other "Colard men, (legal voters)" from Ohio, who desired the "priverlige of fighting—and (if need be dieing) to suport those in office who are our own choise."[28] From Pittsburgh came an offer from the captain of the Fort Pitt Cadets, a black militia company formed in 1860, to furnish 200 "able-bodied" men "of unquestionable loyalty to the United States of America."²⁹ The Reverend Garland H. White, the former body servant of Georgia senator Robert Toombs, who had escaped from slavery and was "stoping in canada for awhile" in the hope of eventually returning home, echoed the sentiment. White offered the services of men willing "to serve as soldiers in the southern parts during the summer season or longer if required. our offer is not for speculation or self interest but for our love for the north & the government at large, & at the same time we pray god that the triumph of the north & restoration of peace if I may call it will prove an eternal overthrow of the institution of slavery which is the cause of all our trouble."³⁰ Abolitionists such as Frederick Douglass also pressed the case, viewing the war as the opportunity for which the antislavery movement had labored for decades. Notwithstanding these appeals, the government moved haltingly toward employing African Americans in any capacity, much less as soldiers. Officials in Washington and the various Northern states assumed that either free men of African ancestry had no interest in the outcome or, even if they did, the whites-only provision of the Militia Act of 1792 precluded them from bearing arms in the nation's defense.³¹ Such logic flatly denied the connections between the war and slavery and between military service and citizenship rights that African Americans took for granted.

Lincoln's Preliminary Emancipation Proclamation of September 1862 signaled the clear emergence of emancipation as a federal war aim. The Confiscation Acts of 1861 and 1862, as well as the Militia Act of 1862, employed increasingly clear language to the effect that the Union's military and political strategists intended to employ African American manpower in the struggle against secession. In November 1862, in a momentous opinion that overturned the Dred Scott decision and undercut the proscriptions of the Militia Act of 1792, U.S. attorney general Edward Bates ruled that free persons of African descent were citizens.³² Insofar as the final Emancipation Proclamation of January 1, 1863, authorized the unqualified employment of blacks in suppressing the rebellion, African American leaders pressed the case for enlistment with renewed vigor. In an editorial in the *Weekly Anglo-African*, Robert Hamilton exhorted: "Let us organize one regiment in every large northern city, and send our offer of services directly to the President or the Secretary of War. We have been pronounced citizens by the highest legal authority, why should we not share in the perils of citizenship? What better field to claim our rights than the field of battle? . . . A century may elapse before another opportunity shall be afforded for reclaiming and holding our withheld rights."[33]

In a similar vein, Sattira Douglas encouraged black men to enlist, predicting that "now is offered the only opportunity that will be extended, during the present generation, for colored men to strike the blow that will at once relieve them of northern prejudice and southern slavery."[34] "If our government succeeds," Meunomennie Miami assured his wife, "then your and our race will be free. The government has torn down the only barrier that existed against us as a people. When slavery passes away, the prejudices that belonged to it must follow."[35] In July 1863, a convention of colored men meeting in New York to promote the enlistment of black men adopted resolutions that, among other things, placed the struggle in world-historical terms. U.S. soldiers, they observed, "are not contending for a party, nor for the spoils of war, but Empire—for universal Human Right and Liberty—to maintain intact the heritage bequeathed to the ages by the men of '76; to make this continent in very truth the same refuge for the oppressed of all lands in spite of caste, complexional differences, wealth, poverty, sect, or creed."[36]

Progressive Northern politicians, led by Massachusetts governor John A. Andrew, also viewed the Emancipation Proclamation as the dawn of a new day with regard to enlisting black soldiers and began recruiting black volunteers to serve in separate regiments commanded by white officers. Andrew did so with the express assurances from Washington officials that the men would be treated equally. In a letter to George T. Downing, a prominent African American caterer from Rhode Island, Andrew assured that black soldiers would be on exactly the same footing as all other volunteers: "Their present acceptance and muster-in, as soldiers, pledges the honor of the Nation in the same degree and to the same rights with all other troops. They will be soldiers of the Union—nothing less and nothing different."[37]

Within a matter of months Andrew's pledge came undone, and black soldiers contended with military and government officials as well as the Confederate enemy. By not removing the legal and administrative marks of inequality, the government compromised its claim to the full allegiance of the men. In organizing to achieve equality, the men and their allies employed the language of citizenship and its emphasis on reciprocal rights and responsibilities to make their case. They learned valuable strategic and tactical lessons from the campaign. The quest for equal pay, for example, united soldiers, their loved ones, abolitionists, and elected officials in a concerted effort to force Congress to change the provisions of the Militia Act of 1862 whereby black soldiers were paid at approximately half the rate of white soldiers. James Henry Gooding, a corporal in the 54th Massachusetts Volunteers and an eloquent partisan of equality, wrote to President Lincoln in September 1863, begging pardon for "the presumption of an humble individual like myself, in addressing you, but the earnest Solicitation of my Comrades in Arms, besides the genuine interest felt by myself in the matter is my excuse, for placing before the Executive head of the Nation our Common Grievance." In setting forth the case for equal pay, Gooding cited the loyalty and steadfastness of the black volunteers: "Obedient and patient, and Solid as a wall are they." Gooding assured the president that his intercession would give new life to their patriotism despite "the evident apathy displayed in our behalf." Identifying the central dilemma that inferior pay posed for the men, he concluded: "We feel as though, our Country spurned us, now we are sworn to serve her."[38] Stephen A. Swails, a sergeant in the 54th Massachusetts Volunteers, wrote to the adjutant general of the army in early 1864, claiming that he had enlisted under the expectation of equality with regular army troops, particularly with regard to pay and allowances. From the time of his enlistment, he had "performed the duty of a soldier, and . . . fulfilled my part of the contract with the Government." But because the government "failed to fulfill its part of the agreement, in as much as it refuses me the pay, and allowances of a Sergeant of the regular Army," Swails demanded a discharge.[39] In protest against the government's policy, the black volunteers from Massachusetts refused to accept the offer of inferior pay, and men from other units of colored troops engaged in similar protests.

By the summer of 1864, as the resultant hardships intensified, men in the 55th Massachusetts Volunteers put a sharper point on their quest for justice. Writing to President Lincoln, they noted that they had spurned the offer of the state of Massachusetts to "make up all Deficiencys which the general Government Refused to Pay" on the grounds that "the Troops in the general service are not Paid Partly By Government & Partly By State." But they also claimed the higher ground of principle: "To us money is no object we came to fight For Liberty justice & Equality. These are gifts we Prise more Highly than Gold For these We Left our Homes our Famileys Friends & Relatives most Dear to take as it ware our Lives in our Hands To Do Battle for

God & Liberty." In light of their obvious enlistment "under False Pretense," they demanded "our Pay from the Date of our inlistment & our immediate Discharge."[40]

In pursuing equality, black soldiers came to articulate a relationship with the federal government that superseded their relationship with the states from which they had enlisted. If at times they used the language of contracts to enumerate the rights and responsibilities of the respective parties, they increasingly situated their claims within the framework of citizenship. The struggle for fair treatment in the army planted the seed for the concept of national citizenship, which flowered after the war in the landmark legislation of the Reconstruction period.

The Confederacy's mistreatment of captured black soldiers also helped advance the sense of national citizenship. A number of reports of summary executions of black men, often by hanging, had reached Union lines even before the widespread press coverage of the assault on Battery Wagner by the 54th Massachusetts Infantry in July 1863 made the practice a rallying cry among white as well as black Northerners. Indeed, orders by high officials in the Confederate government authorized the enslavement of captured black soldiers and sailors even if not their summary execution. After months of considering an appropriate response, in July 1863 President Lincoln at last prescribed retaliation for the mistreatment of captives, but the order was not enforced. An anonymous black sailor in the South Atlantic Blockading Squadron reported that his comrades considered the government's unwillingness to retaliate "a burning shame." "If protection is not guaranteed, if the authorities do not intend taking any notice of these acts committed by these ruffian murderers as they are in every sense of the word, why then they cannot expect us to fight for the flag."[41]

Hannah Johnson of Buffalo, New York, wrote to Lincoln expressing her concerns over the reported ill-treatment of captured black soldiers. Her son served in the 54th Massachusetts Volunteers, she reported, and had "fought at Fort Wagoner but thank God was not taken prisoner, as many were." Only the assurances (from friends apparently) that "Mr. Lincoln will never let them sell our colored soldiers for slaves" overcame her misgivings about letting her son enlist. In light of the alleged abuses, she asked: "Now Mr Lincoln dont you think you oght to stop this thing and make them do the same by the colored men?" She urged the president not to fear the appearance of cruelty, for "a just man must do hard things sometimes, that shew him to be a great man." "Will you see that the colored men fighting now, are fairly treated," she asked. "You oght to do this, and do it at once, Not let the thing run along meet it quickly and manfully, and stop this, mean cowardly cruelty. We poor oppressed ones, appeal to you, and ask fair play."[42]

Black soldiers from throughout the North took the lead in opposing every manifestation of inequality in military service. "We came out to be true union soldiers the Grandsons of Mother Africa Never to Flinch from Duty," noted three soldiers in the New York–raised 20th U.S. Colored Infantry in making the case for equal treatment.[43] An anonymous black soldier from Maryland expressed a similar view: "We have come out Like men & we Expected to be Treeated as men but we have bin Treeated more Like Dogs then men. . . . [I] Supose that because we are colored that they think that we Dont no any Better. . . . [I]f we Ever Expect to be a Pepple & if we Dont Reply to some one of a thourety we Shall for Ever be Troden Down under foot of man."[44] By 1864, soldiers increasingly viewed the right of suffrage as both a fitting reward for their sacrifices and an indispensable safeguard for African American interests.

The closely contested presidential contest of fall 1864 played an unexpected part in galvanizing interest in the suffrage. Working closely with military officers intent upon securing Lincoln's reelection, Republican political operatives took pains to record the votes of soldiers, often with complete disregard for the voter's complexion and other particular circumstances. A private in the 20th U.S. Colored Infantry had the opportunity "as a freehold cittizon of the state of New York to cast my vote on a ritten form for that purpose for the first time for the candidate of my choice," even while under arrest in a military prison.[45] For formerly enslaved as well as formerly free black soldiers, the 1864 election made palpably clear the importance of the elective franchise in the political future of the nation.

The soldiers' demands upon the federal government for full citizenship ran fast into the principle of federalism whereby individual states had jurisdiction over most of the associated rights and privileges. In fact, black leaders had pursued a strategy of pressing state governments for their rights during the antebellum period, but for the first year of the war they minimized agitation along these lines. By 1862, however, they resumed the struggle, hoping that the political leaders and voting populations of the various Northern states had begun to understand the link between slavery, the war, and abridged citizenship rights of African Americans.

In perhaps the most notable of the state-level campaigns for civic equality, black men in Illinois agitated for the repeal of the infamous black code, originally enacted when the territory achieved statehood in 1839. Among other things, the code required black newcomers to the state to register and post a hefty bond to assure that they would not become a public burden. The code also disqualified them from the suffrage and denied access to various public services such as schools. Energized by the successful incorporation of Colored Troops into the war against slavery, veterans of the prewar convention movement and of the mobilization of black soldiers aimed to demolish these invidious distinctions. John Jones, a wealthy Chicago property owner, who had been born a slave in Tennessee and had worked with Frederick Douglass and Martin R. Delany in recruiting men to serve in black regiments, led the effort to persuade the governor and the state legislature to repeal the code. While humbly petitioning those officials, Jones laid claim to the rights all Americans enjoyed. In February 1865, the legislature responded favorably to the campaign and repealed the black code.[46] In Indiana, a similar campaign achieved success in early 1866.[47]

In Iowa, a coalition of white and black Republicans had by the start of the war been gaining ground in their effort to repeal the territorial black code and its odious provision excluding black persons from settling in the state. The events of the war added new momentum. Specifically, under the auspices of the Union army's effort to relocate contrabands from Arkansas to the states of the upper Midwest, a former slave who settled in Iowa was arrested early in 1863 for violating the law. With legal representation, he contested the constitutionality of the law and won. As the case awaited appeal to the state supreme court, the state legislature lifted the ban against black settlement.[48]

The campaign for equal rights in California followed a similar pattern. From the mid-1850s, black Californians had organized to repeal the state's discriminatory legislation, particularly the law prohibiting black persons from testifying in court cases involving white persons. Like similar campaigns in other Northern states, the organizers targeted the state legislature, appealing, as one leader explained, "to the hearts and consciences of our rulers, not to their passions and prejudices" and "to their sense of right and justice, not to their feelings of pity and commiseration."[49] In 1863 the legislature capitulated, opening the courts to black testimony.

In Philadelphia, the chronicler of the Underground Railroad, William Still, helped lead a campaign for unrestricted access to the privately operated streetcars that provided public transportation.[50] As early as 1862, a committee submitted a petition to the board of presidents of the city passenger railroads bearing the signatures of "three hundred and sixty highly respectable citizens of Philadelphia, praying that the rules indiscriminately excluding colored people from the inside of the cars be rescinded." When, after two more years, the board had taken no action, the committee reissued the plea, arguing that exclusion caused "very serious inconveniences and hardships" and observing that Philadelphia, alone among "the principal Northern cities," observed the discriminatory practice. "Why then," they asked, "should they be excluded in Philadelphia, in a city standing so preeminently high for its Benevolence, Liberality, Love and Freedom and Christianity, as the City of Brotherly Love?"[51] The leaders pursued a number of tactics, including public meetings, negotiations with the streetcar companies, and court action. By late 1864, several of the companies began offering separate "negro cars," which some black Philadelphians celebrated as "a stepping-stone" to unrestricted access, according to one observer.[52] Wishing to assure continuing progress, organizers went to court after a conductor removed a black woman from a car and in late 1866 received a favorable judgment. Building upon that victory, organizers applied the strategy of their counterparts in Illinois to lobby the state legislature for a legal prohibition against racial discrimination in public transportation. In March 1867, state leaders approved the legislation, but a second court case was necessary to bring the streetcar companies into compliance.[53]

The complexity of individual circumstances created some dissent in the pursuit of equal rights, and black leaders of the Civil War era proved no more adept at resolving these contradictions than have leaders of popular movements in other times and places. Specifically, activists on behalf of integrating such private businesses as barbershops and restaurants frequently met resistance from the African American proprietors and workers. In Cleveland, Ohio, for example, barbers rejected the plea of black leaders that they serve customers "without respect to caste or color." Given their dependence on white patronage, the barbers feared a backlash that would leave "them and their families to starve." In light of the barbers' unwillingness to capitulate, a mass meeting resolved to "discountenance all persons who make color a mark of distinction."[54] Similar encounters in Pennsylvania prompted a resolution at a state convention condemning the actions of "all proprietors of barber shops, restaurants and other places of business kept by colored men who exclude people of their own complexion from privileges they extend to white men."[55]

The race riots in Detroit and New York in the spring and summer of 1863 underscored the importance of full citizenship rights as a shield against popular reactions to emancipation and equality, particularly on the part of Irish immigrants.[56] In light of these events, Robert Hamilton of the New York *Weekly Anglo-African* demanded "immediate emancipation with affranchisement," denouncing what he described as "gradual emancipation," that is, "the process which the blacks have been undergoing in the so-called free States for the last fifty years." "With the name, and some of the privileges of freemen," he argued, "we have been, and are still undergoing, the oscillating process of gradual emancipation—today decked with laurels for the well-won victory, and tomorrow, hung at the lamppost because we are not white."[57]

By 1864 a consensus had emerged among soldiers and civilians alike that voting rights held the key to the political future. The premier expression of this sentiment was the National Equal Rights League, formed in Syracuse, New York, in October 1864. John S. Rock summarized the purpose of the league succinctly: "All we ask is equal opportunities and equal rights."[58] Agitation for the suffrage as the chief symbol of equality spread throughout the Northern states and Union-occupied areas of the Confederacy, such as Louisiana and Tennessee. Louisiana freemen pressed state-level leaders and Lincoln himself for the vote, and by the spring of 1864 the president had begun considering qualified suffrage for black veterans.[59] A convention of colored men meeting in Nashville, Tennessee, in January 1865, built the case for equal rights on the foundation of black military service. The delegates claimed devotion "to the principles of justice, of love to all men, and of equal rights on which our Government is based, and which make it the hope of the world." They continued:

> We know the burdens of citizenship, and are ready to bear them. We know the duties of the good citizen, and are ready to perform them cheerfully, and would ask to be put in a position in which we can discharge them more effectually. We do not ask for the privilege of citizenship, wishing to shun the obligations imposed by it.

Near 200,000 of our brethren are to-day performing military duty in the ranks of the Union army. Thousands of them have already died in battle, or perished by a cruel martyrdom for the sake of the Union, and we are ready and willing to sacrifice more. But what higher order of citizen is there than the soldier? or who has a greater trust confided to his hands? If we are called on to do military duty against the rebel armies in the field, why should we be denied the privilege of voting against rebel citizens at the ballot-box? The latter is as necessary to save the Government as the former.[60]

Following the Syracuse convention of the National Equal Rights League, affiliates in the various Northern states jointly pressed the case for civil and political rights.[61]

Like their counterparts in Nashville, delegates to the Pennsylvania state equal rights convention of February 1865 claimed full citizenship as the reward for the service of black troops. John Q. Allen of Philadelphia "hoped that the blood of the Negro, shed upon the fields of this rebellion, would prove sufficient to wash away the obstacles which prevent us from the enjoyment of our political rights," and Aaron Still of Reading argued "that there was some equivalent due to the black man for his life and services, and that we should exert ourselves to receive it."[62] In pressing specifically for the state legislature to overturn the constitutional provision of 1838 that had disfranchised African American voters on the premise that they were not citizens, they cited Attorney General Edward Bates's 1862 opinion that African Americans born in the United States were citizens. By virtue of "the proofs of determined manhood and loyalty manifested by Colored men of Pennsylvania, during the course of the existing unholy rebellion, in defence both of the State and of the Union," they demanded "immediate action in the premises." "Remember," they cautioned, "that your memorialists do not ask for favors. They claim rights."[63] Resolutions of the convention of Ohio colored men in January 1865 cited "the generous ardor of our fellow-citizens, men of color, who have rushed to the standard of their country" in arguing that all state or national laws "that make distinctions on account of color" be repealed and that "in the Territories, in the rebel States, when reorganized, and throughout the entire nation, colored men shall exercise the elective franchise, and be otherwise fully clothed with the rights of American citizens."[64]

Following the end of the war, no African American doubted that full citizenship rights were necessary to assure freedom and achieve equality. In October 1865, a convention of the colored men of California met "to consider and deliberate on subjects connected with our interests as citizens of this state."[65] Like other such bodies, they pressed for the vote, vowing "to petition the Legislature . . . to have the State Constitution so amended as to secure its colored citizens the right of suffrage." They made the case for equal rights on the grounds "that no Christian nation with any real sense of justice or humanity, could ask a class of people to assist in saving the Government from destruction, and after they had sacrificed hundreds and thousands of their lives to that effect, to then deny them of the common rights that nature had endowed them with; rights involving principles upon which the Government founded its political institutions, pronounced by them to be the natural rights of all men."[66]

African American soldiers from Iowa's 60th U.S. Colored Infantry drew upon their exemplary record of service to press for the right to vote when the unit was mustered out of service in October 1865. "Having returned home from the battle field, and feeling conscious that we have discharged our duty as soldiers in defence of our country," they "respectfully urge[d] that it is the duty of Iowa to allow us to use our votes at the polls; believing as we do and must, that he who is worthy to be trusted with the musket can and ought to be trusted with the ballot." In a specific appeal to the people of Iowa, they explained: "We ask no privilege, we simply ask for our own rights, long denied by the misguided and now conquered South, and withheld from us at the North in obedience to the political teachings and demands of slaveholding public opinion." They also sought recognition of "our claim to manhood by giving to us that right without which we have no power to defend ourselves from unjust legislation, and no voice in the Government we have endeavored to preserve. Being men, we claim to be of that number comprehended in the Declaration of Independence, and who are entitled, not only to life, but to equal rights to the pursuit and securing of happiness—in the choice of those who are to rule over us."[67]

By 1868, through the combined efforts of Republican Party strategists and African American leaders, the Iowa legislature agreed to submit to the electorate for approval several amendments to the state constitution that would eliminate the legacy of racial discrimination with respect to voting, legislative apportionment, and militia service. Invoking "the honored name of 200,000 colored troops, five hundred of whom were from our own Iowa," black Iowans voiced support for impartial suffrage. In November 1868, the amendments became law.[68]

The start of the Civil War understandably marked a watershed in the experience of African American Northerners. First and foremost, it signaled the beginning of an armed struggle over the future of slavery in the United States from which they earnestly prayed that freedom would prevail. They aimed to keep the national political focus on the fundamental issue that prompted secession, namely, slavery. They also presumed that military service would clear a path through discriminatory laws and practices to black male suffrage and civic equality for all African Americans.

When the Lincoln administration accepted black volunteers into national service, it inadvertently but necessarily forced a reconsideration of the antebellum definitions of citizenship. The earlier wars in which African Americans participated—specifically the Revolution and the War of 1812—offered few reliable guides. To be sure, politicians in those eras praised the loyalty of the veterans and pledged everlasting gratitude for their service to the cause of liberty. And while the men who served often won freedom from bondage, they witnessed at best only marginal improvements in the overall climate of civil and political rights.

During the Civil War, African American volunteers from the Northern states took up the cause of citizenship rights where the military service of their fathers and grandfathers and the abolitionist and the state convention movements had left it: in full expectation that the government would reward their sacrifices with full freedom, equality, and citizenship. Men and women in civilian life pinned their own hopes on the soldiers, and that faith was not misplaced. Without their combined efforts, the prevailing antebellum concepts of citizenship may not have undergone such scrutiny during the Civil War era. In that case, the monumental legislation that established national citizenship and attendant civil and political rights may well have been delayed into the twentieth century, with profoundly negative implications for American citizens of every color and nationality.

NOTES

1. See Sean Wilentz, *The Rise of American Democracy: Jefferson to Lincoln* (New York: Norton, 2005); Eric Foner, *The Story of American Freedom* (New York: Norton, 1998).

2. See Emory M. Thomas, *The Confederacy as a Revolutionary Experience* (Englewood Cliffs, NJ: Prentice-Hall, 1971); and, particularly with regard to African American slaves and freemen, Bruce Levine, *Confederate Emancipation: Southern Plans to Free and Arm Slaves during the Civil War* (New York: Oxford University Press, 2006); Robert F. Durden, *The Gray and the Black: The Confederate Debate on Emancipation* (Baton Rouge: Louisiana State University Press, 1972); and Charles H. Wesley, "Employment of Negro Troops as Soldiers in the Confederate Army," *Journal of Negro History* 4 (July 1919): 239–53.

3. Most were in three states: Kentucky (225,483), Missouri (114,931), and Maryland (87,180). See Joseph C. G. Kennedy, *Population of the United States in 1860*, compiled from the Original Returns of the Eighth Census under the Direction of the Secretary of the Interior (Washington, DC: Government Printing Office, 1864), 598–99.

4. For succinct overviews of these themes, see Eric Foner, "Rights and the Constitution in Black Life during the Civil War and Reconstruction," *Journal of American History* 74 (December 1987): 863–83; and Phillip Shaw Paludan, *"A People's Contest": The Union and Civil War, 1861–1865* (New York: Harper and Row, 1988), chap. 9.

5. See Graham Russell Hodges, *Root and Branch: African Americans in New York and East Jersey, 1613–1863* (Chapel Hill: University of North Carolina Press, 1999); Milton C. Sernett, *North Star Country: Upstate New York and the Crusade for African American Freedom* (Syracuse, NY: Syracuse University Press, 2002). For the reference to "Colored apprentice for life," see Kennedy, *Population of the United States in 1860*, 599.

6. For a survey of discriminatory legislation in the Northern states, see Leon F. Litwack, *North of Slavery: The Negro in the Free States, 1790–1860* (Chicago: University of Chicago Press, 1961), chaps. 3–4; for New England, see Joanne Pope Melish, *Disowning Slavery: Gradual Emancipation and "Race" in New England, 1780–1860* (Ithaca, NY: Cornell University Press, 1998).

7. Quoted in James M. McPherson, *The Negro's Civil War: How American Negroes Felt and Acted during the War for the Union* (New York: Pantheon Books, 1965), 248.

8. See Stanley W. Campbell, *The Slave Catchers: Enforcement of the Fugitive Slave Law, 1850–1860* (Chapel Hill: University of North Carolina Press, 1970); Don E. Fehrenbacher, *The Dred Scott Case: Its Significance in American Law and Politics* (New York: Oxford University Press, 2001).

9. Quoted in Herbert Aptheker, ed., *A Documentary History of the Negro People in the United States*, 5 vols. (New York: Citadel Press, 1951–93), 1:472.

10. See, for instance, W. Jeffrey Bolster, *Black Jacks: African American Seamen in the Age of Sail* (Cambridge: Harvard University Press, 1997).

11. *Weekly Anglo-African*, September 14, 1861.

12. See especially Aldon D. Morris, *Origins of the Civil Rights Movement: Black Communities Organizing for Change* (New York: Free Press, 1984); John Dittmer, *Local People: The Struggle for Civil Rights in Mississippi* (Urbana: University of Illinois Press, 1994); and Charles M. Payne, *I've Got the Light of Freedom: The Organizing Tradition and the Mississippi Freedom Struggle* (Berkeley: University of California Press, 1995).

13. Among the many studies of this subject, see particularly Alexander Keyssar, *The Right to Vote: The Contested History of Democracy in the United States* (New York: Basic Books, 2000).

14. Frederick Douglass, *Life and Times of Frederick Douglass Written by Himself* (1881; Hartford, CT: Park Publishing Co, 1884), 437.

15. C. Peter Ripley et al., eds., *The Black Abolitionist Papers*, 5 vols. (Chapel Hill: University of North Carolina Press, 1985–92), 5:254.

16. Quoted in Donald Yacovone, ed., *Freedom's Journey: African American Voices of the Civil War* (Chicago: Lawrence Hill Books, 2004), 20.

17. Sattie A. Douglas to Mr. Editor, *Weekly Anglo-African*, June 20, 1863, in Ripley et al., *Black Abolitionist Papers*, 5:212–13.

18. Excerpt from Proceedings of the National Convention of Colored Men, Held in City of Syracuse, New York, October 4, 5, 6, and 7, 1864, quoted in Ripley et al., *Black Abolitionist Papers*, 5:306. The chief recruiter of black soldiers in middle and eastern Tennessee, Colonel Reuben D. Mussey, used similar language to fault General William T. Sherman's reluctance to employ black troops in his command: "I think he is fully two years behind the time—and when I say two years I mean two of those century like years which we are living." Quoted in Ira Berlin, Joseph P. Reidy, and Leslie S. Rowland, eds., *The Black Military Experience*, ser. II of *Freedom: A Documentary History of Emancipation, 1861–1867* (Cambridge: Cambridge University Press, 1982), 111.

19. Ripley et al., *Black Abolitionist Papers*, 5:123.

20. See, for example, Floyd J. Miller, *The Search for a Black Nationality: Black Emigration and Colonization, 1787–1863* (Urbana: University of Illinois Press, 1975); and Robert L. Harris Jr., "H. Ford Douglas: Afro-American Antislavery Emigrationist," *Journal of Negro History* 62 (July 1977): 217–34.

21. *Weekly Anglo-African*, September 14, 1861.

22. George B. Vashon to His Excellency Abraham Lincoln, in Ripley et al., *Black Abolitionist Papers*, 5:152–53. Vashon's letter was published in Douglass's *Monthly* in October 1862.

23. Vashon to Lincoln, in Ripley et al., *Black Abolitionist Papers*, 5:154–55. This view of racial destiny anticipated W. E. Burghardt Du Bois, "The Conservation of Races," *The American Negro Academy Occasional Papers*, no. 2, 1897.

24. Quoted in Aptheker, *Documentary History*, 1:474–75.

25. The number of such men who served in volunteer regiments is difficult to determine precisely, but it is likely that several hundreds, if not several thousands,

did so. Some of these men later transferred into the segregated regiments of Colored Troops, which the War Department began forming in the spring of 1863. H. Ford Douglas, a prominent abolitionist, enlisted in an Illinois volunteer regiment and later commanded an all-black independent light-artillery battery that he organized in Kansas. See Harris, "H. Ford Douglas," 228–30. Douglas described his circumstances in a letter to Congressman Owen Lovejoy in these terms: "Although I am respected by my own Regiment and treated kindly by those who know me and the motives that induced me to enlist[,] still there are those in the other Regiments with whom I have to come in contact who have no regard for my feelings simply because I have the hated blood coursing in my veins." Douglas to Lovejoy, February 3, 1863, in Ripley et al., *Black Abolitionist Papers*, 5:179. In other cases, the men remained with their original regiments. In a letter to his wife, a black man serving in a Connecticut volunteer regiment alluded to "the mean treatment which your dearly beloved husband has suffered at the hands of some of his fellow soldiers." See Meunomennie L. Miami to My Dear Wife, *Weekly Anglo-African*, April 18, 1863, in Ripley et al., *Black Abolitionist Papers*, 5:187–88.

26. Miami to My Dear Wife, 5:187–88.

27. Quoted in Aptheker, *Documentary History*, 1:463.

28. Boyd and Alston to Hon. Simon Cameron, November 15, 1861, in Berlin et al., *Black Military Experience*, 80. The men wrote to the secretary of war after first having communicated their plan to Salmon P. Chase, a fellow Ohioan who was Lincoln's secretary of the Treasury.

29. Rufus Sibb Jones to Hon. Edwin M. Stanton, May 13, 1862, in Berlin et al., *Black Military Experience*, 84.

30. Garland H. White to E. M. Stanton, May 7, 1862, in Berlin et al., *Black Military Experience*, 82.

31. "An Act more effectually to provide for the National Defence by Establishing an Uniform Militia throughout the United States," May 8, 1792, 2nd Cong., 2nd sess., chap. 33, *The Public Statutes at Large of the United States*, vol. 1 (Boston: Charles C. Little and James Brown, 1845), 271–74.

32. For Attorney General Bates's opinion, see Edward McPherson, *The Political History of the United States of America, during the Great Rebellion*, 2nd ed. (Washington, DC: Philp and Solomons, 1865), 378–84.

33. *Weekly Anglo-African*, January 17, 1863, in Ripley et al., *Black Abolitionist Papers*, 5:175–76.

34. Sattie A. Douglas to Mr. Editor, *Weekly Anglo-African*, June 20, 1863, in Ripley et al., *Black Abolitionist Papers*, 5:212–13.

35. Miami to My Dear Wife, 5:187–88.

36. *Record of Action of the Convention Held at Poughkeepsie, N.Y., July 15th and 16th, 1863, for the Purpose of Facilitating the Introduction of Colored Troops into the Service of the United States* (New York: Frances and Loutrel, 1863), 10; see also Ripley et al., *Black Abolitionist Papers*, 5:224–28, esp. 227.

37. Andrew to Downing, March 23, 1863, in Berlin et al., *Black Military Experience*, 88–89.

38. Corporal James Henry Gooding to Abraham Lincoln, September 28, 1863, in Berlin et al., *Black Military Experience*, 385–86.

39. Sergt. Stephen A. Swails to Col. E. D. Townsend, January 14, 1864, in Berlin et al., *Black Military Experience*, 376–77.

40. Sergt. John F. Shorter et al. to the President of the United States, July 16, 1864, in Berlin et al., *Black Military Experience*, 401–2.

41. "Rhode Island" to the Editor, *Weekly Anglo-African*, January 23, 1864.

42. Hannah Johnson to Hon. Mr. Lincoln, July 31, 1863, in Berlin et al., *Black Military Experience*, 582–83. Coincidentally, Lincoln ordered retaliation upon Confederate prisoners for the ill-treatment of black prisoners on July 31, 1863.

43. George Rogers et al. to Mr. President, August 1864, in Berlin et al., *Black Military Experience*, 680–81.

44. Unsigned to Mr. Edwin M. Stanton, October 2, 1865, in Berlin et al., *Black Military Experience*, 654–55.

45. Samuel Roosa to Abraham Lincoln, January 24, 1865, in Berlin et al., *Black Military Experience*, 477–79.

46. *Weekly Anglo-African*, January 7, 1865; January 14, 1865; March 4, 1865. See also McPherson, *Negro's Civil War*, 252–54.

47. McPherson, *Negro's Civil War*, 254.

48. Robert R. Dykstra, *Bright Radical Star: Black Freedom and White Supremacy on the Hawkeye Frontier* (Cambridge: Harvard University Press, 1993), 198–200. See also James. L. Hill, "Migration of Blacks to Iowa, 1820–1960," *Journal of Negro History* 66 (Winter 1981): 289–303, esp. 290–95.

49. Quoted in McPherson, *Negro's Civil War*, 250.

50. Philip S. Foner, "The Battle to End Discrimination against Negroes on Philadelphia Streetcars (Part One): Background and Beginning of the Battle," *Pennsylvania History* 40 (July 1973): 261–91; and Foner, "The Battle to End Discrimination against Negroes on Philadelphia Streetcars (Part Two): The Victory," *Pennsylvania History* 40 (October 1973): 355–79.

51. William Still et al. to the Board of Managers of the various City Passenger Cars, in Aptheker, *Documentary History*, 1:502–3.

52. Letter from "Observer," December 26, 1864, *Weekly Anglo-African*, January 7, 1865.

53. See also McPherson, *Negro's Civil War*, 255–61.

54. *Weekly Anglo-African*, March 4, 1865, reprinting an account from the *Cleveland Leader* of a meeting in held on February 3, 1865.

55. Quoted in Philip S. Foner and George E. Walker, eds., *Proceedings of the Black State Conventions, 1840–1865*, 2 vols. (Philadelphia: Temple University Press, 1979–80), 156.

56. For accounts of these events, see McPherson, *Negro's Civil War*, 69–76; and Ripley et al., *Black Abolitionist Papers*, 5:229–38; Aptheker, *Documentary History*, 1:501–2. See also Barnet Schecter, *The Devil's Own Work: The Civil War Draft Riots and the Fight to Reconstruct America* (New York: Walker, 2005); and Iver Bernstein, *The New York City Draft Riots* (New York: Oxford University Press, 1990).

57. *Weekly Anglo-African*, September 26, 1863, in Ripley et al., *Black Abolitionist Papers*, 5:256–57.

58. Excerpt from Proceedings of the National Convention of Colored Men, Held in City of Syracuse, New York, October 4, 5, 6, and 7, 1864, quoted in Ripley et al., *Black Abolitionist Papers*, 5:305.

59. LaWanda Cox, *Lincoln and Black Freedom: A Study in Presidential Leadership* (Columbia: University of South Carolina Press, 1981).

60. Andrew Tait et al. to the Union Convention of Tennessee, January 9, 1865, quoted in Berlin et al., *Black Military Experience*, 812.

61. See accounts of these meetings in Foner and Walker, *Proceedings of the Black State Conventions*, vol. 1 (Pennsylvania, Michigan, and Ohio) and vol. 2 (New Jersey). Accounts of the various conventions of the Pennsylvania State Equal Rights League also appear in the *Christian Recorder*, February 18, August 26, September 2, and November 18. 1865.

62. Quoted in Foner and Walker, *Proceedings of the Black State Conventions*, 1:140.

63. Quoted in Foner and Walker, *Proceedings of the Black State Conventions*, 1:166.

64. Quoted in Foner and Walker, *Proceedings of the Black State Conventions*, 1:349, 351.

65. Foner and Walker, *Proceedings of the Black State Conventions*, 2:168.

66. Ibid., 176.

67. *Christian Recorder*, November 18, 1865.

68. Dykstra, *Bright Radical Star*, 218–19, 223–24.

ABOUT THE CONTRIBUTORS

STEPHEN D. ENGLE is Professor and Chair of History, Florida Atlantic University. His publications include *Yankee Dutchman: The Life of Franz Sigel.*

WILLIAM MCKEE EVANS is professor emeritus at California State Polytechnic University. His publications include *To Die Game: The Story of the Lowry Band, Indian Guerrillas of Reconstruction.*

DAVID T. GLEESON is Reader in History at University of Northumbria in Newcastle. He is the author of several works, including *The Irish in the South, 1815–1877.*

ANDREA MEHRLÄNDER is Executive Director of Berlin's Checkpoint Charlie Foundation. She is the author of several studies on Germans and the Confederacy.

JOSEPH P. REIDY is Professor of History and Associate Dean of the Graduate School of Arts and Sciences at Howard University. He is the author of several works and the coeditor of the first four volumes of *Freedom: A Documentary History of Emancipation, 1861–1867.*

ROBERT N. ROSEN, Esq., is an attorney at Rosen Law Firm in Charleston, South Carolina. His publications include *The Jewish Confederates.*

SUSANNAH J. URAL is Associate Professor of History at the University of Southern Mississippi. She is the author of *The Harp and the Eagle: Irish-American Volunteers and the Union Army, 1861–1865.*

INDEX

CPSIA information can be obtained
at www.ICGtesting.com
Printed in the USA
FSOW01n0035300816
24379FS